Updated and Reprinted 2003, 5th Edition
Copyright © 1992 by Douglas F. Warring, Ph.D.
Published by Leadership, Inc., of Scottsdale, Arizona 85260

All rights reserved. No part of this manual may be reproduced in any form without express written permission from the author, except for brief passages in connection with a review.

Requests for permission or further information should be addressed to Leadership, Inc., of Scottsdale, 7418 E. Helm Drive, Scottsdale, Arizona 85260. Please call (602) 443-2727 or (612) 962-4877.

ISBN 0-9630772-4-4

Printed in the United States of America.

10 9 8 7 6 5 4 3 2 1

## *Acknowledgements*

pp.102,3 Ellen Goodman, "The Tricky Equation of Skills and Luck," © 1987, The Boston Globe Newspaper Company/Washington Post Writers Group, reprinted with permission.

pp.104,5 Ellen Goodman, "A Grateful Wife Has Second Thoughts," © 1987, The Boston Globe Newspaper Company/Washington Post Writers Group, reprinted with permission.

pp.142,3 "Countering Ageism," from *Truth About Aging,* AARP, 1980. © 1980, The American Association of Retired Persons. reprinted with permission.

pp.185,6 From "Body Ritual Among the Nacirema," by Horace Miner. Reproduced by permission of the American Anthropological Association from *American Anthropologist* 58:3, 1956. Not for further reproduction.

# PREFACE

The study of human relations and multicultural education is an integral part of learning for living. People, by the very tenets of human nature, strive for interactions in a variety of settings. This creates a specific need for understanding at all levels within a pluralistic multicultural society.

The following pages represent an attempt to compile articles, exercises and supplemental materials on human relations/multicultural issues that may at first appear to be somewhat different but are in fact integrally related. It is through the application of the concepts and principles of these materials that understanding can occur.

The objectives are to achieve and demonstrate the following:
(1) Understand the contributions and life styles of various racial, cultural and economic groups in our society.
(2) Recognize and deal with dehumanizing biases, prejudices and discrimination.
(3) Create environments, which contribute to the positive self-image of persons and to positive interpersonal relations;
(4) Respect human diversity and personal rights.
(5) Develop multicultural overall inclusive approaches.
(6) Move to an education that is multicultural and works for anti-bias.
Remember, multicultural education consists of many components and can not be reduced to one or two items.

In the study of multicultural education we need to be mindful of the diversity that exists within all social/ethnic groups. This includes groups that are often categorized as African-Americans, Asian-Americans, European-Americans, Hispanic/Latino(a)-Americans, Native Americans/American Indians. These terms are in reality geopolitical labels often used for convenience. While there are commonalities between and within groups, differences also exist.

There is some degree of sense in linking all white people and all people of color to examine ethnocultural identity, which is often perceptual, and race based. Resistance to this is often linked to denial, escapism, silence, and a collective unconscious designed to maintain the status quo. But to consistently categorize in this way contributes to the illogical fallacy of racial identification and collective homogeneity.

In dealing with multicultural issues we need to remember that illiteracy, poverty, prejudice, violence, hunger, and other problems occur among all groups of people. No matter where we live or what groups we 'belong to' problems exist. However, some groups face greater challenges to existence.

The challenges we each face in our struggles to embrace multicultural education require that we are able to think analytically about current developments and examine options for the implementation of possibilities. We must continue to examine relationships between culture, ethnicity, bias, and learning as well as other factors. Learning from this study and discussion will enable us to build new systems that are inclusive.

The readings, charts, exercises and activities contained in this publication are designed as a starting point for understanding and dealing with the complexities of everyday interactions. It is the hope of the author/editor that through increased understanding of individuals, groups and societies we can create positive change in an ever-changing multicultural world.

# CONTENTS

**Preface** .................................................................................................................. iii

**Contents** ................................................................................................................. iv

### SECTION I
### OVERVIEWCULTURAL PLURALISM AND ETHNOCENTRISM

**Rationale and Objectives** ........................................................................................ 1

**Introduction** ............................................................................................................ 2

**Multicultural On-Going Process** ............................................................................ 8

**Definitions** .............................................................................................................. 9

### SECTION II
### COMMUNICATIONS UNDERSTANDING AND INTERACTING WITH OTHERS

**Rationale and Objectives** ...................................................................................... 13

**Multicultural Bingo** ............................................................................................... 14

**Group Process** ....................................................................................................... 15

    Roles and Responsibilities ................................................................................. 17

    Group Expectations ............................................................................................ 18

### SECTION III
### ANALYZING CULTURE AND SOCIETY

**Rationale and Objectives** ...................................................................................... 19

**Knowledge Bases for Diversity** ............................................................................ 20

**Reflection** .............................................................................................................. 21

**What's The Name of The Game** ........................................................................... 30

**Culture and Its Impact on Education** .................................................................... 32

### SECTION IV
### PERCEPTION AND MISUNDERSTANDING IN HUMAN RELATIONS/MULTICULTURAL EDUCATION

**Rationale and Objectives** ...................................................................................... 43

**I Am...** ................................................................................................................... 44

| | |
|---|---|
| **Me Bags** | 45 |
| **Identity Development** | 46 |
|     Stages of OTAID | 50 |
|     Group Identity Development | 51 |

## SECTION V
## ATTRIBUTION LABELING AND IDENTITY

| | |
|---|---|
| **Rationale and Objectives** | 53 |
| **Educational Priorities Checklist** | 54 |
| **American Creed** | 55 |
| **Hidden Curriculum** | 56 |
| **Forces Influencing Behavior at Work** | 57 |
| **Prejudice** | 58 |
| **Motivation** | 61 |
| **Attribution** | 62 |
|     The Tricky Equation... | 63 |
|     Behavior Labeling | 64 |
|     Teachers Don't Want... | 65 |

## SECTION VI
## FOUNDATIONS OF OPPRESSION AND THE COLOR BLIND PERSPECTIVE

| | |
|---|---|
| **Rationale and Objectives** | 67 |
| **Power** | 68 |
|     Analyses | 69 |
|     Group Structure | 70 |
| **Affirmative Action** | 71 |
| **Foundations of Oppression** | 74 |
|     Grids | 75 |
|     Race Relations | 76 |
|     White Privilege | 77 |

# SECTION VII
# SOCIOECONOMIC STATUS AND POVERTY

**Rationale and Objectives** ............................................................................ 80
**Poverty** .......................................................................................................... 81
    Perceptions and School Behavior.................................................................. 85
    The Truth About Welfare .............................................................................. 89

# SECTION VIII
# SEXISM, HETEROSEXISM, GENDER FAIR ISSUES, SEXUAL HARASSMENT, HOMOPHOBIA, AND RELATED ISSUES

**Objectives and Rationale** ............................................................................ 90
**Gender** .......................................................................................................... 91
    Semantic Derogation..................................................................................... 96
    Myths and Realities ...................................................................................... 97
    Education and Income................................................................................... 99
**Status of Women**........................................................................................... 99
    Businessman...Businesswoman .................................................................. 101
    A Grateful Wife... ......................................................................................... 102
    Story About a Young Woman ..................................................................... 104
**Sexual Harassment** ..................................................................................... 106
    Legal Implications ....................................................................................... 110
    Court Decisions .......................................................................................... 111
    Case Studies ............................................................................................... 115
    Examples .................................................................................................... 119
    Effects Chart .............................................................................................. 120
    Rights and Responsibilities ........................................................................ 121
    Stopping, Unwanted... ................................................................................ 122
    Complaint Procedure .................................................................................. 123
    Test, Facts and Myths ................................................................................. 124
**Gay, Lesbian, Bisexual, and Transgendered** ............................................ 125
**Dealing With Homophobia** ........................................................................ 126

    Glossary of Terms ............................................................................................... 128

    Statistics on GLBT Youth .................................................................................. 129

    Preventing Homophobia in School ..................................................................... 130

    Index of Homophobia ......................................................................................... 133

    Attitude Scale ..................................................................................................... 135

    General Knowledge Review ............................................................................... 136

**Heterosexual Privilege** .............................................................................................. 137

## SECTGION IX
## AGE AND AGE BIAS

**Rationale and Objectives** ........................................................................................... 138

**Age and Age Bias** ...................................................................................................... 139

**Countering Ageism** .................................................................................................... 142

**Consideration for Illustrations** ................................................................................... 145

## SECTION X
## APPLYING EDUCATION THAT IS MULTICULTURAL AND ANTI-BIASED

**Rationale and Objectives** ........................................................................................... 146

**Learning Styles, Multiple Intelligences, etc.** ............................................................. 147

**Models of Curriculum and Organizational Levels** .................................................... 151

**Preliminary Screening Form** ...................................................................................... 152

**Curriculum Analysis Questionnaire** ........................................................................... 155

**Checklist... Sexism In Materials** ............................................................................... 162

**Cultural Bias In Materials** .......................................................................................... 163

**Evaluation Criteria** ..................................................................................................... 165

**In The Classroom** ....................................................................................................... 167

**Different Views of America's Ethnic** ........................................................................ 168

**School Checklist...Racism and Sexism** ..................................................................... 170

## SECTON XI
## MISCELLANEOUS READINGS, REFERENCES, AND RESOURCES

**Minnesota Public School Guidelines** ........................................................................ 183

**Body Ritual Among the Nacirema** ............................................................................... 185

**Appendices**

    **A. Multicultural Project** ............................................................................. 187

        Lesson Planning ......................................................................................... 188

        Lesson Plan ................................................................................................ 191

    **B. Sample of Sources** ................................................................................. 192

    **C. Community Resources** ......................................................................... 193

    **D. Southeast Asian Resources** .................................................................. 197

    **E. American Indian Resources** ................................................................. 198

    **F. Local Stores** ........................................................................................... 201

    **G. Community Newspapers** ..................................................................... 202

    **H. Internet Resources** ............................................................................... 203

    **I. Case Study Format** ................................................................................ 210

# SECTION I

# OVERVIEW OF CULTURAL PLURALISM AND ETHNOCENTRISM

***Rationale***: We live in an increasingly complex and diverse society. Yet our socialization into a particular culture and lifestyle induces us to accept certain values, attitudes, and beliefs as universally correct and valid. This ethnocentrism serves to limit the effectiveness of interpersonal relationships across diverse groups.

***Objectives***
1. To develop an understanding of the differences between cultural pluralism and assimilation.
2. To be able to distinguish between the individual, social groups, and society and to identify the effects of each on interpersonal relationships.
3. To explain how ethnocentrism and unconscious ideology operate.
4. To broaden perspectives to include global options.
5. To understand culture, ethnicity, boundaries, borders, and other related terms.
6. To understand ethnocentrism and its impact.

# INTRODUCTION

The world is growing smaller on a daily basis as migration and other factors contribute to the increasing diversity in the United States of America (USA). During the past century, important movements calling for recognition of the rights and needs of people of color, women, and other oppressed groups have surfaced in this country. In the early 1900's the average American was 21 years old with a life expectancy rate of 47 and the infant mortality rate in New York City was 50% according to Hodgkinson (2002). Compare that with today where the average American is now 38 with a life expectancy of 78. Over three-fourths of the immigrants now come from countries other than Europe and we are experiencing a rapid aging. Nothing is distributed evenly across the nations, not jobs, not race, not age, not wealth, and not even crime.

The women's movements and the civil rights movements during the past 60 years have brought together groups focusing on social change. The focus has been on the inclusion of groups that have been previously omitted from the mainstream of American education. It is important to examine the connection between the concern for the rights of others and the concern about educational issues. This places the focus for discussion with the educational environment. Most educational endeavors have been void of course work on these issues, or have peripherally dealt with them, so it is quite readily apparent that the persons who are preparing to teach for the most part have not had adequate training to assist in the preparation of future global citizens. This includes the understanding and support for a multicultural environment.

Education has been one of these closed systems. Many reports and other indicators have called for, and continue to call for educational reform. When you analyze these reports be sure to read between the lines. They don't often state their desired final outcomes, only partial examples based on biased analysis.

In an effort to assist teachers and other school personnel in understanding the changes in society Minnesota enacted legislation mandating all educators and prospective educators to take a course or series of competencies in Human Relations. The course competencies consisted of work in the following areas:
1. Understand the contributions and lifestyles of various racial, cultural, and economic groups in our society;
2. Recognize and deal with dehumanizing biases, prejudices, and discrimination;
3. Create environments which contribute to positive self-esteem of persons and to positive interpersonal relations; and
4. Respect human diversity and personal rights. This has more recently expanded to include more specific aspects of multicultural education.

This requirement has evolved slightly over the years and several other states have since added comparable requirements. Most of the requirements now speak to the area of multicultural education.

As teachers and professionals in all fields we have an intellectual and ethical responsibility to provide our students and others with the most current and accurate information possible. A more inclusive education will have a number of important effects on students. It will expand their worldview by exposing them to the life experiences of people both similar to, and different from themselves. It will make them more cognizant of interesting variables including culture, ethnicity, and gender, which are important variables for everyday life. It will also make students aware of the significant contributions of members of groups who have been omitted from the American mainstream, as well as provide them the skills to recognize and deal with dehumanizing bias, prejudice, and discrimination. This will help students to benefit from an increased appreciation of diversity in any of their future roles as parents, teachers, community leaders, coworkers, employers, and citizens. This should facilitate the changes in climate necessary to ensure change.

Diversity is inevitable and continues to increase. Mobility and migration patterns throughout the world continue to bring people into contact with others they never thought would be possible. One of the consequences of this is the opportunity to become more multicultural and manage diversity in constructive instead of destructive ways. This new diversity poses challenges and opportunities for all.

In order to understand others better and interact with them in more positive ways it is essential to understand your own culture and cultural identity. Examine the generalized identity you have constructed over time and start to analyze each part. Of special interest are factors that contribute to intersecting variables such as race/ethnicity, gender, socioeconomic status, religion, and other similar identities. This will assist you in understanding your worldview. As you progress on your journey remember that your identity development and understanding your culture are works in progress.

**Models For Education**

As a model for education we could utilize some of the current programs that are either in existence or being created at the local levels. Minnesota is in the process of moving in that exact direction for all of its K-12 programs. To that end the Minnesota State Board of Education adopted a plan for all school districts in Minnesota regarding Multicultural and Gender-Fair Disability Sensitive (MCGFDS) Curriculum and is working on integrating global issues as well.

Several years ago the State of Minnesota passed a law requiring all teachers in the state to successfully complete a Human Relations course. Continuing from that point, the school board in each district is now required to adopt a written plan to assure that curriculum is evaluated and developed for use in each district school establishes and maintains an inclusive educational program. Specific objectives are designed to achieve the following outcomes in addition to the Knowledge, Practice, and Assessment Standards. An inclusive educational program is one that employs curriculum developed and delivered so students and staff:

1. Gain an understanding and appreciation of the contributions and life styles of various racial, cultural, and economic groups in our society:
2. Recognize and deal with dehumanizing biases, prejudices, and discrimination,
3. Create environments, which contribute to the positive self-image of persons and to positive interpersonal relations,
4. Respect human diversity and personal rights,
5. Develop multicultural, approaches, and
6. Incorporate education that is multicultural as a regular ongoing process throughout the educational realm.

Minnesota now requires all K-12 Schools to have a Multicultural, Gender-Fair, Disability Sensitive Plan for all curriculum areas. Obviously these need to be regularly updated. Where is your school in this process? How effective is this committee/plan in facing new challenges? Examine the field of multicultural education for more information.

Multicultural Education has been defined as an idea, an educational reform movement, and as a process (Banks, 2001). According to Banks, (2001) the goal of multicultural education is to change the structure of educational institutions to improve the chances for equal educational opportunity and academic and social achievement for all students. Education must be anti-biased and seek for change. Change is already occurring so don't change just for the sake of change, make it count.

MCGFDS education is education which values cultural pluralism, and reflects the view that schools should <u>not</u> seek to melt away cultural differences through forced assimilation, but should be a process of shared acculturation. Multicultural education programs for teachers, staff, and students must permeate all areas of the educational experience.

Multicultural education is developmental and emergent. It is a process for impacting upon the totality of the educational enterprise. The salient feature of these programs is the use of a systematic approach to the design, development, and implementation of a pluralistic anti-biased framework. This should provide a significant level of cognitive sophistication for all involved.

What is needed is to integrate concepts and to examine the impact of specific elements (intersecting variables) such as race, class, gender, lifestyles, and exceptionality. This is where variables intersect to impact each other. These are inextricably interwoven characteristics. Some of these status variables can be more successfully dealt with in modified learning environments.

Instructional strategies include the use of cooperative learning with a basic understanding of values and differences seen as positive and brought out in the classroom. Specific pedagogical techniques are essential to integrating factual information about people of color and women into the classroom. A cooperative instructional system utilizes cooperative task structures in which students spend much of their time in heterogeneous groups earning recognition, praise, and rewards based on the academic performance of their respective groups (Johnson & Johnson 2002. Cohen 1986 & Slavin 1983).

Since the State of Minnesota (Minnesota Department of Education, 1974) requires all prospective teachers, administrators, counselors, social workers, community educators, and school personnel to take course work in "Human Relations", the Multicultural Gender-fair curriculum component for all school districts is a natural and necessary step. This needs to be evaluated regarding the significance of impact and if shown to be successful, be implemented in all institutions of higher learning which are the agencies offering the course work. This will undoubtedly lead to significant changes in the attitudes and behaviors of those persons who are employed in higher education, thus creating a change in the climate and curriculum in higher education. This will in turn assist in the achievement of some societal goals such as:
1. Reduce prejudice,
2. Reduce discrimination,
3. Provide equal opportunity,
4. Create an anti-biased education, and
5. Provide social justice for all.

This is a process in the move to foster education that is multicultural and anti-biased.

**Education that is Multicultural and Anti-biased**
Education must move to a practice that is inherently multicultural and intentionally anti-biased. Without doing so it remains biased. There are many reasons educational inequality exists. Some of the most significant reasons are listed here.
1. There is a lack of diverse educational resources.
2. Most teachers know very little about cultural traits, behaviors, values, and attitudes of diverse populations.
3. Most curriculum designs and instructional materials are Eurocentric and show other signs of bias.
4. The environments in which students live and in which they learn often differ significantly.
5. Most educators do not teach students how to survive and succeed in schools.

**Guidelines for Teaching**
In order to be more effective in meeting the needs of all learners cultural scripts need to be written and analyzed that consciously cause an analysis and reanalysis of teaching and the entire educational process. Some of the guidelines that will assist all school personnel in becoming more effective are listed here. Look at these and be truthful about what you are presently doing and what you would like to accomplish.
1. Knowledge, attitudes, and skills of the teacher-teacher as important variable,
2. Knowledge about cultural, racial, gender, ethnic, and other groups,
3. Sensitivity to one's own culture, attitudes, and behavior,
4. Convey positive images of all groups,
5. Be sensitive to culture, attitudes, and beliefs of your students and their families,
6. Choose teaching materials carefully,
7. Use supplemental materials,
8. Be sensitive to the controversial nature of some materials,
9. Be sensitive to the developmental level of your students,

10. View all students as winners,
11. Differentiate education from schooling-most parents want an education for their children,
12. Use cooperative learning techniques and group work to promote integration and positive interaction,
13. Make sure that school plays, pageants, cheerleading squads, and school publications are integrated.

Characteristics of Education that is Multicultural in the USA

The entire educational process has a primary focus on the students. Students are individuals who are also members of various clubs, groups, organizations, and cultures. All members of any society need multicultural education to assist them in operating effectively in a democratic manner. Some of the essential elements that schools should understand and operationalize include:

1. Elimination of stereotypes and biases,
2. Use of inclusive materials (all cultural diversities reflected),
3. Teaching from perspectives and values of all groups,
4. Fostering respect and appreciation for cultural diversity,
5. Validating every individual regardless of race/ethnicity, gender and/or ability,
6. Integrating diversity into every subject area,
7. Exhibiting a sense of belonging for all students,
8. Reflecting student achievement patterns equitably across race/ethnicity and gender, and
9. Utilizing cooperative learning techniques where appropriate.

**Schools As Social Systems**

We must remember that we are all members of social systems. Social systems operate in interesting ways in our schools. These systems create, maintain, and/or change CULTURE. Change is an ongoing process while growth is an option. Will you be a change agent? CULTURE consists of knowledge, concepts, values, beliefs, symbols and interpretations.

The essence of culture is how members of groups interpret, use, and perceive these elements. People within a culture usually view things similarly (paradigm). An appropriate paradigm to develop is one that utilizes a pluralistic, multidimensional process. This will in turn create a new culture, one which includes the gradually evolving knowledge and ideas that are accumulating as the society faces new problems or as it develops in anticipation of future survival problems.

A major goal of multicultural education is to change teaching and learning approaches so students of both genders, from differing economic strata, and from diverse cultural and ethnic groups will have equal opportunities to learn and succeed in education. Empowerment is the key.

**Summary and Recommendations**

A major goal of the educational environment should be to help students acquire the knowledge, skills, and dispositions (attitudes) needed to function effectively within the national macroculture, their own microcultures, and within and across other microcultures.

Multicultural Education seeks to reform the total schooling process for all students through changes in the curriculum, instruction, and co-curricular programs. Since teaching is an interactive process that flows throughout the entire educational endeavor learning is not confined only to the classroom. The entire educational learning community should have

1. An awareness of diversity,
2. An acceptance of diversity,
3. An affirmation of diversity,
4. An appreciation of diversity, and should all
5. Interact and teaching with diverse perspectives.

Characteristics of the School that is Multicultural include:
1. High expectations and positive attitudes for all students,
2. Curriculum reflects diversity,
3. Teachers use different teaching styles,
4. Respect is shown for all languages and dialects,
5. Materials used show and respect diversity,
6. Assessment and testing procedures are culturally sensitive,
7. The hidden curriculum reflects diversity,
8. Counselors have high expectations for all students,
9. Parent/guardian family involvement is high, and
10. A plan that is multicultural and non-biased is adopted by the board and supported by all of the school personnel.

When these are in place and functioning well, education will be multicultural and anti-biased and the students, their families, and our communities will all benefit.

**References**
Banks, J., & Banks, C. (2001). *Multicultural education: Issues and perspectives.* New York, NY: Wiley and Sons.
Banks J. (1997). *Multiethnic education: Theory and practice*: Allyn and Bacon, Boston, MA.
Bronstein, P. & Quina, K. (1988). *Teaching A psychology of people: Resources for gender and sociocultural awareness.* Washington, D.C: American Psychological Association,
Cohen, E. (1986). *Designing groupwork.* New York: Teachers College Press.
Grant, C. (Ed.), (1992). *Research and multicultural education: From the margins to the mainstream.* Washington, D.C.: The Falmer Press.
Hodgkinson, H. (2002). Demographics and teacher education: An overview. *Journal of Teacher Education, 53 2 102-105.*
Johnson, D. W., Johnson, R. T., & Holubec, E. J. (1998). *Cooperation in the classroom (6$^{th}$ ed.).* Edina, MN: Interaction Book Company.
Johnson, D. W. & Johnson, R. T. (2002). Multicultural education and human relations: Valuing diversity. Boston, MA: Allyn and Bacon.
Minnesota Department of Education (1974). *Human Relations Guide: Inter and Intracultural Education.* St. Paul, MN.
Minnesota State Board of Education (1988). *Multicultural and gender-fair curriculum.* Minnesota Rules Part 3500.0550, St. Paul, MN.
Nieto, S. (2000). *Affirming diversity: The sociopolitical context of multicultural education.* New York: Longman.
Slavin, R. (1983). *Cooperative learning.* New York: Longman.
Sleeter, C. (1992). *Keepers of the American dream: A study of staff development and multicultural education.* Washington, D.C.: The Falmer Press.
Tiedt, P. & Tiedt, I. (2000). *Multicultural teaching: A handbook of activities, information, and resources* (4th Ed.). Boston, MA: Allyn and Bacon.

---

**Reflection/Discussion Items**
1. In small groups of 3 or 4 discuss where you are in the process of understanding and applying diversity.


2. How does this apply to you and your future profession?

3. What is your knowledge of the educational process and how do these items apply?

4. What other questions or comments do you have at this time?

# Multicultural On Going Process

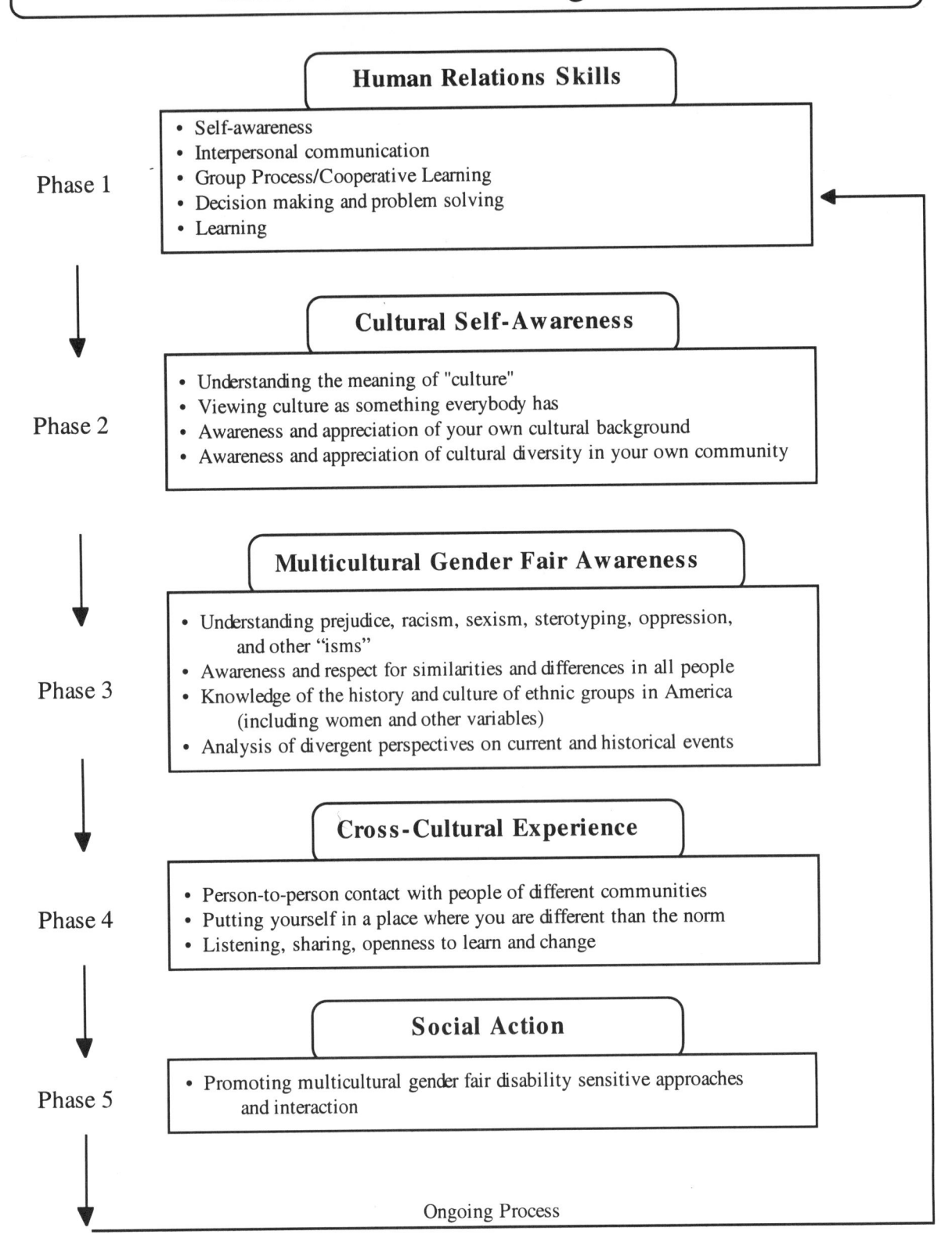

### Human Relations Skills

Phase 1
- Self-awareness
- Interpersonal communication
- Group Process/Cooperative Learning
- Decision making and problem solving
- Learning

### Cultural Self-Awareness

Phase 2
- Understanding the meaning of "culture"
- Viewing culture as something everybody has
- Awareness and appreciation of your own cultural background
- Awareness and appreciation of cultural diversity in your own community

### Multicultural Gender Fair Awareness

Phase 3
- Understanding prejudice, racism, sexism, sterotyping, oppression, and other "isms"
- Awareness and respect for similarities and differences in all people
- Knowledge of the history and culture of ethnic groups in America (including women and other variables)
- Analysis of divergent perspectives on current and historical events

### Cross-Cultural Experience

Phase 4
- Person-to-person contact with people of different communities
- Putting yourself in a place where you are different than the norm
- Listening, sharing, openness to learn and change

### Social Action

Phase 5
- Promoting multicultural gender fair disability sensitive approaches and interaction

Ongoing Process

# DEFINITIONS

It is important to consider alternative definitions and come to agreement on word use. This is one step in the process of creating understanding. Words and language are powerful and give meaning to interactions.

1. **Attitudes** (Feeling – Emotional)
   The "I" portion of one's self-concept. They are our likes and dislikes; our affinity for and our aversion to situations, objects, and persons, etc.

2. **Beliefs** (Knowledge)
   The cognitive component: it is the relationship between two things or between something and a characteristic of it (i.e., I believe in democracy; dogs have four legs). Things we accept as true.

3. **Category**
   An accessible cluster of associated ideas that as a whole has the property of guiding daily judgments.

4. **Differentiated Categories**
   These are categories that are held tentatively, making allowance for variation and subdivision.

5. **Discrimination**
   *Behavioral* – differential treatment of individuals because of their perceived membership in a minority group. May result from prejudicial attitudes held by an individual member of the majority, an institution, or a society, or from conformity.

6. **Ethnic Group**
   A group whose members are bound together by common cultural characteristics (e.g., values, ideas, food habits, family patterns, sexual behavior, modes of dress, standards of beauty, political conceptions, economic forms, and recreational patterns). These are inherently ethnocentric. Its members tend to regard their own cultural traits as natural, superior and correct and to view those of other ethnic groups as odd, inferior, or immoral.

7. **Heterosexism**
   A system that uses heterosexuality as a standard and then assigns roles, rewards, punishments, and all socialization on that standard.

8. **Homophobia**
   A fear of persons perceived to be homosexual, or more appropriately gay, lesbian, bisexual or transgendered (GLBT see page 125). (For more information see the section Dealing with Homophobia on page 126 and glossary on page 128.)

9. **Ideology**
   A systematic body of beliefs or concepts, especially about human life or culture which are often used to guide judgment and reinforce existing systems.

10. **Institutional Racism/Colonialism, etc.**
    Institutional racism is and is a social system in which race is the major criterion of role assignment, role rewards, and socialization. This system is often established through colonialism. After colonial contact occurs, the dominant elite power holders create a monopoly of political, economic, social, cultural, natural, and psychological resources resulting in a social system that is oppressive of all other people. The typical stages in this process are contact, invasion, takeover, system creation, and maintenance of the system through whatever

means necessary. Psychological processes to justify this are rationalization and/or justification. See also minority.

11. **Labels of Primary Potency**
    Out of all the labels that could be attached to an individual, these labels are the most powerful and salient, (Examples: a woman doctor, a blind man, a male nurse), limiting the individual to a biased definition.

12. **Levels of Analysis**
    There are consistently used to evaluate and analyze issues. These are typically: 1. Individual/psychological, 2. Group/social-psychological, 3. Society/societal, and 4. Global/international.

13. **Majority**
    Categories of people who possess special access to positions of power, prestige, and privileges in a society (synonym: dominant elite, super ordinate). They control society's economic, political, psychological, and/or social systems. Examine the topic of white privilege to gain knowledge of an element in the analysis.

14. **Minority**
    Categories of people who possess imperfect access to positions of equal power, prestige, and privileges in a society (synonym: subordinate). Any group that views itself and/or is defined by a dominant power elite as unique on the basis of perceived physical, cultural, economic, and/or behavioral characteristics and is treated accordingly in a negative manner.

    Examples of these include but are not limited to the following real and/or perceived items
    a. Physical – race, sex, age, ability
    b. Cultural – religion, ethnicity
    c. Economic – social class
    d. Behavioral – deviant

    Looking at our society in the United States today and using these definitions:
    Can a minority be racist?
    Can a woman be a sexist?
    Use a theoretical framework and examine levels of analysis.

15. **Monopolistic Categories**
    Categories that become so powerful and rigid that all contradictory information is rejected.

16. **Non-Conscious Ideology**
    A set of beliefs that we accept implicitly but because we cannot even conceive of alternative conceptions of the world, much as a fish is unaware that its environment is wet, we do not question.

17. **Power**
    Power is the ability to accomplish a task.
    There are often two types of power that are used to discuss issues:
    Individual power: the ability to mobilize one's own resource to accomplish a task, and
    Societal power: the ability to influence the behavior of others or to influence control and the means
    to enforce that influence. Power in and of itself is neither good nor bad.

18. **Prejudice: "Hardening of the Categories"**
    An unwillingness to change one's biased beliefs and attitudes after being presented with new contradictory information. Do not confuse this with refencing (#24).

19. **Principle of Least Effort**
    This is based on the fact that, as a rule, monopolistic categories are much easier to form and to hold than are differentiated categories. A common process is either/or thinking.

20. **Psychological Clowning**
    Exaggerating a trait (i.e., exaggerating the Black accent) and affecting the traits ascribed to one's group to enjoy some pragmatic reward. People have often been rewarded for "playing a role" in society.

21. **Race**
    The perception of an individual or group, which is defined as different from the elite and from others on the basis of perceived physical criteria. *Important:* race is not truly a physical group, but one that is perceived and defined as different on the basis of physical criteria (i.e., skin color, hair type, etc.). Race is socially constructed.

22. **Racial Prejudice**
    This is an attitude toward an individual or a group predicated upon traits or characteristics that are, or are erroneously believed to be, racial in origin, but without any adequate foundation in fact or experiential acquaintance. This is a common form of response based on a stereotype.

23. **Racism/Sexism**
    When an elite (dominant) group develops a social system in which race/sex is the major criterion of role assignment, role rewards, and socialization and has the power to enforce those decisions. A similar process occurs in reference to other factors. (See Section VII for more information).

24. **Refencing Device**
    (Yes, but ... syndrome) A common mental device that permits people to hold to their prejudgments even in the face of much contradictory evidence, admitting exceptions, see Gordon Allport's The Nature of Prejudice.

25. **Stereotype**
    An exaggerated belief associated with a category is a stereotype. The attribution of identical characteristics to any person in a group, regardless of the actual variation among members of that group is an example.

26. **Two-Valued Judgments**
    Evaluations of the world in terms of two values; i.e., something is either all good or all bad. These are a function of monopolistic categories and a result of an inability to utilize perspective taking skills.

27. **Wishful Thinking/Self-Deception**
    Because we believe something to be desirable, we persuade ourselves that it is true.

**Classifications and Ideologies**
People have some innate need to categorize things by size, shape, color, etc. This carries over into the realm of human interaction and becomes a spontaneous event. Inferences are then drawn and traits ascribed on the basis of these inferential decisions. Impressions are then formed of others based on extremely limited information. An element often involved in this process is an ideology.

An ideology provides answers to everyday problems of living, thereby reducing uncertainty and offering broad principles that give meaning and purpose to life. The answers often lie in the fundamental beliefs of an ideology, namely those beliefs that are to be accepted on faith and not to be questioned by persons sharing that ideology. Thus, an ideology can act to relieve pressure from and increase comfort of committed believers. Persons who see ideologies as generally negative view the complacency created by ideologies as an escape from freedom or the avoidance of taking personal responsibility for continually having to cope with the everyday problems of living.

This process is part of and can lead to stereotyping. Stereotypes are exaggerations and allow for the inference of anything from anything without any facts. Individuals then form opinions and take actions on these biased beliefs. Individuals tend to overestimate the similarity of the behavior of out-group members and overestimate the similarity of themselves to other in-group members.

Remember, stereotypes and prejudices can change. One way to do this is engage in fact finding. Learn as much as you can about the other person or persons. Seek to find similarities as well as differences. This will result in the breakdown of preexisting categories and lead to enhanced interactions based on fact rather than fiction.

---

**Reflection/Discussion Items**

1. Examine the definitions for majority, minority, prejudice, racism/sexism, and ideology. How is this different than any prior learning?

2. What is your first memory of interaction with culture/ethnicity different from your own?

3. Where did you acquire your first stereotypes?

4. What other observations and questions do you have?

# SECTION II

# UNDERSTANDING AND INTERACTING WITH OTHERS

***Rationale***: Communication occurs at different levels through our perceptions, interactions with the media, and with other people. Our interpersonal effectiveness is largely dependent upon our skills and abilities as sensitive and responsive communicators.

***Objectives***
1. To understand the communication process and how it is culturally impacted.
2. To examine verbal and nonverbal communication.
3. To understand and work effectively in small groups.
4. To understand our own personal methods of "screening" communication.
5. To understand and utilize constructive and effective communication (feedback, gestures, touching, empathy, listening, group process, and hidden agendas).
6. To examine the role of perception.
7. To understand the self and culture with regard to communications.

# MULTICULTURAL BINGO

**RULES:**
1. Get the signature from a person who can answer the question or is or has done or knows the answer.
2. Each person may sign your sheet only once.
3. Each person signs his or her own sheet in the middle square.
4. If you are competitive you may play the first "Bingo" will be the winner. *

| has visited Europe? *Jeane* | has some item of sports equipment from another country? *Colleen* | has ever attended a workshop with a multicultural theme? | buys gas for the car by the liter? | speaks more than one language? *Claudia* |
|---|---|---|---|---|
| has corresponded with someone from a country in Asia? | attended the Festival of Nations in St. Paul? *Jon* | has visited a country in Asia? *Asia* | owns a pair of binoculars made outside the U.S.? *Dave* | know what the initials OPEC stand for? |
| has a name that is not European? | belongs to an international organization? | operates in a multi-cultural manner? | was born in a state other than Minnesota? *Jack* | has visited a country in Africa or the Middle East? |
| is a parent or guardian? | has visited a country in Latin America? *Adrienne* | has recently eaten in an ethnic restaurant? *Anne* | has relatives living in a country other than the U.S.? | recently read a book written by a person of color? *Sara* |
| knows a game played in more than one culture? *Susan* | has prepared an ethnic meal in the last month? | is wearing a piece of clothing representative of cultural diversity? *Jocline* | has attended a play/concert performed by a multicultural group? *Brandi* | knows a contribution made to math by more than two cultural groups? |

**Reflection/Discussion Item**
*What can you remember about each person who signed your sheet?

# GROUP PROCESS

Group process skills are essential in the formation of highly productive work groups. Absenteeism, satisfaction, and productivity impact schools as well as other societal organizations and elements of group process are present. In order to foster productivity and provide an equitable learning opportunity, understanding and applying positive group process are important. We all work with and in different groups and need to be conscious of these as we interact. If we can interact successful it increases our ability to understand each other and our cultures and as a result maximize our potential and that our of work group. As you read over the following items consider how they apply to your groups and continually assess your progress. The following defense mechanisms are adapted from the 1972 Annual Handbook for Group Facilitators.

## Defense Mechanisms—Behaviors to Avoid

1. *Fight Defenses:* These are based on the premise that "the best defense is a good offense."

*Competition with the Facilitator:* The person who struggles to control the group or "outdo" the trainer may be attempting to prove his/her group prowess in order to avoid dealing with his/her own behavior.

*Cynicism:* This may be manifested by frequent challenging of the group contact and goals, skeptical questioning of genuine behavior, and attacks on stronger, threatening members.

*Interrogation:* A barrage of probing questions keeps one on the defensive. An individual who habitually cross-examines others in the group under the guise of getting "helpful information and understanding" may be fighting to get the spotlight safely away from himself or herself.

2. *Flight Defenses:* These are the most frequently used means of avoiding honest, feeling-level involvement in the group process.

*Intellectualization ("head trips," dime-store psychology):* These are processes by which an individual deals with his or her emotions in an objective, diagnostic, or interpretative way, so that he/she never comes to grips with his or her gut-level feelings, e.g., "I guess I'm angry with you because you remind me of my older sister."

*Generalization:* Closely related is the tendency to make general, impersonal statements about group behavior instead of applying them directly to self or specific participants. For example, a tense person states, "People can really get anxious when there are long silences," when he really means, "I am very uptight with this silence."

*Projection:* Here the individual attributes to others traits that are unacceptable in himself or herself; e.g., someone competing for attention in the group may attack another person for using more than his share of the group's time.

*Rationalization:* This is an attempt to justify maladaptive behavior by substituting "good" reasons for real ones: e.g., "I'm not getting very much out of this group because there are not enough people of my age, and I just can't relate with the group members."

*Withdrawal:* This defense may vary in intensity from boredom to actual physical removal of one's self from the group. Consistently silent persons may be passive learners, but they are not grouping interpersonally.

**3.** *__Group Manipulation Defenses:__* Participants frequently maneuver other members into specific kinds of relationships in order to protect themselves from deeper involvement or confrontation.

*Pairing:* Members seek out one another, or seek out one or two supporters and form an emotional subgroup through which they protect and support each other.

*Red-Crossing:* This may occur within or outside subgroups. In conflict or confrontation situations, the member mediates or defends the person under fire. The assumed contract is "Let's keep it safe I'll come to your aid if you come to mine."

*Focusing on One:* An entire group may find itself spending excessive amounts of time and energy on one individual. By keeping the spotlight on one single person for an extended time period, the opportunities increase for a large number of participants to fall silent or keep the action away from themselves.

**Summary**

As you consider these and the additional roles and responsibilities for groups on the next page please be aware of specific cultural behaviors and do not assume all members are alike or will in fact operate in a similar manner. When we internalize multiple cultures they will be our guides, as we become more fully multicultural.

In schools more than any other setting opportunities exist to have a close and regular interaction with a wide variety of people. As we work with others it is helpful to take the opportunity to learn from and about them and their culture according to Cushner, McClelland, and Safford (2003). The path to change is begun by understanding some of the information of which we are unaware. From this a person may proceed to gain awareness and build a knowledge base from which to draw. Combs (1965) stressed the importance of examining an individual's perceptions about themselves, their beliefs, and patterns of behavior in the change process. These can be impediments or provide impetus.

It is only when the individuals see themselves as active participants that change can occur on more than a small scale. Allport (1954) examined change and developed a contact theory outlining factors for successful change. These include: equal status contact, long-term meaningful contact, contact that negates or violates stereotypes, and pursuit of a common goal,

When these are in place a change will occur.

**References**

Allport, G. (1954). The nature of prejudice. Reading, MA: Addison-Wesley.
Combs, A. (1965). *The professional education of teachers.* Boston, MA: Allyn and Bacon.
Cushner, K., McClelland, A., & Safford, P. (2003). *Human diversity in education: An integrative approach* (4th Ed.) Boston, MA: McGraw Hill.

---

**Reflection/Discussion Items**
1. What has been your previous experience working in and with groups?

2. If you enjoyed it, process why and discuss it with a small group?

3. If you disliked it, process and discuss it with a small group?
---

# ROLES AND RESPONSIBILITIES OF GROUP MEMBERS

1. *All members of the group share responsibility for the group*. Identify with the group and its goals; if the group fails it's your fault – not the "group's" fault.

2. *The group should always make decisions*. They are not made by the leader, any individual, or any clique. Rotate the leadership and other roles. The group should decide all important policies.

3. *Use methods that will allow as many as possible of the group to participate*. Let the group discuss frequently in subgroups to bring out individual opinions by asking frequent questions of group members. Don't force the chair to do all the work. If there is a silent member in the group, try to involve that person. Likewise, if there is a dominating member, sidetrack the talkative one by interrupting when that person takes a breath or directing a question to another member of the group.

4. *Listen critically and thoughtfully to others*. Try hard to get the other person's point of view and see what experience and thinking it rests on. See if you can learn from that person. Perspective taking is valuable.

5. *Don't monopolize the discussion*. Make your point in a few words. Give others a chance.

6. *Don't let the discussion get away from you*. If you don't understand where it is going, say so. Ask for examples, cases, and illustrations until you really understand.

7. *Group members should be conscious of the importance of the roles they play in the group*. Study the different roles that people can play, analyze the roles you play, consciously play roles that are helpful to group progress.

8. *Rotate roles within your group*. The same person should not always be the chair or recorder.

9. *Analyze and utilize culture*. Cultural perspectives are always present in the group. Seek first to understand others and their perspectives and then seek to be understood.

10. *If you need assistance ask.* If you think the group is bogged down or you need some assistance, ask your professor.

# GROUP EXPECTATIONS

Reflection items for you and your future groups.
1. Things I would like to understand better about the groups in which I work or with whom I associate.

2. Things I would like to learn how to do better in various groups.

3. Feelings I have in some groups that I would like to change or improve.

4. Why do I remain silent in some group situations?

5. Why do I talk a lot in some group situations?

6. What cultural factors impact groups?

7. What other items about groups is important or concerns you?

# SECTION III

# ANALYZING CULTURE AND SOCIETY

***Rationale***: An important component of human relations in a multicultural society is an understanding of the context in which human interaction takes place. In order to assist in the development of a multicultural society in the broader objective of respecting human diversity and personal rights, the parameters of American society are explored, including its institutions and the hierarchical structure of the existing socioeconomic levels. Given this context, the student is assisted in better understanding the structure of the society in which he/she lives, his/her role in the dominant society, and an awareness of the forces shaping his/her identity. Educators also need to be aware of how schools, as institutions for the transmission of culture, reflect the power structure of the dominant society and how they can also be agents of change. Reflection is a significant component for understanding actions.

### *Objectives*
1. To be able to use a models to analyze the dominant society (understand ups and downs).
2. To demonstrate an understanding of how the interrelationships of people impact individual behavior.
3. To show and explain how the dominant society perpetuates itself through the educational institution.
4. To describe the cultural elements that impact an individual in their life.
5. To be able to define and explain the relevance of terms and concepts relating to the analysis of the dominant society.
6. To understand the social formation of categories and the intersection of variables.
7. To describe how schools can become agents of change.
8. To explore reflective practice.

# KNOWLEDGE BASES FOR DIVERSITY

A knowledge base on theory, research, and practice is a grounding to enable individuals to better understand and teach multicultural populations (Smith, 2000-2001). A knowledge base consists of theory, research, and practice whose aim is to provide a better model for application to each area of teaching and learning. When these are in place according to Smith, (2000-2001) teachers and other school personnel will be more effective in meeting the needs of diverse student populations. Diversity in this case refers to learners who are linguistically and culturally different as well as those who are similar to the norm in any learning environment.

The following fifteen knowledge bases were identified by Smith (1998) and (Smith, 2000-2001). As you read these assess your level of knowledge and think about ways you can improve your knowledge base in the others.

1. Foundations of Multicultural Education
2. Sociocultural Contexts of Human Growth and Development in Marginalized Ethnic and Racial Cultures
3. Cultural and Cognitive Learning Style Theory and Research
4. Language, Communication, and Interactional Styles of Marginalized Cultures
5. Essential Elements of Cultures
6. Principles of Culturally Responsive Teaching and Culturally Responsive Curriculum Development
7. Effective Strategies for Teaching Minority Students (those who are other than the prevailing school culture)
8. Foundations of Racism (add other "isms" such as sexism, heterosexism, etc.)
9. Effects of Policy and Practice on Culture, Race, Class, Gender, and Other Categories of Diversity
10. Culturally Responsive Diagnosis, Measurement, and Assessment
11. Sociocultural Influences on Subject-Specific Learning
12. Gender and Sexual Orientation
13. Experiential Knowledge
14. Foundations of Identifying and Teaching Special Needs Students (Exceptionality)
15. Foundations of International and Global Education

There is a natural tendency of some people to skip this first fourteen and look only at number fifteen, which can be a classic avoidance technique. International and global education are important considerations as the world grow smaller each day however be sure you are competent in the others. It is often easier to protest what is happening in South America or establish pen pals in another country than to confront the areas of bias around us. The United States of America is comprised of numerous cultures and subcultures. As you read and progress through this book increase your knowledge base and assist others in doing the same. We all learn from each other and our experiences, although sometimes similar, are uniquely different. Extend and challenge yourself on your journey.

**References**

Smith, G. P. (1998). *Common sense about uncommon knowledge: The knowledge bases for diversity.* Washington, DC: American Association of Colleges for Teacher Education.

Smith, G. P (2000-2001). Relationships among knowledge bases for diversity in teacher education, critical pedagogy, critical inquiry, and story. Journal of Critical Inquiry Into Curriculum and Instruction 2(3) 26-30

| Reflection/Discussion Items |
| --- |
| 1. Think about your knowledge and background in these areas. Which ones are you comfortable with now? |
| 2. Which ones do you need more work on understanding and applying? |
| 3. What additional ones would you add? |

# REFLECTION

This section will highlight the use of reflective practice in the promotion of social justice and educational equity. In order to accomplish this teacher educators will share the lens of race, class, gender, and other intersecting variables with their perspectives as it impacts learners. The goal is to develop educators with solid pedagogical foundations who are effective reflective practitioners and culturally responsible professional educators. In order to become an effective teacher, students must understand their own experiences, thoughts, and feelings surrounding those experiences. This will enable the integration of critical, reflective thinking within and across courses to facilitate movement toward becoming culturally responsible professionals.

A key element for successful critical reflection is the identification of a specific process involving the social hierarchy. These processes include the use of perceptions, assumptions, experiences, attributions, and reflections. All participants need to identify and/or establish a baseline for later comparison. They must identify the perceptions and initial assumptions they bring to any situation. Since education is neither apolitical nor neutral it is important to draw the comparison to the concept of Liberating Education by Paulo Freire. This encourages students to take risks, be curious, and ask questions. The critical reflection can occur either in writing or by sharing in a trusted community the new awareness gained through this process. Structured questions are of greatest benefit in this part of the process.

**What is Reflection?**
Reflection is one of the many teaching strategies that can be successfully utilized in courses on topics such as multicultural education. Reflection is critical step in understanding actions. It is especially crucial in assisting persons to function in a multicultural society through understanding issues and thinking critically. Three types of reflection that have been identified as crucial in the research are anticipatory reflection, reflection in action, and reflection on action (Loughran, 1996).

Anticipatory reflection is attempting to make decisions while predicting what a situation will demand prior to its actual occurrence. In reflection-in-action, the individual recognizes a problem, is able to "name" what needs to be addressed, and frames the context in which it will be attended to. This is an important process since many decisions are non-logical processes. Reflection-in-action occurs as skillful judgments, decisions, and actions are undertaken spontaneously, often without being able to state the rules or procedures followed. One example is an athlete or performer who has a successful performance and responds with the statement, "I was in the groove." Although it is often difficult to make it verbally explicit, by observing and reflecting on actions it may be able to make a description of the tacit knowledge implicit in the acts. It must be remembered that descriptions of knowledge-in-action are always constructions and as such they are attempts to put into explicit, symbolic form a kind of intelligence that begins by being unspoken and spontaneous. Constructions are often based upon cultural reality, which is socially developed based upon personal development.

Descriptions most often are conjectures therefore it is beneficial to examine those actions in light of current developments. Knowing-in-action is dynamic, and facts, procedures, rules, and theories are static. Knowledge-in-action is revealed when we have learned to do something and we can execute smooth sequences of activity, recognition, decision, and adjustment without real conscious thought. In reflection-in-action, the individual recognizes a problem, is able to "name" what needs to be addressed, and frames the context in which it will be attended to. This process of problem setting is fundamental to reflection.

Reflection on action occurs after an experience. Looking back on experience, or retrospective reflection, offers opportunities to make better sense of past experiences and to develop new or deeper understandings of that situation. A useful perspective on reflective practice in education emphasizes learning by doing and coaching or mentoring. These concepts focus on promoting proficiency in reflection-in-action through learning to recognize good practice, building images of competence, and thinking while acting. The use of dialogue among teachers and prospective teachers is encouraged to improve proficiencies. It is important to consider current research while learning applications under the tutelage of a professional. These three types of reflection and related issues are in the following Table 1 Types of Reflection and Related Issues.

**Table 1 Types of Reflection and Related Issues**

**Anticipatory Reflection**
Looking forward to or foreseeing what is about to happen.

Potential errors
1. Inadequately assessing impact or lack of impact upon learning strategies to objectives.
2. Unforeseen events will disrupt or change course of actions.
3. Lack of awareness or understanding of cultural variables *.
4. Others

**Reflection In Action**
Recognizing what is presently occurring (success/failure) while in the course of taking some form of action.

Potential errors
1. There are intuitive elements in action whereby people may not be able to explain actions and events.
2. May need to stop and take extra time to process as not all people process at same rate.
3. May be an immediacy of events that only allow for reactions and not processing.
4. Lack of awareness or understanding of cultural variables *.
5. Others

**Reflection On Action**
Recognizing what has transpired (success/failure) after taking some form of action.

Potential errors
1. Events may be indescribable (intuitive knowing).
2. Inability to recognize success or failure in a situation (metacognition).
3, Others

**Issues**
These are common to all three types of reflection
1. Time element may not allow for reflection.
2. Complexity of an issue takes time for analysis and may interrupt smooth flow of events.
3. Interruptions impede reflection.
4. Rewards and punishments within systems create differential focus.
5. Lack of control over some goals or objectives within bureaucracy.
6. Lack of awareness or understanding of cultural variables *.
7. Others

*Cultural Variables are often referred to as elements of culture or intersecting variables.

This model is especially useful in courses such as multicultural education or social justice. Teachers and prospective teachers are expected to be able to reflect upon why they make certain choices of practice and determine how institutional, social, and historical factors may constrain or influence their choices. They are asked to thoughtfully examine how the context and cultural elements influences teaching and learning. Moral and ethical criteria are now, or should be, incorporated into the discourse about practical action where the central questions ask which educational goals, experiences, and activities lead toward forms of life which are mediated by concerns for justice and equity. Critical reflection "involves questioning that which is otherwise taken for granted and involves looking for unarticulated assumptions and seeing from new perspectives.

**Role of Reflection**
Reflection is critical in understanding actions and issues. A central role of teacher educators is to understand strategies that examine judgments, actions, and decisions people undertake spontaneously without understanding their cultural constructions. Many decisions are non-logical processes such as knowledge-in-action which occurs as skillful judgments, decisions, and actions we undertake spontaneously, without being able to state the rules or procedures we follow. Although it is often difficult to make it verbally explicit, by observing and reflecting on our actions we may be able to make a description of the tacit knowledge implicit in the acts. It must be remembered that our descriptions of knowledge-in-action are always constructions and as such they are attempts to put into explicit, symbolic form a kind of intelligence that begins by being tacit and spontaneous. Constructions are often based upon our own cultural reality, which is socially developed based upon personal interactions. Our descriptions are conjectures; therefore, it is beneficial to examine those actions in light of current developments. Knowledge-in-action is revealed when we have learned to do something and we can execute smooth sequences of activity, recognition, decision, and adjustment without real conscious thought.

In reflection-in-action, the individual recognizes a problem, is able to "name" what needs to be addressed, and "frames" the context in which it will be attended to. This process of problem setting is fundamental to reflection. Reflection on action occurs after an experience. Looking back on experience, or retrospective reflection, offers opportunities to make better sense of past experiences and to develop new or deeper understandings of that situation.

A useful perspective on reflective practice in education emphasizes learning by doing and coaching or mentoring. These concepts focus on promoting proficiency in reflection-in-action through learning to recognize good practice, building images of competence, and thinking while acting. The use of dialogue among teachers and prospective teachers is encouraged to improve proficiencies. It is important to consider current research while learning applications under the tutelage of a professional. As noted this is especially useful in courses such as multicultural education. Teachers and prospective teachers are expected to be able to reflect upon why they make certain choices of practice and determine how institutional, social, and historical factors may constrain or influence their choices.

Critical reflection involves questioning that which is otherwise taken for granted and involves looking for unarticulated assumptions and seeing from new perspectives. The presenters will share models that are useful in teaching courses and conducting this type of action research.

**Research on Reflection**
The first perspective on reflective inquiry focuses exclusively on teaching strategies and does not examine the content, context, and goals of teaching. Donald Cruickshank's (1987) concept of a reflective teaching model is an example of this perspective. Cruickshank describes reflective teaching as an opportunity to apply principles and theories of teaching and learning developed through scientific inquiry to real situations. (Adler, 1994, p.52) In his initial work, preservice and inservice teachers taught a predetermined "content-free" lesson to a small group of peers. The teachers then assessed the extent to which the participants had learned. They determined the effectiveness of their teaching through discussion with participants. The focus of this kind of reflective inquiry is on how well teachers replicate teaching behaviors deemed effective by empirical research. It is assumed that such reflection will enable teachers to improve their teaching skills in the future. (p.52) Freire (1970) defines praxis as connecting theory with reflection and action. He further examines this as a more inclusive and expansive way to develop multiple perspectives and put that learning into action.

Davidman & Davidman (2001) and Nieto (2001) state that learning occurs when based on the real life experiences of the students. This moves from content knowledge to application and reflection upon the applications, which are also underlying elements of critical pedagogy. Multicultural education ties this to the development of action for social justice.

Schön (1983, 1987) presents a perspective on the reflective practitioner as "one who can think while acting and thus can respond to the uncertainty, uniqueness, and conflict involved in the situations in which professionals practice" (Adler, 1994, p.52). Schön's concepts of reflection are framed around tacit knowledge in action and reflection. Schön and vanManen (1991) present three types of reflection: anticipatory reflection, reflection in action, and reflection on action.

Schön (1987) describes tacit knowledge as a process of recognition or appreciation. He states that in using tacit knowledge, "we are usually aware of no antecedent reasoning" (p. 23). He suggests that "the immediacy of our recognition" suggest that an elaborate reasoning process did not occur (p. 23). Tacit knowledge can take the form of normative judgements. Schön contends that "in the very act by which we recognize something, we also perceive it as 'right' or 'wrong'" (p. 23). People must be able to view issues and events from multiple perspectives or the reflective processes become extremely limited. Freire (1985) insists that people must have the ability or permission to take risks, and question so they can develop their own answers in order to be liberated. Without the ability to develop perspective taking skills reflection is severely limited to a repetition of a monocultural perspective.

Knowledge-in-action refers to "the sorts of know-how we reveal in our intelligent action – publicly observable, physical performances like riding a bicycle" (p. 25). The knowing is in the action and we reveal it by our spontaneous, skillful execution of the performance (p. 25). A central question to consider is how do educators know if learners have applied or can actually apply the material.

Chester Barnard (1938/1968) describes non-logical processes such as knowledge-in-action as "skillful judgements, decisions, and actions we undertake spontaneously, without being able to state the rules or procedures we follow" (in Schön, 1983, p. 24). Although it is often difficult to make it verbally explicit, Schön suggests that "by observing and reflecting on our actions" one may be able to make a description of the tacit knowledge implicit in the acts (p. 25). He contends, however, that our descriptions of knowledge-in-action are always constructions. "They are always attempts to put into explicit, symbolic form a kind of intelligence that begins by being tacit and spontaneous.

An athlete or performer may successfully accomplish a task but upon questioning be unable to explain why they were successful. Their descriptions are in reality conjectures. For knowing-in-action is dynamic, and 'facts,' 'procedures,' 'rules,' and 'theories' are static" (p. 25). Knowledge-in-action is revealed when we have learned to do something and we can execute smooth sequences of activity, recognition, decision, and adjustment without real thought (p. 26).

In reflection-in-action, the individual recognizes a problem, is able to "name" what needs to be addressed, and "frames" the context in which it will be attended to (Schön, 1983, p. 40). This process of problem setting is integral to reflection according to Schön.

Reflection on action occurs after an experience. "Looking back on experience, or retrospective reflection, offers opportunities to make better sense of past experiences and to develop new or deeper understandings of that situation" (Loughran, 1995, p. 13).

Schön's perspective on reflective practice in education emphasizes learning by doing and coaching (Adler, 1994, p. 53). His concepts focus on promoting proficiency in reflection-in-action through learning to recognize good practice, building images of competence, and thinking while acting. He encourages the use of dialogue among teachers in improving proficiencies. Schön asserts, "professional knowledge, in the sense of knowledge developed through research, is secondary," one learns by doing under the "tutelage of experienced practitioners" (Schön, 1987, p. 16).

The following Table 2 Model of Reflective Practice demonstrates basic elements of the types of reflection and rudimentary thought process at each level. (See Table 2)

Table 2 Model of Reflective Practice*

| *Anticipatory Reflection* | *Reflection in Action* | *Reflection on Action* |
|---|---|---|
| Type of students | **Monitor class** | **Evaluations** |
| Prior knowledge | Adjust as necessary | Application of evaluations |
| Goals and Objectives | **Awareness of actions** | Honesty of evaluators |
| Strategies to be utilized | | Varieties of evaluations |
| **Examples** | | |
| Teacher | Teacher | Teacher |
| Assign paper | Clarify process as it unfolds | Evaluate outcome (assign grades) Accept or assign re-write after discussion |
| **Student** | **Student** | **Student** |
| Read about and listen to assignment | Ask for clarifications and work on assignment, complete and turn in | Evaluate outcome (grade received) Accept or re-write if an options |

This is not a linear process. Looping occurs throughout the model as people question actions and often seek clarification. Another key element to remember is that not all people progress at all let alone at similar rates so some are unable to move to an accurate reflection on action. If as Huber states (2002), we do not have a culturally responsive pedagogy and understand knowledge bases for diversity we miss crucial cultural elements in the teaching and learning process.

**Levels of Reflection**

Zeichner (1987) identifies three levels of reflection, which are technical, reflectivity, and critical reflection. He draws on the work of Schön (1983) and Tom (1985) in distinguishing the levels. At the technical level, "the dominant concern is the efficient and effective application of educational knowledge for the purposes of attaining ends which are accepted as given. At this level, neither the ends nor the institutional contexts of the classroom, school, community, and society are treated as problematic" (p. 24). It is an examination of the effectiveness of teaching strategies in enabling students to achieve a given set of objectives (Adler, 1994, p. 53).

The second level of reflectivity "places teaching within its situational and institutional contexts. Teachers are expected to be able to reflect upon why they make certain choices of practice" and determine "how institutional, social, and historical factors may constrain or influence their choices." They are being asked to thoughtfully examine how context influences teaching and learning (Adler, 1994, p. 53).

Critical reflection is the third level. Zeichner (1987) suggests that moral and ethical criteria are now incorporated into the discourse about practical action (p. 25). "At this level the central questions ask which educational goals, experiences, and activities lead toward forms of life which are mediated by concerns for justice, equity, and concrete fulfillment, and whether the current arrangements serve important human needs and satisfy important human purposes" (Tom, 1985 and Zeichner & Liston, 1987, p. 25). In critical reflection, the ends and means of teaching and the surrounding contexts are viewed as "as value-governed selections from a larger universe of possibilities" (p. 25). Critical reflection "involves questioning that which is otherwise taken for granted and involves looking for unarticulated assumptions and seeing from new perspectives" (Adler, 1994, p. 54). This is also referred to as a step in the movement toward critical pedagogy, which is based on the experiences and viewpoints of the individuals utilizing the process according to Nieto (2001). See table 3 Levels of Reflection outlines basic functions for each of the levels.

**Table 3 Levels of Reflection**

| |
|---|
| **Technical reflection** |
| Application of educational knowledge only |
| Effectiveness in meeting goals and objectives without question |
| |
| **Reflective reflection** |
| Examining situational, contextual and institutional factors |
| Understanding what constraints are placed on education and why |
| |
| **Critical reflection** |
| Utilizing a framework based on intersecting cultural variables |
| Examining moral and ethical criteria in the educational process |
| Demonstrating a concern for justice and equity |

Critical reflection can and should serve as an overlay to anticipatory reflection, reflection in action and reflection on action. When applied to the field of teacher education examples can be drawn from the principles of culturally relevant teaching and the critical perspective which sees school functioning in order to serve the dominant members of the society (Pai & Adler, 1977). The research of Ladson-Billings (1995) describes some of the basic principles of culturally relevant teaching. First students must experience academic success, which is essential in developing positive self-esteem. Second, students must develop cultural competence. This is best accomplished by using the student's home culture as a vehicle for learning. And third, students must develop a sense of critical consciousness, which is related to critical reflection. This is also critical culturally responsive pedagogy described by Huber (2002).

Power relations must be addressed for it is the power holders who most often determine the options presented to schools and students. As a result schools serve the role of reproducing the dominant culture. Critical reflection can be a tool to assist teachers in the continuing need to question what is often taken for granted if it is infused with an understanding of cultural variables and how they intersect to impact each and every one of us. These processes can result in self-reflection, critical interrogation, knowledge deconstruction, critical reflection, knowledge reconstruction, meta-cognition, and development of multiple perspectives rather than a one best way approach.

As Dinkelman (2003) states, reflection and self-study become powerful tools in the preparation of teachers. It is essential to determine which techniques work best and why if we strive to create in teachers the ability to critically reflect.

**Summary and Applications**
Successful teachers are those who engage students in meaningful activities whereby students are empowered through studying their own culture and subsequent interactions. They are also empowered by developing an understanding of other cultures how they intersect to form many intricacies in the knowledge construction process.

Questions to consider in reflection upon learning and teaching.
1. Do the materials build a natural progression in relation to identified course outcomes and have learners critically reflecting upon knowledge-in-action?
2. Are the activities sufficient to support the learning of desired outcomes and have the learners critically reflecting upon knowledge-on-action?
3. Are the activities and other course materials based on situational contexts and likely to be of interest to the learners?
4. Do the activities build an understanding of the cultural content and concepts embedded within the course (understanding intersecting variables and QLE)?
5. How are situational cultural contexts utilized to promote positive applications for all students?
6. Are the readings and other assignments integrated and accurately assessed?
7. Can the learning be sufficiently assessed in line with stated course outcomes?

8. Does the course utilize a holistic curriculum with quality learning experiences for all based on situation contexts?
9. Does the course guide the students into action for social justice and help them to develop an ability to apply the lens of cultural indicators (intersecting variables)?
10. Others

Examples of Activities/Techniques

These are examples of assignments that can be integrated into any class. We have found them especially useful in the development of critically reflective individuals who are on a journey to become or to continue to grow in their understanding of multicultural education. These can be used at different points in a course and can be modified to suit any specific needs of the course. It is an ongoing process.

1. Write and discuss

Placing a question on the board for learners prior to class enables them to think about (recall, question and apply information) the assigned readings and questions for that class period or a continuation of the discussion from a previous class. In order to facilitate processing of the individual's ideas, the learners are asked to write down a brief answer/response to the question and make applications from their context. They are then placed in dyads and asked to discuss their answers and take into consideration the answers of the other person. They are then placed in quads and asked to discuss their answers and take into consideration those of all members of their group. Then some elements are discussed in the entire large group and tied into the discussion topic for the day.

2. Writing reactions to readings enables the learners to critically question previously held beliefs and to personalize and apply multiple perspectives to the materials and their learning.

3. Culture paper

Writing a culture paper forces the learners to examine their own cultural frames and reflect on their personal realities in relation to the formation of the mainstream worldview in the United States of America. It also has them examine power relationships and the cultural socialization of race, gender, class, etc as it applies to them and their lives and schools.

4. Interviews

Conducting an interview with a person who self-identifies as a member of a different socially constructed racial/ethnic category and reflecting on the discussion topics enables the learners to engage in a productive dialogue with members of the community. The focus is on discussing similar and different perceptions of school based experiences to have the participants develop an understanding of common assumptions that are often made. (These are designed to be highly structured initially and free flowing after that point depending on the person they are interviewing.) Upon completion of the interview and completing a written report the students are assigned to small groups and asked to verbally share their learning.

5. Case studies/Vignettes

Reading and discussing case studies/vignettes allows the learners to apply the material as they discuss their perceptions and hear options from others. Depending upon the structure of the course a case study could be written while conducting and observation. If this is used it is often helpful to have more than one person conducting a written evaluation on the same subject so elements of attribution can be addressed as they will invariably define behavior differently.

6. Worksheets and lesson plans

Worksheets, lesson plans, videos with worksheets, and other similar course assignments force the learners to assemble their thoughts on paper and critically reflect on perceptions as they are shared with others.

7. Presentations and reflection after presentations

Reflecting upon the group presentation and writing an individual assessment that no one except the instructor will view after its completion allows the learner to critically evaluate (reflection-on-action) the effectiveness of their project group, group presentation, and individual contribution. There must be an understanding that no one except for the instructor will read the reflection. This allows for a more honest response.

**Conclusion**
Examining the ongoing process through the use of critical reflection is invaluable for students and teachers alike. For students it helps them see the value in critical reflection and the growth and development that can occur over one term. It also helps to set the stage for development of the understanding that the process is always ongoing and is never finished. Following up on this in other classes, in which the students are enrolled if possible, is a continuation of the developmental process for them and the instructor.

The process is both conscious and unconscious as Zozakiewcz, Writer, and Chávez Chávez (2002) speak to in their article. This is a process that by its very nature needs to be developmental in order to move from the more mechanistic technical reflection to the level of critical reflection. It is beneficial to assist in the process of moving the unconscious to the conscious through critical reflection. And as Nieto (2001) states, the curriculum and pattern of instruction is considered critical pedagogy when among other things, the learning process moves from knowledge to reflection in action. To be more fully understood items should be written down and then discussed in diverse groups.

The ability of teachers to scrutinize their practice according to National Board for Professional Teaching Standards (1999) is a crucial element for improvement. They (NBPT) rely heavily on this ability to analyze their practice and to reflect on what might improve their teaching in the certification process. The National Board Certification process requires intense self-reflection and analysis of one's own practice. And purposes of instruction, reflections on what occurred support candidates' works, and the effectiveness of the instruction (NBPT).

For the instructor the ongoing process clearly demonstrates the growth some students have made and in other cases may in fact suggest changes that are necessary for the instructor make in the course in order to be more effective. Critical reflection is a vital process in which to engage so that productivity in meeting stated course outcomes could be enhanced. There is much work to be done in the continual process of critical reflection to transform practice.

**References**
Adler, S. (1994). *Reflective practice and teacher education.* Washington D.C.: National Council for the Social Studies. (ERIC Document Reproduction Service No. ED 3733014).
Banks, J. & Banks, C.M. (2001). *Multicultural education: Issues and perspectives.* Needham Heights, MA: Allyn and Bacon.
Brookfield, S. (1995). *Becoming a critically reflective teacher.* San Francisco, CA: Jossey-Bass.
Canning, C. (1991). What teachers say about reflection. *Educational Leadership,* 8(6), 18-21.
Cruickshank, D. (1987) *Reflective teaching: The preparation of students of teaching.* Reston, VA: Association of Teacher Educators.
Davidman, D. & Davidman, P. (2001). *Teaching with a multicultural perspective: a practical guide, 3$^{rd}$ edition.* New York: Longman.
Delpit, L. (1995). *Other people's children.* New York: New Press.
Dewey, J. (1933). *How we think: A restatement of the relation of reflective thinking to the educative process.* Chicago: D.C. Heath.
Dindelman, T. (2003). Self-study in teacher education: A means and ends tool for promoting reflective teaching. *Journal of Teacher Education,* 54(1), 6-18.
Freire, P. (1970). *Pedagogy of the oppressed.* New York: Seabury Press.
Freire, P. (1985). *The politics of education: Culture, power, and liberation.* South Hadley, MA: Bergin & Garvey.
Grant, C.A. & Zeichner, K. (1984). On becoming a reflective teacher. In *Preparing for reflective teaching,* edited by C.A. Grant. Boston: Allyn and Bacon.
Huber, T. (2002). *Quality learning experiences for all students.* San Francisco: Caddo Gap.
Ladson-Billings, G. (1995). "But that's just good teaching!" The case for culturally relevant pedagogy. *Theory Into Practice,* 34(3), 161-165.

Loughran, J. (1996). *Developing reflective practice: Learning about teaching and learning through modeling.* London: Falmer.

National Board for Professional Teaching Standards (1999). *What teachers should know and be able to do.* Washington, DC: Author.

Nieto, S. (2001) *Affirming diversity: The sociopolitical context of multicultural education.* New York: Longman.

Pai, Y. & Adler, S. (1977). *Cultural foundations of education, 2nd ed.* Columbus, OH: Prentice Hall.

Schön, D. (1983). *Educating the reflective practitioner toward a new design for teaching and learning in the professions.* San Francisco, CA: Jossey-Bass.

Schön, D. (1983). *The reflective practitioner.* New York: Basic Books.

Shade, B.J. (Ed.). (1989). *Culture, style, and the educative process.* Springfield, IL: Charles C. Thomas.

Tom, A. (1985). Inquiry into inquiry-oriented teacher education. *Journal of Teacher Education,* 36(5), 35-44.

Zeichner, K. & Liston, D. (1987). Teaching students to reflect. *Harvard Educational Review*, 57(1), 23-47.

Zozakiewcz, C. Writer, J. & Chávez Chávez, R. (2002). Conscious and unconscious multicultural practices of new teachers: Rethinking teacher education as a reflective circle. In *Research on Preparing Teachers Who Can Meet the Needs of All Students: Teacher Education Yearbook XI* p9-30, edited by J. Rainer Dangel & E. M. Guyton. Dubuque, IA: Kendall/Hunt.

---

**Reflection/Discussion Items**

1. Reflect on knowledge bases and this section on reflection and discuss how they apply to you and your profession.

2. Which knowledge bases for diversity are you comfortable in applying to education?

3. Which knowledge bases will you need to work on in order to become more proficient in education?

4. How will you approach the topic and task?

5. What can others do to assist you in this process?

6. Which level of reflection are you most confident in?

7. How can you maximize your potential in all areas of use of reflection?

8. What other questions or observations do you have?

# WHAT'S THE NAME OF THE GAME

Have you ever heard two European males having an excited conversation in their native language? Have you ever noticed an Asian Indian woman in a long sari walking down the street? Perhaps you have seen someone in flowing robes. Or maybe you have seen an Amish couple riding in a horse-drawn buggy along a country road. If you have, can you remember how you felt or what you thought? Were you curious? Did you stare? Were you a bit frightened and eager to hurry away?

First impressions of people who are different from you are very important. Curiosity and fear are two common reactions to strangers and these first impressions may be a strong influence on how you judge them. But are first impressions the best way to judge something or someone new? Usually they are based on what is apparent only on the outside. Stereotypes are likely to result from judgments made about people based only on first impressions. You do not like it when you, your school, or your friends are judged on the basis of one incident or what someone else says. You want people to understand you before they make a judgment on you.

By learning more about other people and the way they live, you can understand them better. But you may still misunderstand people with different cultures if you fail to recognize your own ethnocentrism. Most people think that their culture's way of doing things is the best, most logical, most beautiful, etc. Many people in the United States might think that people who do not live in a modern life full of cars, appliances, and factories are "backward." However, those same people may consider Americans backward because they manufacture the tools of their own destruction. Many cultures might judge the way people in the United States put old people in nursing homes as cruel and uncivilized.

When people are ethnocentric, they not only overlook the weaknesses of their own culture; they also judge all other cultures by their own standards. Sports can be used to illustrate how this can cause real problems. Would anyone, for instance, expect a football player to hit home runs? Is it fair to judge the player's ability by the rules of another game? In the same way it is unfair to judge another culture by the standards of your culture because each has its own unique set of rules, or values.

As you read about other people and cultures in this course, try to remember this idea. Work to minimize your stereotyped thinking and ethnocentrism and maximize your understanding of other people and why they do the things they do. For it is only when you have learned the name of the game that you can know what rules apply.

1. Define the following terms in your own words:

    *Ethnocentrism*_____
    _____

    *Culture*_____
    _____

    *Stereotype*_____
    _____


2. What is meant by the statement, "It is only when you have learned the name of the game that you can know what rules to apply?" _____
    _____

# THE NAME OF THE GAME EXERCISE

Read the statements below. Mark those statements that are ethnocentric with an E (evaluative). Mark those that are a stereotype (an exaggeration) with a S. Mark those that are statements of fact with an F (true or mostly true).

_____ 1. Many groups of people live on the earth today.

_____ 2. People in India are poor, starving, and have big families.

_____ 3. All people, everywhere in the world, raise their children to be like themselves.

_____ 4. The Eastern religions of Buddhism and Hinduism are not popular in the West.

_____ 5. The family is the primary social group in most cultures.

_____ 6. It's uncivilized to eat raw fish.

_____ 7. The United States government should send volunteers to help other countries improve their culture.

_____ 8. Japanese and Chinese cultures are the same.

_____ 9. Americans are richer and better educated than people in other cultures are.

_____ 10. Cultures are in the process of constant change.

_____ 11. Southern Europeans are basically lazy people.

_____ 12. Each culture on earth is different from all other cultures.

_____ 13. The United States is the greatest country in the world.

_____ 14. You can always tell Scandinavians by their blond hair and blue eyes.

_____ 15. All cultures have ways of expressing artistic feelings.

_____ 16. Latin Americans put off until tomorrow what they could do today.

_____ 17. All cultures have standards about what is right and wrong.

_____ 18. People in other countries should learn English in order to communicate on an international level.

_____ 19. Russians are short, stocky people with wide faces.

_____ 20. Africans live in small tribal villages and celebrate festivals with exotic dances.

# CULTURE AND ITS IMPACT ON EDUCATION

According to Nance & Dixon, (1991) race and schooling are two of the most critical social issues in our society. As educators in community education, K-12, and colleges/universities, we have an intellectual and ethical responsibility to provide people with the most current and accurate information possible. This should result in the move toward a more inclusive program. A more inclusive community education program will have a number of important effects on community members. Kerns (1989) states that all communities of tomorrow will have access to a comprehensive lifelong learning system. It will expand their worldview by exposing them to the life experiences of people both similar to, and different from themselves. It will make them more cognizant of culture, ethnicity, social class, and gender as important variables for everyday life. It will also make community members aware of the significant contributions by individuals and groups who have been omitted from or underrepresented in the American mainstream, as well as provide them the skills to recognize and deal with dehumanizing bias, prejudice, and discrimination (Tiedt & Tiedt, 2002). This will help students to benefit from an increased appreciation of diversity in their current and future roles as parents, teachers, community leaders, co-workers, employers, and citizens. This should facilitate the changes in the community necessary to provide increased access for all.

Another consideration of this model would be to have advisory councils or committees would be made up of representatives from community organizations, parents, community members, teachers, social workers, counselors or psychologists who would meet on a regular basis to discuss any problems or concerns that need to be addressed. This should help the schools to be more sensitive to community concerns, which in turn translates into more community ownership of schools and the educational process. When this occurs you will find increased participation and a decrease in dropouts from our traditional programs. If we look at models somewhat similar to this in some of the European countries, we find a higher rate of success for all students, which should be a model vision.

As teachers and community leaders we have an intellectual and ethical responsibility to provide our students with the most current and accurate information available. A more inclusive education will have a number of important effects on students. It will expand their worldview by exposing them to the life experiences of people both similar to, and different from themselves. It will make them more cognizant of culture, ethnicity, and gender as important variables for everyday life. It will also make students aware of the significant contributions of members of groups who have been omitted from the 'American mainstream', as well as provide them the skills to recognize and deal with dehumanizing bias, prejudice, and discrimination.

Minnesota has also been in the national forefront with legislation and programming in community education. This extends education from the belief in the formal K-12 classroom to the entire community. This helps to build communities and helps students to benefit from an increased appreciation of diversity in any of their future roles as parents, teachers, community leaders, co-workers, employers, and citizens. This also should facilitate an awareness of and appreciation for the positive community climate necessary to ensure ongoing change.

In order to meet this goal it is best to fully integrate information about women, people of color,, and other types of intersecting variables into traditional and non-traditional courses and onto advisory councils. This is necessary in order to achieve cultural balance, and to totally transform the entire curriculum to become community based and inclusive (Warring, 1991 b). Ideally, diversity can be appreciated with different cultural values and practices accorded validity and respect. The integration approach will provide more legitimacy for the inclusion of diversity throughout the entire curriculum in a multidisciplinary approach rather than the difference often noted with separate and distinct courses. When this is carried into social action this will lead to increased respect and empathy for the community and global concerns now being faced.

The goal of multicultural education is to change the structure of educational institutions to improve the chances for equal educational opportunity and academic and social achievement for all students (Banks, 2001). This is in concert with the community education philosophy.

**Goal Achievement**

Since the State of Minnesota requires all prospective teachers, administrators, counselors, social workers, community educators, and school personnel to take course work in "Human Relations", the Multicultural Gender-fair curriculum component for all school districts is a natural and necessary step. This needs to be evaluated regarding the significance of impact and if shown to be successful, be implemented in all institutions of higher learning which are the agencies offering the course work. This will undoubtedly lead to significant changes in the attitudes and behaviors of those persons who are employed in higher education, thus creating a change in the climate and curriculum in higher education as well as local community levels. This will in turn assist in the achievement of some societal goals such as:

1. reduce prejudice,
2. reduce discrimination,
3. provide equal opportunity, and
4. provide social justice.

When the climate changes, the number of community members accessing programs will also increase. This will ultimately lead to an increase in community participation in the educational enterprise. This is necessary to forming bridges with local communities.

**Culture and Values**

Within the next ten-twenty years, 40-60 percent of the students attending public schools in the United States will be non-European Americans (Hodgkinson, 2002). They will be students from various ethnic and cultural backgrounds including people from a variety of specific groups within the broader categories of African-Americans, American-Indians, Asian-Americans, Hispanic/Latino(a)-Americans, and others. Before our educators can begin to teach, we must first have at least a basic understanding of the student's ethnicity and culture. Otherwise, the expectations will be invalid and we will be guilty of ethnocentrism and enculturation (Warring 1991 b). In addition to these challenges, educators should consider the many educational opportunities of working with an increasingly diverse population of students.

The first step, however, is for all educators to learn about their students' cultures and the community cultural influences on their education. This should help broaden the definition of education to include all pertinent experiences occurring in and outside the confines of the 'formal' classroom structure. In many states students of color will comprise the majority of the student population. These demographic changes have brought both unique and diverse needs to America's colleges and universities, along with many opportunities.

Culture is a social system that represents an accumulation of beliefs, attitudes, habits, values, and practices that are a filter for groups of people. Culture is traditionally dispensed within the family structure of all groups. Generally speaking, there is a unity and shared togetherness experienced by many people who believe it is imperative to work for the good of the group. Common indicators include statements such as "A life well lived should be lived for the family and others in your clan and community".

Recognizing that there are many options, traditional cultures often promote a sense of group kinship. Students learn about this kinship from their parents/guardians, extended family and peers while they are growing up. They acquire a sense of cooperation within the community and work for the good of the group. There is a sharing and cooperative effort functioning in the lives of many cultural people. A person's status may be determined by the good he or she does for the family and other members of the community. This is a natural tenet of community education, which must be embraced to deal with a sense of community.

One cultural expectation that coincides with the group dynamics is that of sharing. This includes sharing food, ideas, knowledge, material wealth and time with others in the family, work place or school. And, it is further expected that others will reciprocate. Generally speaking, there is a unity and shared togetherness experienced by minority people who work for the good of the group (Warring, Hunter, & Zirpoli, 1992). For example, one can see this group oriented philosophy of American Indians, in this Ojibwe phrase "We honor a man for what he has done for the people rather than for what he has done for himself".

Similarly, Asian parents teach their children to think of themselves as part of the group. They put greater emphasis on teaching their children to be loyal to their group—whether family or nation—than on individual rights or responsibilities. Consider the Japanese value of working for the good of one's society, which is a long-term goal, similar to the American Indian philosophy of gaining honor by serving your people.

Personal dignity and pride are important elements to the Hispanic character. Sharing and helping others within the community are common interactions. Thus, Hispanic children are usually comfortable within cooperative learning environments and may perform poorly in situations demanding individual competition.

Personal dignity and pride are important elements to the Hispanic character. Sharing and helping others within the community are common interactions. Thus, Hispanic children are usually comfortable within cooperative learning environments and conversely, may perform poorly in situations demanding individual competition. This is a trait or quality not fully understood by most of the individualistic majority in our society. Here, mainstream values clash with many cultures and sub cultures.

Since an individualistic rather than a collective, cooperative learning environment exists in most institutions, the students must first unlearn or modify their own culturally sanctioned interactional and behavioral styles if they wish to be rewarded in the school context and subsequently achieve academic success. This is a very difficult choice for most students of color. What also occurs is an authoritarian power structure in most schools that must be modified.

The following are elements of examples of traditional cultures and interactions that often occur within and by them. They are not meant to stereotype, but are illustrated as options for discussion. It is often helpful to understand some cultural traits often associated with groups while remembering that all people are individuals and the intersection of variables causes an impact as well. As you read this keep in mind that even though there are some general traits that apply to groups of people we are all individuals with our own idiosyncrasies.

**African American Culture and Teaching**
(Based on assistance by and discussions with Dr. Kerry Dean Frank as well as other references.)
African Americans came to what is now the United States with the earliest European settlers and worked as indentured servants until they could purchase their freedom. All eventually became free and self-supporting. A significant number of free African Americans existed in the colonies prior to the creation of slavery. They had a highly developed and advanced civilization prior to this enslavement.

Despite persistent beliefs and many misunderstandings about African Americans, they were and are a diverse people. According to Marshall (2002) ethnic diversity was an inherent characteristic due to the varied diversified of their origin. It has been estimated that as many as 75-90 percent of Black Americans have White ancestors and about 25 percent have Native American ancestry (Tatum, 1997). Slavery in America was a unique institution designed to dehumanize Africans and enable whites to maximize profit as well as reinforce white supremacy. This institution maintained itself until after the Civil War when changes began sweeping the US. Thus, the culture of African Americans is an amalgamation of their African origins and the assimilation of various Anglo-European orientations to which they were exposed.

Some present day African Americans have entered the middle class, which has created social and economic variations along with other intersecting variables. The common bond still shared is the continuing experience of institutional racism and discrimination. This reinforces a sense of identity and peoplehood according to Banks (2003). With the current immigration from different portions of Africa terminology has once again been a crucial element. Preferences will range from African Americans to Blacks to citizens of the US. According to Salzman, et al (1996) African Americans who operate in a traditional manner are more likely to operate in certain ways. Some of these are listed here.

**African Americans are likely to:**
Look away while listening.
Stand close to others when talking.
Be reluctant to talk about family problems and personal relationships.
Prefer to work in groups

Place a high value on nonverbal communication.
Seek ways to express self-identity.
Be concerned with present more than the future goals.
Consider family and extended family as very important.
Be influenced by many adults within the family and extended family.
Consider Mother's role as the most significant in family.
Live in a female-headed household.
Consider elderly members of the community especially important and respected.
Consider religion an important part of life and the church minister as the most influential member of the community.
Embrace cultural norms if they are living in low SES conditions than if they live in middle or upper class conditions.
Believe that most individuals within the white culture do not understand or want to understand their culture.
Find it difficult to operate within predominantly Black settings if they grow up in white, middle-class settings.

Variations in how these characteristics are manifested depends in large measure on whether the person participates in the church or on the streets. Both of these institutions serve to instruct in addition to the family. These are not meant to stereotype, but are illustrated as options for discussion. It is helpful to understand some cultural traits often associated with groups while remembering that all people are individuals and the intersection of variables causes an impact as well. It is a challenge to become aware of factors that influence perceptions regarding content and process of learning. Popular culture must be understood and further evaluated to effectively teach students who are members of this racial and ethnic group. If teachers are unaware of cultural aspects they may inadvertently create situations that are not affirming.

A culturally responsive pedagogy builds on the premise that how people are expected to go about learning may differ across cultures. Cultural differences present both challenges and opportunities for teachers. To maximize learning opportunities, teachers must gain knowledge of the cultures represented in their classrooms and then translate this knowledge into instructional practice. Culturally responsive pedagogy alone is not enough to mediate the effect of historical inequity on involuntary minorities and methods by themselves do not suffice to advance their learning. A "humanizing pedagogy," advocates valuing the students' background knowledge, culture, and life experiences and creates contexts in which students and teachers share power. This power sharing and valuing of students' lives and cultures may provide a positive counterforce to the negative sociocultural experiences of students; it can enable them to see themselves as empowered within the context of school and allow them to retain pride in their cultural heritages.

According to Marshall (2002) it is crucial for teachers to be aware of their perceptions and expectations for students because these impact the decisions they make about content and pedagogy. Assess learning styles and use ones that foster involvement in the learning process. Maintain high expectations and work with students to achieve them. Make connections between the classroom and the community. These are a few of the ideas that will greatly enhance the learning of students who are part of this group. To assist in this process of understanding four of the predominant cultural/ethnic groups and some general traits are presented.

**Traditional Asian American Culture and Teaching**
Asians are one of the most diverse groups of people in the United States based on ethnic and national origin. As Asian Americans they have a highly diversified ethnic group and vary greatly in terms of cultural and physical characteristics (Banks, 2003). Although quite diverse they have had some different and similar experiences in the United States. They have often been called the Model Minority but this is a generalization that does not apply to all members of the group. There is tremendous economic, ethnic, and racial diversity within the Asian American community. This coupled with other intersecting variables adds to this diversity.

The history of immigration and the laws related to it form the basis for a complicated analysis of American thought regarding Asians. Person of Asian ancestry were negatively impacted by immigration legislation (Marshall, 2002). The study of Asian Americans should include early immigration from 1785 through immigration status and internment camps to the new elements of racism that began to occur in the 1980's shortly after the Vietnam War ended. The understanding and belief of teachers regarding immigration and refugees will directly impact their teaching and ability to work with students from these groups. Economic challenges and blame coupled with the state of affairs in the United States led to some nasty incidents.

When studying Asian Americans be sure to break down the analysis into different groups and examine the impact of intersecting variables as well. Remember that the generalizations presented to do not apply to all groups of Asian Americans, as they are one of the most diverse groups in the world and within the United States. Some of the traditional ways Asian Americans operate, according to Takaki (1998) are listed here.

**Traditional Asian Americans are likely to:**
Not shake hands with each other (women) or with men.
Consider the touching of strangers as inappropriate.
Consider eye-to-eye contact between strangers is considered shameful.
Smile or laugh to mask other emotions or avoid conflict.
Consider emotional restraint, formality, and politeness as essential for appropriate social behavior.
Show deference to others and try to be non-confrontational.
Hide emotional expressions and personal feelings as these are seen as a sign of immaturity.
Consider time as flexible and not hurry or consider it important to be punctual except in very important cases.
Consider family and extended family as very important.
Consider the behavior of an individual member of a family as a reflection of the entire family.
Respect learning and have high educational standards.
Be very modest.

Individuals within this group place a high value on family and will maintain both personal and family honor and status. There is a high respect for elders and a strong commitment to fulfill obligations. There is often a great deal of ritual in specific subgroups such as the Hmong community and the concept of harmony is an important value. These are not meant to stereotype, but are illustrated as options for discussion. It is helpful to understand some cultural traits often associated with groups while remembering that all people are individuals and the intersection of variables causes an impact as well. The diversity within this community has additional implications for teachers.

A wide range of variety will be seen in academic and verbal skills within this group. Teachers may also find a disparity between the culture of the home and school. Another factor inhibiting achievement is the belief that they are passive and uninvolved. This is a classic case of misunderstanding between cultures as nothing could be further from true. The reality is one of respect for educators and a belief in the authority of the educator. Another complicating variable is that of cultural difference as American schools often place a high value on individualism while many members of this group share a more collective cooperative orientation.

In order to be more successful when teaching students from this diverse group teachers should use culturally appropriate instruction A characteristic of this is making connections between the home and school culture. Having high expectations that are realistic and assisting in the development of a positive self-image are also extremely important.

**Hispanic/Latino(a) American Culture and Teaching**
The Hispanic/Latino/a group is the fastest growing ethnic group in the United States. The three major groups comprising a significant number of the members of this group in the United States are Mexican Americans, Puerto Ricans, and Cuban Americans. These diverse groups have significant cultural, racial, and other ethnic differences so they can not all be stereotyped together. Even though most of these groups share a past influenced by Spain, the Spanish occupation, and Spanish language, there are significant historical, racial, and cultural differences among them (Banks, 2003). When these are added to other intersecting variables the complexity of members of the group is extremely vast.

Even though members of these groups made gains in the 1960's, many of the gains were lost in the 1970's and 1980's under conservative political elements in the United States. The various groups worked to form political, cultural, and business organizations that pushed for collective rights and improvements in education and economics.

Since Puerto Rico is part of the United States it should be studied differently than other ethnic groups within this area. Puerto Rico became an American colony in 1898, which has had an enormous impact on its people. Another factor to consider is Puerto Rican populations on the United States mainland are growing faster than the population in Puerto Rico (Population Reference Bureau, 2001). Content about them should be included in the mainstream curriculum according to Banks (2003). Compare and contrast their experiences with other immigrant groups. The concept of race should be studied with racism as it exists within the United States and in Puerto Rico.

Many members of these groups have made significant economic, social, and cultural contributions to the United States. They also seek to maintain their cultural identity. Others have been able to "pass" due to light skin complexion when they change their language and accents. As with other cultural and ethnic groups, the members of this one share many similarities. While not meant to stereotype, some similarities are listed below. Members of this group, according to Carrasquillo (1991) are likely to operate in the following ways.

**Traditional Hispanic/Latino(a) Americans are likely to:**
Touch people with whom they are speaking. May engage in introductory embrace, kissing on the check, or backslapping.
Stand close to people with whom they are speaking.
Interpret prolonged eye contact as disrespectful.
Keep family or personal information from strangers.
Have a high regard for family and extended family.
Treated the elderly with respect.
Help other family members and friends with childcare.
Be non-confrontational.
Be emotionally expressive (especially Hispanic females).
Have traditionally prescribed sex roles for males and females.
Considered children a family priority.
Expect their children to consult parent's advice on important issues.
Be more concerned with present than future time.
Be very modest.

Verbal interactions are very important and the group is an important consideration as working together is highly valued. In communication diplomacy and tact are valued. Spanish is one of the world's great languages and it sill have a very low prestige in most parts of the U.S. People's perceptions are created by their language and it is important therefore to understand language and its use. Individuals who are members of this group identify closely with their family, community, and ethnic group. Within the family and community are status definitions and roles that are clearly defined and should be respected. Achievement is highly dependent upon the cooperation of individuals rather than competition. These are not meant to stereotype, but are illustrated as options for discussion. It is helpful to understand some cultural traits often associated with groups while remembering that all people are individuals and the intersection of variables causes an impact as well. Teachers of students from this group need to have an understanding and knowledge of second language acquisition skills. There are many misconceptions about language use and habits that need to be clarified to avoid common misperceptions and stereotypes.

Teachers also should assess their own attitudes toward this area and work to find ways to adjust instructional strategies to students. (Marshall, 2002). As with other groups, self-image is a basic building block in the educational process that must be fostered. A cultural inconsistency often exists between home and school in the areas of interaction patterns, teaching style, and climate of schools and classrooms. When these are understood and appropriately addressed, learning will be enhanced.

**Native American/American Indian Culture and Teaching**
(This section is based on work by and discussions with Dr. Sally Hunter as well as other references.)
The very first issue to discuss is terminology. Preferences will vary among individuals and when reference is made try to be as specific as possible by use of the name of the clan or band. Many popular images of members of these groups are widespread and often very stereotypical. Modern programs and older ones most typically western movies shown images that are exaggerated and perpetuated these stereotypical images. A major goal of curriculum should be

to assist students in developing a view of the development of the Americas from the point of view of the Native Americans/American Indians (Banks, 2003).

Although the term Indian often invokes images that are stereotypical, Indian peoples are very diverse in all aspects of life. There are over 550 federally recognized groups often referred to as tribes. Most of these have their own distinct language, history, folklore, and other traits. This is the most diverse of any group. Although diverse they are also some similarities. The people who are members of this group are indigenous to the United States and were here when Europeans came. Disease, war, and attempted genocide had a devastating impact on these populations (Marshall, 2002). Areas of residence and economic conditions vary widely. Not all members of this group live on reservations as approximately 1/2 of all American Indians are urban dwellers.

Some of these form the core values of the culture and are based on a deep spirituality. This spirituality influenced all facets of life. Dr. Sally Hunter (1998) provides the following myths and facts.

**Myths and Facts Often Associated with Native Americans/American Indians**

| *Myth* | *Fact* |
| --- | --- |
| Indians are shy. | Indians are taught to be respectful. |
| Indians are stoic. | Indians are taught to keep emotions and feelings to themselves or to share only with family members. |
| Indians are dependent on the government. | Government has never finished paying for Indian land. |
| Indians are wild and aggressive | Indians are generally non-aggressive. |
| Indians are dirty. | Indians bathed daily while the Pilgrims did not. |
| Indians are lazy. | Their land base and natural resources have been diminished. Thus, unemployment is relatively high among the Indian population. |

Living with nature or living in harmony requires individuals to be astute observers. Members of this group see and watch movement as reflected in gestures, facial expressions, or changes in the physical environment. Auditory and visual channels will vary depending on the group and are not used simultaneously. When engaged in conversation one does not interrupt the speaker and avoids a direct gaze or eye contact. Silence is seen as a virtue in most settings and is one sign of respect for others. These are not meant to stereotype, but are illustrated as options for discussion. It is helpful to understand some cultural traits often associated with groups while remembering that all people are individuals and the intersection of variables causes an impact as well. Values and value orientation can be a significant issue in meeting the needs of students from this group. Teachers should not assume that all students think like they do and accept the values of the school system, which are highly competitive and individualistic. These values are contrary to those of many Native American/American Indian students.

Students who are well grounded and have a sense of culture are more successful in schools according to Reyhner (1992). Accept the legitimacy of cultural values and the basic value orientation of students from this group. Use culturally appropriate materials and classroom practices that are not stereotypical. When an overall respect for culture of others is developed teachers will be more successful and so will their students.

In your study be sure to examine similarities and differences in other groups such as European Americans, Arab Americans, Jewish Americans, and others. Consequently, leaders in education must consider new strategies to address the diversity of participatory and learning styles from our multicultural society. Cooperative learning and participatory community decision making address these needs. As you consider those keep in mind the differences between traditional styles of operation and those that are nontraditional. Not all members of a group will operate in the same manner. This is due to the diversity that exists within and across cultures as well as the impact of intersecting variables.

**Strategies**

First learn about the communities from which your students come and something about each individual students. You will be better prepared to deal with the myriad of cultures and ethnic groups now present in our schools. Culture and language are mediators for all learning and interaction, therefore it is important to understand the role of perceptions and power in schools and communities. Appropriate strategies for instruction in schools include the use of cooperative learning and participatory decision making with a basic understanding of values and differences of the community seen as positive and brought out in the classroom and other decision making areas. Specific methodological techniques are essential to integrating factual information about people of color and women into education. A cooperative instructional system utilizes cooperative task structures in which participants spend much of their time in heterogeneous groups earning recognition, praise, and rewards based on the performance of their respective groups. These same principles can be applied to decision making in local schools and communities.

In 1954, Gordon Allport proposed a hypothesis for positive intergroup relations, which included five conditions. Allport's seminal text, The Nature of Prejudice, was devoted to understanding the origins of prejudice, the cognitive processes involved in the development of prejudice, and ways in which intergroup contact could be improved. Allport indicated that contact between members of different ethnic groups was likely to be more effective in changing attitudes and behaviors if certain conditions existed. The five conditions that he mentioned were:
1. Positive interdependence or cooperation,
2. Equal status contact in the pursuit of a common goal,
3. Social norms favoring group equality and egalitarian intergroup association,
4. Attributes of group members that contradict stereotypes, and
5. Contact that promotes interaction on a personal rather than only on a group level.

When these basic principles are applied to decision making and community involvement, positive learning communities will result. These can be applied to any type of community.

Over the years, in an effort to address those efforts delineated by Allport, several cooperative learning strategies were developed. Three such strategies; which are all cited earlier in this manual are the Cohen Model (1986), the Slavin model (1980, 1983), and the Johnson and Johnson Model (1975, 1990) will be discussed. All three models address issues related to positive intergroup contact, increased participation and achievement. In addition to classroom applications, these principles work in community team building.

The Cohen Model (1986) advocates establishing conditions in the classroom and in meetings which contradict expectation of low competence. Cohen indicated that persons, who are assumed to be of high status (e.g., middle class, attractive white, neat, attractive) are also expected to have high competence. Expectations of high competence tend to result in self-fulfilling prophecies in the classroom and in other meetings because students/participants who are expected to be of high competence are treated as though they possess certain abilities whether these abilities exist or not. The opposite exists for students/participants who are assumed to be of low status (e.g., lower class, minority, different in certain respects). Expectations of low competence also result in self-fulfilling prophecies where contributions are either ignored or discounted.

Cohen's methods to address these expectations include two approaches 1) expectations training and 2) establishing multiability classrooms/groups. Expectations training involves bringing in those persons expected to be (or perceived by others) of low competence into the desired setting prior to the beginning of the project and teaching them a skill which they would subsequently teach to or use with their peers. The skills advocated would be those skills that would not perpetuate stereotypes. Setting up multiability environments includes involving all citizens in cooperative groups, working together to achieve a common goal. Cohen's reasoning is that all students/participants have at least one skill that could help accomplish a goal and that no individual possesses all of the skills necessary to accomplish a goal. When diversity of experience is shared, greater flexibility for resolution of problems occurs.

The Johnson and Johnson Model (1975) has often been referred to as Learning Together. More recently, the model is referred to as Circles of Learning (1984). In the Johnson and Johnson Model, a cooperative goal structure is described as one in which there is a group goal (positive goal interdependence), sharing of ideas and materials (resource interdependence), a division of labor (role interdependence), and group rewards (celebration interdependence). In this approach, students/participants work as a group to complete a single group project, share ideas and help each other with answers to questions, make sure all members are involved and understand group answers, and ask for help from each other before asking the teacher/leader. This moves away from traditional authoritarian styles where the leader takes total control. The teacher/leader praises and rewards the group on the basis of group performance. The Johnson and Johnson Model advocates the utilization of nine different kinds of positive interdependence. According to this model, however, all groups must have goal interdependence. While this is discussed in terms of learning environments, it also has proven effective in team building. When community team members feel a sense of acceptance and inclusion, our educational environments will also improve.

**Why Diverse Learning Communities Do Not Exist**
Some of the fundamental blocks to creating successful diverse learning communities include:
1. There is a lack of diverse educational resources,
2. Most educators know very little about cultural traits, behaviors, values, and attitudes of diverse populations,
3. Most curriculum designs, instructional materials, and institutional structures are Eurocentric,
4. The school and home environments in which students live and learn differ significantly, and
5. Most traditional educators do not teach students how to survive and succeed in schools and communities.

These are critical factors that need to be addressed to eliminate some of the current blocks that exist. When these are dealt with a new culture can emerge. The essence of culture is how members of groups interpret, use, and perceive these elements. People within a culture usually view things similarly (paradigm). An appropriate new paradigm to develop is one that utilizes a pluralistic, multidimensional process. This will in turn create a new culture, one which includes the gradually evolving knowledge and ideas that are accumulating as the society faces new problems or as it develops in anticipation of future survival problems. One of the keys to the cultural transmission process is the language of the social group. Language needs to be changed to be more inclusive.

A major goal of multicultural education is to change teaching and learning approaches so that students and community members of both genders and from diverse cultural and ethnic groups will have equal opportunities to learn and succeed in educational institutions. Multicultural (Gender-Fair) Education seeks to reform the total educational process for all students and community members through changes in the curriculum and instruction program as well as in the governance structures.

**Summary**
Generally speaking, most researchers on multicultural issues agree that only by reforming the entire school environment will any substantive changes occur in attitudes, behavior and social and academic achievement. The entire culture of the school learning community must undergo significant change. Teachers must modify instruction to facilitate academic achievement among students from diverse groups thus creating an equity pedagogy.

As noted, most educational endeavors have been void of course work on multicultural issues and inclusive participatory and teaching strategies. It is apparent that most persons who are preparing to teach or administer at the K-12 and college/university level have not had adequate training to assist in them in the preparation of future global citizens. Appropriate instructional and facilitation strategies include the use of cooperative learning and participatory decision making with a basic understanding of differing values and cultures being seen as positive. These values need to be examined and positively integrated into the K-12 and college/university educational programs to create effective learning communities.

As educators we have an intellectual and ethical responsibility to provide our community members with the most current and accurate information available. A more inclusive educational community will have a number of important effects on our communities. It will expand their worldview by exposing them to the life experiences of people both similar to, and different from themselves. It will make them more cognizant of culture, ethnicity, and gender as important variables for everyday life. It will also make students aware of the significant contributions of members of groups who have been omitted from the American mainstream, as well as provide them the skills to recognize and deal with dehumanizing bias, prejudice, and discrimination. This will help community members to benefit from an increased appreciation of diversity in any of their current or future roles as parents, teachers, community leaders, co-workers, employers, and citizens. This should facilitate the participation in the process and in the educational climate necessary to ensure change.

If we look at existing models and ask ourselves what do we really want for the children and adults in our immediate areas, we need to address the resources that are available and how we can best meet the needs of the persons in our community. Some of the benefits of this model according to Warring, (1991b) are:

1. Parents/guardians and community members are empowered with knowledge about what is happening in system.

2. A strong advisory council is available to deal with issues that come up on a regular basis.

3. The cohorts gather on a regular basis to support each other.

4. There is a greater sense of ownership by the community members, the teachers of the programs and the students in the programs.

5. There is an increased amount of participatory decision making.

6. The students in the program feel a greater sense of community and are more willing to work as volunteers in the community.

7. We hopefully will prepare more qualified persons to meet needs that exist in the world for today and tomorrow.

8. Children and youth at risk will benefit from early identification and ongoing continuous interventions.

9. Funding for this program should be adequate since all persons are involved and share in its success.

10. It will strengthen the need cited by the Carnegie Commission on Education for cooperative work and consensus building among employees (community members).

11. Individuals will have a heightened capacity for posing and analyzing problems and evaluating outcomes having worked on shared decision making, cooperation, and problem solving.

12. All personnel in the community will have a greater understanding of education and what it means for connecting with the work place and the broader attitudes, values, and talents involved in the community as a whole.

If these are employed and people are involved in committed relationships with others who are diverse we will then have effective learning communities for all.

**References**

Allport, G. (1954). *The nature of prejudice.* Boston, MA: Anchor.

Banks, J. (2003). *Teaching strategies for ethnic studies.* (7th ed.), Boston, MA: Allyn and Bacon

Banks, J. (2001). *Multicultural education: Issues and perspectives* Boston, MA: Allyn and Bacon.

Banks, J. (1997). *Multiethnic education: Theory and practice.* Boston, MA: Allyn and Bacon.

Bronstein, P, & Quina, K. (1988). *Teaching a psychology of people: Resources for gender and sociocultural awareness.* Washington, DC: American Psychological Association.

Carrasquillo, A. L. (1991). *Hispanic children and youth in the United States.* New York, NY: Garland.

Cleary, L., & Peacock, T. (1998). *Collected wisdom: American Indian education.* Boston, MA: Allyn and Bacon.

Cohen, E. (1986). *Designing groupwork.* New York: Teachers College Press.

Fitzpatrick, J. P. (1987). *Puerto Rican Americans: The meaning of migration to the mainland* (2nd ed.). Englewood Cliffs, NJ: Prentice-Hall.

Hodgkinson, H. (2002). Demographics and teacher education: An overview. *Journal of Teacher Education, 53* 2 102-105.

Hunter, S. (1998). Discussions with Dr. Hunter, a professor at the University of St. Thomas. Based on work from Warring, D., Hunter, S. & Zirpoli, T. (2001). "*Understanding cultural influences on behavior*" chapter in Zirpoli, T. & K. Melloy Behavior Management For Teachers (3rd ed.).

Johnson, D., & Johnson, R. (1996). *Learning together and alone (3rd ed.).* Englewood Cliffs, NJ: Prentice-Hall.

Johnson, D., Johnson, R., & Holubec, E. (1995). *Circles of learning: Cooperation in the classroom.* Edina, MN: Interaction Book Company.

Kerns, M. (1989). *The evolution and the vision.* St. Paul, MN: St. Thomas Community Education Center.

Marshall, P. (2002). *Cultural diversity in our schools.* Belmont, CA: Wadsworth.

Minnesota Department of Education (1974). *Human relations guide: Inter and intracultural education.* St. Paul, MN: Author.

Minnesota State Board of Education (1988). *Multicultural and gender-fair curriculum.* Minnesota Rules Part 3500.0550, St. Paul, MN: Author.

Nance, E., & Dixon, D. (1991). *School Desegregation and community education: Effects and opportunities.* Community Education Journal Vol. 18, No. 2. Alexandria, VA.

Population Reference Bureau (2001, May). *2001 world population data sheet of the population reference bureau* (Book ed.). Washington, DC: Author.

Reyhner, J. (1992). Teaching American Indian students. Norman, OK: University of Oklahoma Press.

Salzman, J., L., Smith, D. L., & West, C. (Eds.), (1996). *Encyclopedia of African-American culture and history* (5 volumes). New York: Macmillan.

Slavin, R. (1983). Cooperative Learning. New York: Longman.

Stephan, W. (1999). *Reducing prejudice and stereotyping in schools.* New York: Teachers College Press.

Takaki, R. (1998). *Strangers from a different shore: A history of Asian Americans*, (Rev. ed.). Boston, MA: Little, Brown.

Tatum, B. D. (1997). *Why are all the Black kids sitting together in the cafeteria?* New York, NY: Basic Books.

Tiedt, P. & Tiedt, I. (2002). *Multicultural teaching: A handbook of activities, information and resources* (5th Ed). Boston: Allyn and Bacon

Warring, D. (1991a). *Human relations and multicultural education manual.* Acton, MA: Copley.

Warring, D. (1991b). An integrative model for restructuring schooling as an educative community, *(National) Community Education Journal, Vol. 18, No. 3.*

Warring, D., Hunter, S. & Zirpoli, T. (2001). "*Understanding cultural influences on behavior*" chapter in Zirpoli, T. & K. Melloy Behavior Management For Teachers (3rd ed.).

---

**Reflection/Discussion Items**

1. How do traits become stereotypes for individuals who are members of groups?

2. What will you do to separate traits from stereotypes?

3. What information do you have access to that will assist you in this process?

4. How can you apply this learning to your future profession?

5. How can you become an ally?

# SECTION IV

# PERCEPTION AND MISUNDERSTANDING IN HUMAN RELATIONS AND MULTICULTURAL EDUCATION

***Rationale:*** The psychological and interpersonal processes that interact on a regular basis impact basic human interactions. Human Relations – particularly interpersonal contact across intersecting variables (racial, sexual, economic, ethnic, and others areas) – is a very complex and volatile issue. In this unit the psychological components of prejudice, sexism, racism, and other "isms" are examined. Students will be exposed to research findings, to various psychologically oriented theories regarding prejudices and their functions, and to current policies, practices, and events. Discussions will be held where students will be given the opportunity to speculate on the psychological and interpersonal goals they desire to uphold for their own classrooms and possible methods for accomplishing these. It is important to explore the intersection of multiple variables as they all impact each other (e.g. race, ethnicity, class, gender, disability, economics, religion, affectional orientation, and others).

## ***Objectives***
1. To develop an understanding of an individual's sensory limitations and the idiosyncratic nature of perception; to acknowledge the ambiguity of social reality and the possibilities for misunderstanding in interpersonal relations.
2. To become aware of an individual's categorization processes with particular emphasis on the personal/ social consequences of using labels and stereotypes.
3. To be able to recognize monopolistic versus differentiated thinking patterns and to achieve a thorough understanding of the advantages and disadvantages of each.
4. To understand the differences between normal prejudgment and prejudice.
5. To become aware of how social perceptions become the formation of judgments about the qualities of others.
6. To examine personal value systems. How does one feel about differences between people? How do race, religious preference, ethnic background, etc., affect a choice of friends, life partner, etc.?
7. To understand the functional significance of individual definitions of self.

# "I AM...." EXERCISE

This activity is an example of a Projective Assessment based on work by Kuhn & McPortland.

It has been designed to explore individual identity and self-image, and to show locus of control. To estgablish a pattern or develop consistency it is best to complete this activity four or five times over a six month span and compare lists.

Write 20 "I am...." statements. (Using 20 statements pushes you and forces you to explore, and possibly exhaust, the self-identification possibilities for a number of categories.)

With the help of the facilitator <u>classify</u> the statements and attempt to define the "sources" from which the messages (insights) are to be generated.

Ask yourself who or what influences your identity or self image: self-concept or self-esteem. (Peers, family, institutions, etc.)

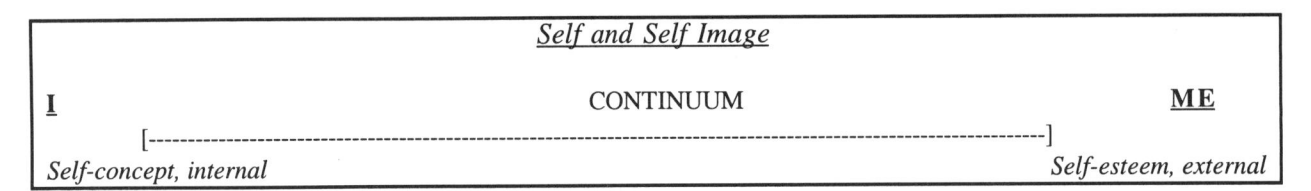

```
                        Self and Self Image
I                           CONTINUUM                                    ME
[-----------------------------------------------------------------------------]
Self-concept, internal                                   Self-esteem, external
```

## Suggested Categories for Classifying Statements

1) <u>Demographics (census-type information, adjectives)</u>. Pertains to religion, nationality, geographic location, age, size/shape/weight/height, etc. Talks about what is important - heavy, small, short, tall, fat, skinny, attractive, etc.

2) <u>Roles</u>. Relates to how people see themselves involved in relationships with others rather than as individuals, i.e., mother, teacher, and caretaker. Also shows what roles are important to them, i.e., a 45-year-old who still sees herself/himself as a daughter or son. Other roles: parent, doctor, teacher, etc.

3) <u>Activities</u>. Includes work activities, career activities, hobbies. Usually involve doing something. (more active terms).

4) <u>Positive/negative statements</u>. Usually self-depreciating statements are negative, and laudatory statements are positive. (more specific).

5) <u>Feeling Statements</u>. Express happiness, depression, elation, sadness, etc.

6) <u>Personal Characteristics</u>. Intelligent, creative, kind, compassionate, generous, non-artistic, etc.) (more general overall category).

---

**Reflection/Discussion Items**

1. Classify your statements into one or more of these categories and then total how many you have in each separate one. How many are in each? Why?

2. What did you include? Why?

3. What did you leave off your list? Why?

4. What is the impact of intersecting variables?

# ME BAGS

Who are you? How do you define yourself? Understanding yourself and being able to share something positive about your own background with others is a necessary step in improving interpersonal relations.

"Me Bags" is an idea that promotes understanding for both the person placing items in the bag, and the person(s) the information is shared with. It gives the people a chance to share their heritage and/or interests with others.

This is one of the many activities that can be utilized with all age students. It should help to improve race relations and reduce prejudice by developing a contextual base for understanding others. When using this activity it is important to focus on similar and different interests as positive. Diversity is strength and needs to be communicated to all.

When we discover more about ourselves (our own history, beliefs, values, and attitudes) as well as those of others, we learn how to respect ourselves and others more.

---

**Reflection/Discussion Items**

1. What is in your pocket, backpack, wallet, or purse right now?

2. What would you bring out to show to us and what would it say about you?

3. What would you prefer not to share with us and why?

4. How might others interpret it?

5. What other types of activities could you use to examine some similar issues for yourself and/or students?

# IDENTITY DEVELOPMENT

Who we are is a complex interaction of many variables operating multi-dimensionally. From prenatal through our physical death multiple factors continuously interact at a conscious and sub (non-) conscious level. Culture, background, training, historical, social, community and all factors and experiences as well as the ability to reflect on these has an impact on identity development. Three of the most significant are race, gender, and socioeconomic status. This is not to say others are not important because they are and do impact these three in a number of ways.

While most researchers in this area have focused more recently on racial identity development, Cass (1979) was one of the first to explore issues of affectional orientation in relation to this model. The model developed dealt specifically with identity formation. Many self-theorists in both psychology and sociology specifically believe that self and self-concepts have meaning based on interaction and relationships with other people and groups (Niedenthal & Beike, 1997).

**Identity Construction**
Early on we are impacted by perceptions of others that affect our self-esteem and to a lesser extent or self-concept. Self-esteem is our view or ourselves as others see us and is quite subjective. It remains fluid and is quite subjective. Because of this fluidity it is unstable and susceptible to change.

As we mature we are impacted more by our self-concept. Self-concept is more stable and consists of our view of ourselves interpreted by us. It is much more concrete and objective. Because of this objectivity is it less susceptible to change.

Identity construction is a term used by many researchers who discuss approaches as a process of progression throughout life. This progression is not a normal process contingent upon one's age. It is **not** a function of age, but of life experience and an awakening of awareness of those experiences. A healthy personal identity will assist learners in doing well educationally because it is rooted in a positive feeling of self.

Parham (1989) proposed a different process than typical stage theory, that of going through cycles in the process of identity construction. The theory of passing around a circle is an interesting way to conceptualize this model of stages of progression. Some cultures believe physical life to be one stage in a cycle while others view it differently. Another theorist, Helms (1989) suggests that racial theories may be additive, successive, or representative of a unique restructuring of experiences.

Noel (2000) builds a strong case for examination of the identity (development) construction process with respect to a person's ability to understand multicultural education. This sheds some very interesting light on the topic as to why some people embrace multicultural education. While some may reject multicultural education others examine and pose various theories within its overall field. As can be seen people are at different stages in their development.

**Bi of Two and Multi of Many**
People are combined of many facets. Most psychologists and earlier stage theorists knew little of racial identity development. They often studied biased samples and examined only stage theories based on age.

So it is no wonder that schools often ignore biracial/multiracial and/or biethnic/multiethnic students. The people who set up and run the schools are often ignorant in that same respect. The special concerns and often even the very existence of bi-racial or multi-racial persons is denied. These terms are used here to identify persons who cross more than one ethnic group and/or more than one racial category.

An additional problem according to Yeh & Huang (1996) is that many theories of ethnic identity are over simplistic due to their failure to account for issues such as social context and the malleability of identity within these and other frameworks. In reality all of these are impacting the interrelationship of race, gender, class, affectional orientation, religion, ethnicity, et al., and combinations within and between. They are not easily separated although most theorists dealing with self-image and identity development attempt to separate them.

Identity is a dynamic ongoing process involving historical, social, cultural, and differential group identification processes. Identity formation depends on a process of exploration within these contexts. This will vary dramatically based on numerous factors. If a child is bicultural and raised in a family system which values one above the other or in fact ignores both, the developmental process will be much different than that of a child raised in a family system that truly values both cultures. As James Baldwin often said, "not everything that is faced can be changed, but nothing can be changed until it is faced."

Similarly impacted, according to Hollingsworth (1997), are the developmental processes including racial identity and self-image, which is highly impacted by self-esteem in transracially/transethnically-adopted children. Age has also been noted to be a significant factor in these studies. The fields of psychology and psychiatry have shown more interest in identity formation and demonstrated increased cultural sensitivity by incorporating cultural considerations in their diagnostic and statistic manual (Takeuchi, 2000).

**Integrative Identity**
Individuals who are members of more than one group can often identify with each group. When this is done in fairly equal amounts a synthesized identity will often result. This is often the case for those expressing a pluralistic identity. These individuals often recognize the commonalities among reference groups and at the same time appreciate the differences (Daniels, 1996). This is an integrative yet pluralistic identity (Cross, 1991).

Cultural reference group, language spoken, cultural, or other factors in development, involvement with culture of origin, involvement with host culture, cultural explanations of behavior, cultural norms, psychosocial environment, sociocultural, sociohistorical, and interrelated issues all impact identity development. This mosaic is constantly changing and is valuable in understanding contextual issues.

When we understand the context in which a behavior is occurring or the context utilized based on an individual's reality we are better equipped to engage in appropriate activities.

An example of some of these factors is shown in the following figure Levels of Influence and Factors Impacted. Influence flows from the societal level through the group and to the individual. Some of the numerous factors impacted are race, gender, and class. Obviously many other factors can be placed in here as well. Three of the most significant considerations impacting these factors are listed here: history, power, and perceptions.

## Levels of Influence and Factors Impacted

**Influence** ---------------------------------------------------------------------→

| *LEVELS/ FACTORS* | SOCIETAL | GROUP | INDIVIDUAL |
|---|---|---|---|
| **HISTORY** <br> Race <br>  Gender <br>   Class <br>    Etc. | | | |
| **POWER** <br> Race <br>  Gender <br>   Class <br>    Etc. | | | |
| **PERCEPTIONS** <br> Race <br>  Gender <br>   Class <br>    Etc. | | | |

(Etc. - Add other intersecting variables and compute the factors' impact).

This model outline some of the key elements impacting persons in our society in the United States today and does not imply that the other factors are unimportant. Other intersecting variables are extremely important in relation to the alternatives a person has in any given situation at any given time and in any given place, as are all factors.

In order to assess this you must first define the situation and your position in relation to it. However, when taking history, power, and perceptions into account in the model, race stands out in our society. This is not inclusive or exhaustive, as there are other significant factors that can also be applied to this model as well. Start to examine the intersecting variables and their relative impact at each level and consider the historical implications of the underpinnings of life in the United States.

Why is race that significant? Historically in what is now the United States of America you had to be a white male who was free (not indentured) owned land, and was a member of the accepted religion in order to be considered worthy. That in part is why when the founding fathers wrote all men are created equal they did not mean **all** people in society. Remember what has consistently happened to indigenous peoples when colonization occurred in any part of the world. As Ghandi said, "we need to be the change we want to see happen."

**Summary**
Constructing our own identities is a very complex process. In order to assist in understanding identity development two models are shown on the following pages. Keep in mind the multiplicity of factors and how these models are similar for most people depending on issues with which they struggle. Examining these models should help in understanding and applying the concept of identity development and the impact of the intersecting variables. This helps in understanding contextual factors involved in the interaction and learning processes.

# References

Cass, V. (1979). Homosexual identity formation: A theoretical model, *Journal of Homosexuality 4 (13) 219-235*.

Cross, W. E. (1991). *Shades of Black: Diversity in African-American identity*. Philadelphia, PA: Temple University Press.

Daniels, G. (1996). *Black and white identity in the new millennium: Unsevering the ties that bind.* In M. P. P. Root (Ed.), The multiracial experience: Racial borders as the new frontier (pp. 121-139). Thousand Oaks, CA: Sage.

Helms J. (1989). Considering some methodological issues in racial identity counseling research, *The Counseling Psychologist, 17 (2) 227-252*.

Helms, J. (1995). *An update of Helm's white and people of color racial identity models*. In J. G. Ponteroto, J. M. Casas, L. A. Suzuki, and C. M. Alexander (Eds.), Handbook of multicultural counseling. Thousand Oaks, CA: Sage Publications.

Hollingsworth, L. (1997). Effect of transracial/transethnic adoption on children's racial and ethnic identity and self-esteem: A meta-analytic review, *Marriage and Family Review, 25 (1-2) 99-121*.

Niedenthal, P. and Beike, D. (1997). Interrelated and isolated self-concepts, *Personality and Social Psychology Review 1 (2) 106-128*.

Noel, J. (2000). *Developing multicultural educators*. New York: Longman.

Parham, T. (1989). Cycles of psychological nigrescense, *The Counseling Psychologist, 17 (2) 187-226*.

Takeuchi, J. (2000). Treatment of a biracial child with schizophreniform disorder: Cultural formulation, *Cultural Diversity & Ethnic Minority Psychology 6 (1) 93-101*.

Terry, R. (1970). *For whites only*. Grand Rapids, MI: Erdmans Publishing.

Yeh, C. and Huang, K. (1996). The collectivist nature of ethnic identity development among Asian-American college students, *Adolescence, 31 (123) 645-662*.

# STAGES OF OTAID
## (Optimal Theory Applied to Identity Development)

1. Absence of Awareness: "Life is inherently good."
   There is no awareness other than to view one's own experience. This is based on the view that all a child knows is its own sense of self.

2. Individuation: "The world is just fine the way it is."
   Individuals lack awareness of the dominant culture's view of the self and rarely assign particular meaning or value to any aspect of their identity. Individuals may lack awareness of the part of self that is devalued by others. They may move from a "family" view to broader community view.

3. Dissonance: "The world is not the way I thought it was."
   Individuals effectively experience those aspects of self, which is devalued by others. This experience triggers conflict between the familiar self-image and the newly experienced feelings of anger, guilt, confusion, insecurity or sadness, which may accompany the encounter with the devalued aspects of self. This may be triggered by an act of discrimination.

4. Immersion: "The world is so unfair to people like me."
   Individuals fully embrace others like themselves who are devalued. This acceptance enables people to appreciate the devalued aspects of themselves. Individuals may "immerse" themselves, directly and/or vicariously, in the culture of the devalued group. *This is often toughest for teachers and other school personnel to understand. *

5. Internalization: "The world does not define who I am; I feel good about myself and more accepting of others."
   Individuals have effectively incorporated feelings of worth associated with the devalued aspects of self- resulting in an increased sense of security. The devalued part of self is recognized as just one of many components of self-identity.

6. Integration: "With my deeper understanding of the world, I want to overcome oppression for everyone."
   (Global Awareness) Individuals' sense of self has developed to a stronger place of inner security so that relationships and perceptions of others reflect this degree of inner peace. Individuals' sense of community has expanded due to a connection to more groups of people because differences are accepted.

7. Transformation: "We are one." Global Acceptance
   The self is redefined toward a sense of personhood that is multidimensional, focusing on internal control and self-mastery. Individuals experience a shift in worldview based on the realization of the interrelatedness and interdependency of all things. All forms of life are accepted and valued for their contribution to the greater good of the whole; all are unique manifestations of the spirit as they define it.
   (Others to consider include L. Myers, B. Cahil, E. Adams, and others)

**Reference**

Cahil, B. & Adams, E., *Identity and engagement in multicultural education*. In Speaking the unpleasant: The politics of (non) engagement in the multicultural education terrain by Rudolfo Chávez Chávez and James O'Donnell (eds.). Albany, NY: Suny, 1998.

# GROUP* IDENTITY DEVELOPMENT MODEL

| Stages of Group Development Model | Attitude toward self | Attitude toward others of the same group | Attitude toward others of different group | Attitude toward dominant group |
|---|---|---|---|---|
| STAGE 1- CONFORMITY | self depreciating | group depreciating | discriminatory | group appreciating |
| STAGE 2- DISSONANCE | conflict between self-depreciating and appreciating | conflict between group-depreciating and group-appreciating | conflict between dominant-held views of minority hierarchy and feelings of shared experience | conflict between group appreciating and group-depreciating |
| STAGE 3- RESISTANCE & IMMERSION | self appreciating | group appreciating | conflict between feelings of empathy for other minority experiences and feelings of culturo-centrism | group depreciating |
| STAGE 4- INTRO-SPECTION | concern with basis of self-appreciation | concern with nature of unequivocal appreciation | concern with ethnocentric basis for judging others | concern with the basis of group depreciation |
| STAGE 5- SYNERGETIC ARTICULATION & AWARENESS | self-appreciating with understanding | selective group-appreciating | selective group-appreciating | selective appreciation |

*Group is used here to identify in-groups often labeled by race, culture, religion, SES, gender, affectional orientation, et. al.

Interestingly most groups, including models of white, multiracial, and gender awareness and identity development parallel these models.

## References

Salet, E., and Koslow, K. (Eds.), (1994). *Race, ethnicity, and self: Identity in multicultural perspective.* Washington DC: National Multicultural Institute.

Also see:
Helms, J., (Ed.), (1990). *Black and white racial identity: Theory, research, and practice.* Westport, CT: Greenwood.

**Reflection/Discussion Items**

1. What significant factors have impacted your identity development?

2. Separate specific variables and analyze them, for an example what is the impact of gender in U.S. society today?

3. What is the impact of race tied to class in society in the U.S. today?

4. What is the impact of race tied to gender in society in the U.S. today?

5. What is the impact of gender tied to class in society in the U.S. today?

6. How are power and history intricately involved in these processes?

7. What other variables do you wish to consider at this time?

8. At what level would you estimate your identity typically operates?

# SECTION V

# ATTRIBUTION, LABELING, AND IDENTITY

***Rationale***: The assignment of individuals into negatively valued, "deviant" categories radically affect the social interactions between that individual and other members of society. This categorization (typically made by members of the dominant group and based on stereotypes) tends to exclude individuals from full participation in American society – social, economic, and political. This significantly impacts one's sense of self or identity. In order to facilitate the student's development of the objective of respecting human diversity and personal rights, the role of the dominant group in the creation and maintenance of deviance, the relativity of definitions of deviant behavior, success/failure models, identity development, and the functionality of diversity are examined.

***Objectives***
1. To understand the functions and dysfunctions of labels for social systems.
2. To explore of the consequences of rule-breaking for the social system.
3. To be able to distinguish between deviance and deviant behavior.
4. To understand the process of attribution.
5. To explore the social processes of labeling and stigmatization.
6. To achieve a cognitive understanding of the concepts of labeling related to identity and outcomes.
7. To identify the hidden curriculum.
8. To recognize the implications of success and failure for social interactions.
9. To explore the student's own attitudes, feelings, and behaviors with respect to others.
10. To explore the similarities and differences between groups.
11. To understand the impact professionals can have on students and others with whom they work.

# EDUCATIONAL PRIORITIES CHECKLIST

Rank the following items in order of their importance in education, with 1 being the most important and 15 being least important. If an item has no relevance to you, throw it out of the rankings and put an X in front of it.

If something is not on this list you may add your own priorities if you wish.

_____ objective grading

_____ interpersonal relationships (student to student)

_____ students learning to think

_____ order and discipline

_____ creative thinking and thinking skills

_____ students understanding basic concepts (standardized testing)

_____ teaching values

_____ interpersonal relationships (teacher to teacher)

_____ making the subject relevant to the students' lives

_____ fostering an open learning environment

_____ making the subject occupationally relevant

_____ making learning fun

_____ importance of extra/co-curricular activities

_____ lifelong learning

_____ multicultural education

_____ others

---

**Reflection/Discussion Activity**:

1. Prioritize what you believe is important.

2. When you have your list develop a rationale for your top ten.

3. Next form a small group (3-5 people) who are in similar licensure areas and develop a list of your top 5 priorities with a supporting rationale. Be prepared to share the results with the class.

4. How similar or different were your priorities from members of your group?

5. How similar or different were your priorities from other members of the class?

# AMERICAN CREED (Myrdal, 1962)

In his discussion of the nature of values in U.S. society, Myrdal (1962) contends that a major ethical inconsistency exists in U.S. society. He calls this "The American Dilemma". Most Americans value equality and human dignity but fail to understand or act upon them. This creates a dilemma. The creed is a set of values in general, abstract language to which most Americans would proclaim allegiance and commitment, including the following:

- the worth and dignity of the individual
- equality
- inalienable rights to life, liberty, property, and pursuit of happiness
- Consent of the governed
- majority rule
- rule of law
- due process of law
- Community and national welfare
- rights to freedom of speech, religion, assembly, and private association

Such values are fundamental to the American system. They are continually reaffirmed in justification of public policy, forming the nucleus of what may be considered America's constitutional morality. Other, less constitutionally oriented values include the following:

- brotherhood
- charity
- mercy
- nonviolence
- perseverance, hard work
- efficiency
- competence and expertise
- competition, rugged individualism
- compromise
- cooperation
- honesty
- loyalty
- integrity of personal consciences

Myrdal further describes the impact of such values in American life:

> America is continuously struggling for its soul. These principles of social ethics have been hammered into easily remembered formulas. All means of intellectual communication are utilized to stamp them into everybody's mind. The schools teach them, the churches preach them, and the courts pronounce their judicial decisions in their terms. They permeate editorials with a pattern of idealism so ingrained that writers could scarcely free themselves from it even if they tried. They have fixed a custom of indulging in high sounding generalities so splendidly gifted for the matter-of-fact approach to things and problems. Even the stranger, when he has to appear before an American audience, feels this, if he is sensitive at all, and finds himself espousing the national Creed, as this is the only means by which a speaker can obtain human response from the people to whom he talks.

## Reference
Myrdal, G. (1962). *An American Dilemma,* New York: Harper & Rowe.

---

**Reflection/Discussion Items**
1. What was Myrdal saying?
2. How does this apply to education in school and society?
3. Examine culture, identity development, values, and the hidden curriculum in light of Myrdal's American Dilemma. What are the implications for your school?

# HIDDEN CURRICULUM/NON-CONSCIOUS IDEOLOGIES

The hidden curriculum is any part of the curriculum that hasn't been examined for what it is teaching. Each and every professional needs to look at the curriculum and their objectives and see if they are consistent. In most schools an inconsistency in practice leads to a different curriculum being learned by students than many professionals believe they are teaching or exists in their school.

Some common examples include:

- A. Punctuality – bells, etc. (Is the teacher late or not ready?)
    1. Unfair expectations
    2. Role models that are selective

- B. Conformity
    1. To whose standards?
    2. For what purpose?

- C. Obedience – (Will the learning transfer from threat to no-threat situation?) Is obedience good in all situations? Some examples from the research for consideration are listed here.
    1. Milgram experiment
    2. Deviance (Rosenhan)
    3. Others that demonstrate obedience?

- D. Respect for property and rights of others
    1. Personal lockers
    2. Desks
    3. Backpacks, etc.

- E. Responsibility
  How do we teach responsibility? Is having homework in on time showing responsibility? Do teachers always have their tests back on time? Does a double standard exist?

  There are many cases on schools overturning actions of student councils.

  With all of the above, don't argue whether we should have these, but whether they are consistent with what we actually do. Do these represent our objectives in teaching democracy?

Professionals also need to examine the role of instructional materials. Content is important in all books and materials, even those seemingly unrelated to the directed course content.

- F. Multicultural materials

- G. Diversity and pluralism

Other areas for examining the hidden curriculum include pedagogical techniques and classroom and school areas. Some examples are bulletin boards, the school calendar, and parent/guardian – teacher conferences.

- H. Bulletin boards
    1. Make one.
    2. What types of pictures and activities are shown?

- I. Calendar
    1. When does school begin and end?
    2. What holidays are taken?
    3. What holidays are celebrated in the school itself?

Schools can easily alienate students. Professionals in the schools need to examine these and other discontinuities to reflect a curriculum and overall school experience that is more respectful and supportive of the entire community.

More specific ways to analyze these are found on other pages.

# FORCES INFLUENCING BEHAVIOR AT WORK AND IN SCHOOLS

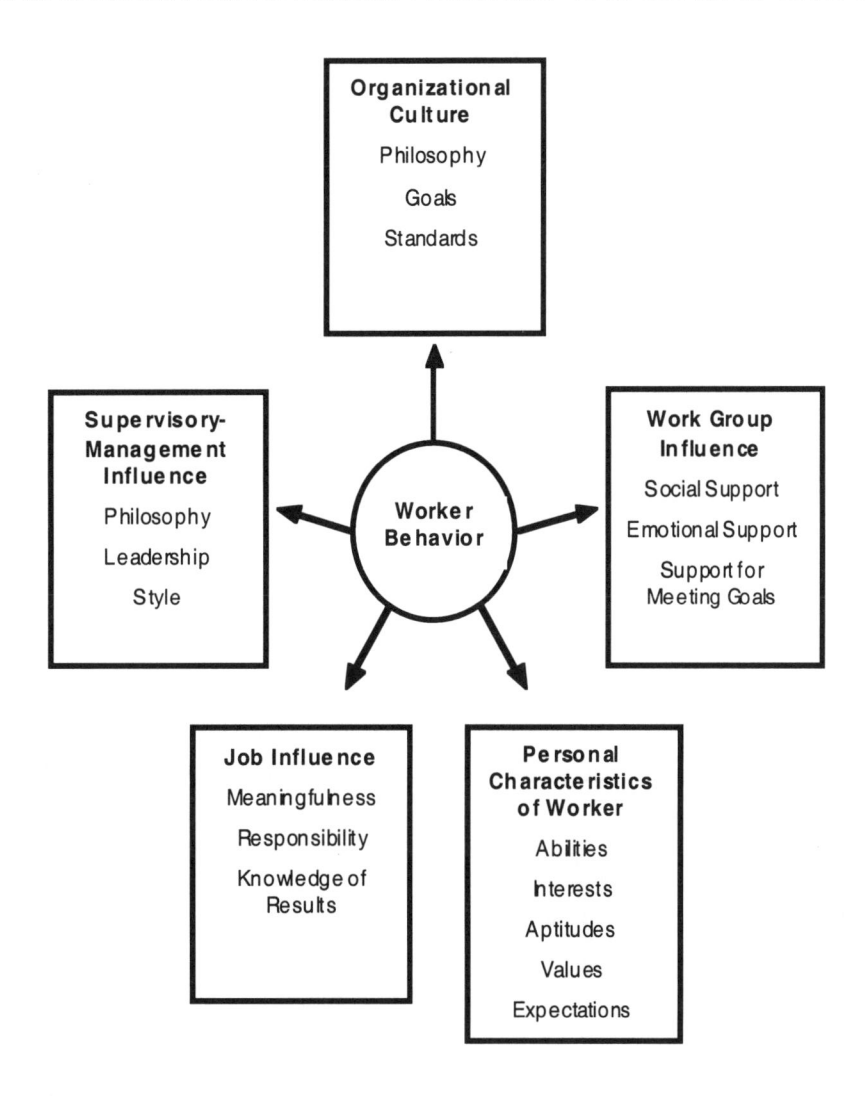

**Organizational Culture**
- Philosophy
- Goals
- Standards

**Supervisory-Management Influence**
- Philosophy
- Leadership
- Style

**Worker Behavior**

**Work Group Influence**
- Social Support
- Emotional Support
- Support for Meeting Goals

**Job Influence**
- Meaningfulness
- Responsibility
- Knowledge of Results

**Personal Characteristics of Worker**
- Abilities
- Interests
- Aptitudes
- Values
- Expectations

---

**Reflection/Discussion Items**

1. How does this model apply to your work environment?

2. If schools reflect and reinforce society, what does this infer about society and societal values?

3. How can school function within the context of society and be agents for change?

# PREJUDICE: HOW THEY SEE IT

The net effect of prejudice is to place the person in a position they do not deserve. Stereotypes produce a generalized picture filled with inaccuracies that are then applied to an entire group of individuals. Although there may be a thread of truth in a stereotype, a person can always find some confirming evidence; the stereotypes always result in someone being a victim or beneficiary without merit. Educators need to understand how this process works and respond appropriately to others. A basic premise to remember is to recognize intersecting variables and understand their importance without turning them into stereotypes.

*Famous authors share their wit and wisdom on a subject that's close to all of us.*

He that is possessed with a prejudice is possessed with a devil, and one of the worst kinds of devils, for it shuts out the truth, and often leads to ruinous error.
*Tryon Edwards*

Prejudice is a mist, which in our journey through the world, often dims the brightest, and obscures the best of all the good and glorious objects that meet us on our way.
– *Tales of Passions.*

He who knows only his side of the case knows little of that.
– *J. Stuart Mill*

All looks yellow to the jaundiced eye.
– *Pope*

Prejudice is the reason of fools.
– *Voltaire*

Ignorance is less remote from the truth than prejudice.
– *Diderot*

Reasoning against a prejudice is like fighting against a shadow; it exhausts the reasoner, without visibly affecting the prejudice. Argument cannot do the work of instruction any more than blows can take the place of sunlight.
– *Mildmay*

Prejudice is the child of ignorance.
– *Hazlitt*

The prejudices of ignorance are more easily removed than the prejudices of interest; the first are all blindly adopted, the second willfully preferred.
– *Bancroft*

The confirmed prejudices of a thoughtful life, are as hard to change as the confirmed habits of an indolent life. And as some must trifle away age, because they trifled away youth, others must labor on in a maze of error, because they have wandered there too long to find their way out.
– *Bolingbroke*

Beware of prejudices. They are like rats, and men's minds are like traps; prejudices get in easily, but it is doubtful if they ever get out.

There is nothing respecting which a man may be so long unconscious, as of the extent and strength of his prejudices.

Opinions grounded on prejudice are always sustained with the greatest violence.

– *Jeffrey*

The prejudiced and obstinate man does not so much hold opinions, as his opinions hold him.
– *Tryon Edwards*

When the judgment is weak the prejudice is strong.
– *O'Hara*

Every one is forward to complain of the prejudices that mislead other men and parties, as if he were free, and had none of his own. What now is the cure? No other but this, that every man should let alone others' prejudices and examine his own.
– *Locke*

Prejudice and self-sufficiency, naturally proceed from inexperience of the world, and ignorance of mankind.
– *Addison*

Even when we fancy we have grown wiser, it is only, it may be, that new prejudices have displaced old ones.
– *Bruce*

In forming a judgment, lay your hearts void of foretaken opinions: else, whatsoever is done or said, will be measured by a wrong rule: like them who have the jaundice, to whom everything appeareth yellow.
– *Sir P. Sidney*

Some prejudices are to the mind what the atmosphere is to the body; we cannot feel without the one, nor breathe without the other.
– *Gréville*

Every period of life has its peculiar prejudice; whoever saw old age that did not applaud the past, and condemn the present times?
– *Montaigne*

Prejudices may be intense, but their lies are limited. To discover when they are dead and to bury them, is an important matter, and no unseemly tears should be shed at their funerals.

Human nature is so constituted, that all see, and judge better, in the affairs of other men, than in their own.
– *Terence*

He that never leaves his own country is full of prejudices.
– *Goldoni*

To divest one's self of some prejudices, would be like taking off the skin to feel the better.
– *Gréville*

Prejudice is the conjuror of imaginary wrongs, strangling truth, overpowering reason, making strong men weak and weak men weaker. God give us the large-hearted charity which "beareth all things, believeth all things, hopeth all things, endureth all things," which "thinketh no evil"!
– *Macduff*

Prejudice is a mist, which in our journey through the world often dims the brightest and obscures the best of all the good and glorious objects tour way.
– *Shaftesbury*

Instead of casting away our old prejudices, we cherish them to a very considerable degree, and, more shame to ourselves, we cherish them because they are prejudices; and the longer they have lasted the more we cherish them. We are afraid to put men to live and trade each on his own private stock of reason, because we suspect that this stock

in each man is small, and that the individuals would do better to avail themselves of the general bank and capital of nations and of ages.
– *Burke*

Never suffer the prejudice of the eye to determine the heart.
– *Zimmermann*

No wise man can have contempt for the prejudices of others; and he should even stand in a certain awe of his own, as if they were aged parents and monitors. They may in the end prove wiser than he.
– *Hazlitt*

Because a total eclipse of the sun is above my own head, I will not therefore insist that there must also be an eclipse in America also; and because snowflakes fall before my own nose, I need not believe that the Gold Coast is also snowed up.
– *Richter*

Prejudices, it is well known, are most difficult to eradicate from the heart whose soil has never been loosened or fertilized by education; they grow there, firm as weeds among rocks.
– *Charlotte Bronte.*

To lay aside all prejudices, is to lay aside all principles. He who is destitute of principles is governed by whims.
– *Jacobi*

When we destroy an old prejudice we have need of a new virtue.
– *Mad. de Stael*

None are too wise to be mistaken, but few are so wisely just as to acknowledge and correct their mistakes, and especially the mistakes of prejudice.
– *Borrow*

Prejudices are what rule the vulgar crowd.
– *Voltaire*

Moral prejudices are the stopgaps of virtue; and as is the case with other stopgaps, it is often more difficult to get either out or in through them, than through any other part of the fence.
– *Hare*

Prejudice is never easy unless it can pass itself off for reason.
– *Hazlitt*

The great obstacle to progress is prejudice.
– *Bovee*

Prejudice squints when it looks, and lies when it talks.
– *Duchess de Abrantes*

When prejudices arise from a generous though mistaken source, they are hugged closer to the bosom; and the kindest and most compassionate natures feel a pleasure in fostering a blind and unjust resentment.
– *Lord Erskine*

# Motivation

Student motivation and success rates in any activity are positively correlated. There have been a large number of research studies that support this concept. As you read this and the next section on Attribution think about yourself and others you know. How do these concepts apply?

Elements that are often included in the discussion on motivation are theories related to attributions, self-worth, self-image (self-esteem), and needs fulfillment. People who are engaged in a new task are relying upon past performance in similar and unrelated tasks to form a mental image of their projected success or failure. Hence some are success oriented and strive for success while other are failure oriented and will develop strategies (excuses) to explain their failure should it occur. Some of these excuses that are commonly used are setting goals too high, not giving effort, procrastinating, and admitting to a small weakness. All of these establish a pattern to account for a potential failure rather than admitting to a lack of ability.

Self-acceptance is a high priority among human beings and this forms the premise for self-worth theory. Using one's peer culture as a reference point an individual makes a determination on where they fit in. This is why utilizing normative referenced evaluations is so much more unhealthy than criterion referenced. In normative referenced there is always competition with others, which can become unhealthy. Covington (1992) found that there is a tendency to equate success with a level of value, which can be unhealthy. In criterion referenced situations there can be teamwork, cooperation, and sharing to achieve a goal (success).

The tie to attribution theory is how individuals perceive the causes of their success or failure. From the standpoint of attribution, emotions are not fixed and examining and understanding basic attributions can change motivation. According to Seligman (1975, 1991) people learn how to explain their success or failure and have the power to change this belief. So if a person has developed a failure orientation it is possible to change that to a success orientation. On of the ways to accomplish this is through guided practice and success until the individual internalizes the success and begins to take credit for the successful outcome.

Action steps that are recommended by Marzano (2003) include several suggestions. First it is important to provide individuals with timely feedback on their accomplishments. Next provide them with activities or tasks that are engaging. One way to do this is by finding out something about them and attempting to make the item as relevant as possible to them and their situations. Providing opportunities for them to construct and work on long-term projects, which they design increases motivation and relate to them. Another key element is to teach people about motivation and how they are personally impacted by it.

Knowledge of the basic process and how it applies to individuals create more opportunities for involvement and potential successful outcomes. Hopefully this will assist you in the process of understanding and appropriately utilizing attribution. On the next page are three charts that show some of the possible processes involved.

**References**
Covington, M. (1992). *Making the grade: A self-worth perspective on motivation and school reform.* New York: Cambridge University Press.
Marzano, R. (2003). *What works in schools: Translating research into action.* Alexandria, VA: ASCD
Seligman, M. (1975). *Helplessness: On depression, development and death.* San Francisco: Freeman.
Seligman, M. (1991). *Learned optimism.* New York: Knopf.

---

**Reflection/Discussion Items**
1. What motivates you to do well on any task?
2. How is attribution involved in this process?
3. How can you apply this to your profession?

# ATTRIBUTION MODEL

An attribution is an inference drawn based on a behavior and its causes or consequences. People observe a behavior and infer its causes. People seem to have a fundamental need to understand behavior and so this process begins in the early stages of development and continues throughout one's lifetime. Causal attributions are made to explain an outcome, which results in a success or a failure. Attributions then examine causes and outcomes and are used in the attempt to predict future outcomes.

The following charts demonstrate the process as it is attempted and the possible outcomes. Begin on the left and consider the traits a person has or is reported to have. Next consider how a person might think and feel about an upcoming task. How will the person attempt to prepare for this task? After attempting a task and before the results are known the person may attempt to guess what the likely outcome is going to be. This falls into the category of metacomprehension. After the outcome is known the person may make an internal or external assignment of worth. See Charts 2 and 3 for possible outcomes at this point.

| Chart #1 Attributions, Metacomprehension, and Outcomes (Read from left to right and consider all of the options in each category prior to the next column.) ||||||| 
|---|---|---|---|---|---|---|
| Traits | Task Anticipation | Task Preparation | Task Attempt | Meta-comprehension | Perception of Outcome | Self-Worth and Attribution |
| Anxiety | Difficulty or ease | Challenge level | | Know | Success | Internal |
| Ability | | Strategy | | Don't know | Failure | External |
| | Importance | | | Aware | Expectation | |
| | | | | | --Confirmed | |
| | Goals | | | Unaware | --Disconfirmed | |

| Chart #2 Attribution | Stable | Unstable |
|---|---|---|
| Internal | Ability | Effort |
| External | Task | Luck |

| Chart #3 Attribution | Stable | Unstable |
|---|---|---|
| Internal | Ability (S*) | Effort (S*) |
| External | Task (S*) | Luck (S*) |

*Strategy is infused throughout the entire model in this chart #

If success oriented people succeed they take credit for their success. (S ~> S = I)
If success oriented people fail initially, they blame external causes and try again. (S ~> F = E)
If success oriented people fail often enough they may become failure oriented. (S ~> F+ = I)
What happens to failure oriented people? (F ~> F =?), F ~> S =?), (F ~> S+ =?)

## Reference
Warring, D. (1991). Attributions and the implication of strategy in the attribution model. *Journal of Instructional Psychology*, Vol. 18(3), 179-186.

**Reflection/Discussion Items**
1. How can you assist a person who has developed a failure orientation to change that into a success oriented one?
2. What is the impact of different types of praise?

# THE TRICKY EQUATION OF SKILLS AND LUCK
*Adapted from writing by Ellen Goodman*

The three women on the panel described their work histories in orderly sequence--jobs, titles, and dates.

They appeared to be models of proper career women, success stories of five-year plans and life-management courses. Their autobiographies would have impressed any personnel manager or editor of *Who's Who*. Surely they impressed the college audience. Yet later, when they talked alone, different words crept into their résumés. The first woman sheepishly confessed to "luck," the second woman admitted "chance," and the third talked about "accident."

Not one of these women had tipped her hat to luck in her public job description. After all, they were enlightened women. They had all read the research. Hadn't it been proved that most women attributed their success to luck while most men attributed it to their own effort, skills, and talents? They knew that trap and wanted to avoid it. They had expunged luck from their curriculum vitae. At least, said one of them, the younger generation could be spared their self-doubt.

It was the first of two conversations that I heard about luck. The next one occurred last week when a woman who had started out in English criticism and ended up in political research confessed she, too, felt awkward explaining the role of accident in her peculiar progression. One wasn't supposed to talk about that anymore. It had become a cliché, a stereotype to shatter.

But this time, it occurred to me that I wasn't sure anymore. I wondered if "planning" isn't just as much of a cliché and "control" as much of a stereotype to shatter. I wondered which point of view is more realistic. When studies about the differences between men and women filter into popular language we usually begin by seeing men as the norm and women as abnormal. If the topic is success and more men are successful, then we begin by worrying about the female success psyche. We assume that women need to change. Why?

But if more men believe they made their own way deliberately, purposely, and skillfully, is it because these men plan better or because they rationalize better? Is it because of their skills or their egotism? Were their lives more in their control or are they more reluctant to admit a lack of control? What does this say about attributions?

And if more women see fate, luck, accident as a central force in their work lives, is it because they are passive, slow to see and reluctant to admit their own skills? Or is it because they are quick to see and comfortable to admit the reality of chance? The answers depend less on our perception of men and women than on our perception of the truth. It depends on how we determine the tricky equation of luck and skill in a life.

I know there are many things we can't do without acquiring skills, making plans. We cannot, blessedly, do brain surgery without medical training. Few people "luck" into medical school. But there are many things we can't do with planning. We cannot chart a course from English critic to political researcher. We cannot figure out how our interests will change and skills will grow. We don't know when chances will come, including the chance to throw over all our previous plans.

It is always easier to plot our lives backward and discover a straight line than to plot them forward on that line. To make a life, we need a peculiar combination of energy and persistence, skills that make readiness, and a lot of luck. Luck has gotten a bad rap. Those who see luck are tempted to believe that their experience has no meaning for others. It was just luck, after all. Women in particular are tempted to hide the happenstance behind a timetable.

But we're dealing with a younger generation full of anxieties about the future, a generation longing to be told the one true path. Maybe what they really need is people who will give them first-hand accounts of chance. Maybe they need our experience and our wishes for good luck.

# BEHAVIOR LABELING

The following are examples of differential labeling.

If an adult is reinforced for behaving appropriately, we call it *recognition*.

If a child is reinforced for behaving appropriately, we call it *bribery*.

If an adult laughs, we call it *socializing*.

If a child laughs, we call it *misbehaving*.

If an adult writes in a book, we call it *doodling*.

If a child writes in a book, we call it *destroying property*.

If an adult sticks to something, we call it *perseverance*.

If a child sticks to something, we call it *stubbornness*.

If an adult seeks help, we call it *consulting*.

If a child seeks help, we call it *whining*.

If an adult is not paying attention, we call it *preoccupation*.

If a child is not paying attention, we call it *distraction*.

If an adult forgets something, we call it *absentmindedness*.

If a child forgets something, we call it *stupidity*.

If an adult tells his or her side of a story, we call it *clarification*.

If a child tells his or her side of a story, we call it *talking back*.

If an adult raises his or her voice in anger, we call it *maintaining control*.

If a child raises his or her voice in anger, we call it a *temper tantrum*.

If an adult hits a child, we call it *discipline*.

If a child hits a child, we call it *fighting*.

If an adult behaves in an unusual way, we call it *individuality*.

If a child behaves in an unusual way, we refer him or her for PSYCHOLOGICAL EVALUATION!

*Source unknown.*

# TEACHERS DON'T WANT TO BE LABELED

When teaching a graduate course I decided to administer a difficult mid-term test to the class. I wanted the students to "feel" what it was like to take such a test and realize what items we use to measure intelligence. I also thought they might be more aware of the short time it takes to obtain a number, which is regarded as very important by many educators.

The students were told to write their names on the test papers.

The administration of the test required only 2 1/2 hours. The students seemed not to enjoy taking it.

Upon scoring the test I found that the lowest score was 24 and the highest 98 out of a possible 100. The mean for the 48 students was 79. The 24 did not astonish me, even though all of the students had successfully completed the general education courses and student teaching and most were ready to graduate by the end of the term. After all, tests have many limitations.

Then I got an idea. I decided to prepare a report for each student, writing her/his name on the outside and his or her test score on the inside of each. I folded and stapled each paper; after all, test scores are confidential information!

At the next class period I arranged all of the folded papers on a table at the front of the room. I wrote the range and the average score on the chalkboard. Many students snickered at the thought of somebody getting a 24. The students were eager and afraid as I began explaining the procedures for picking up their papers. I made a point of telling them not to tell others their score, because this would make the other person feel as if s/he too had to divulge his/her "total endowment." The students were then directed to come up to the table, row by row, to find their paper. Many opened their mouths with astonishment and then smiled at their friends to indicate they were extremely happy with their scores.

There was dead silence when I began to discuss the implications of the test scores. I explained that in some states a person who scores below 90 on a mid-term test is classified as a slow learner. The fact that group intelligence tests should not be used to make such a classification was stressed. I also told them someone in this class could have been classified as a slow learner and placed in a special class on the basis of this test.

I told how many guidance counselors would discourage a child with low test scores from attending college. Again I emphasized the fact that one person in this room was ready to graduate from college with a Master's Degree, having passed several courses in history, biology, English, and many other areas.

I then went on to explain that the majority of elementary and secondary school teachers believe in ability grouping. This is usually done on the basis of intelligence tests, so I explained that I would like to try ability grouping with this class; again to see "how it feels." Some students objected right away, saying, "I did not want to know their test scores." I calmed them by saying it would be a worthwhile learning experience and assured them that I really didn't believe in test scores.

I told the students not to move at this time, but I would like all of those with a test score below 70 to come to the front so they could sit nearer to me for individual help. I told the students who had an average score (between 71-88) to go to the back of the room and then take the seats in the middle of the class. The students with an above average score were asked to go to the side of the room and take the seats in the back, as they really didn't need much extra help.

"O.K., all those who got a score below 60 can come to the front of the room." The students looked around to find those who scored below 60. I said that I knew there was a 24 and a couple of 50s. Again, there was dead silence.

"O.K., all those students whose score is between 71-88 go to the back of the room." Immediately, to my amazement, 8 or 10 students picked up their books and headed for the back of the room. Before they could get there I said, "Wait a minute! Sit down. I don't want to embarrass you, but you would lie and cheat, the same way we make our students lie and cheat, because you don't want to classified as 'slow'."

The class erupted. It was in an uproar for about five minutes. Some indicated that they needed to use the restroom. All agreed it was a horrifying and yet valuable experience.

I asked them to do one thing for me: Please do not label students because we are all "gifted," "average," and "slow," depending on the task at hand. Everyone is exceptional. They promised.

---

**Reflection/Discussion Items**

1. What is the impact of the use of labels in education?

2. How can you apply the attribution model from these readings to yourself? To your students?

3. How do the success/failure models apply to you? To your students?

4. What is the impact of different types of praise on outcomes for you? For you students?

5. What is the impact of different types of praise on success/failure beliefs in you? In your students?

6. Why do people rely so heavily on the effort hypothesis?

7. What would you have done if you were placed in the situation described in this story?

# SECTION VI

# FOUNDATIONS OF OPPRESSION AND THE COLOR BLIND PERSPECTIVE

*Rationale*: In order for individuals to change biased behavior, they must recognize who owns the problem. They also need to understand that it is in the self-interest of whites in the United States to eradicate personal and institutional white racist behavior. The colorblind perspective is a point of view, which sees racial and ethnic group membership as irrelevant and leads to continued bias. This point of view must be understood for change to occur.

### *Objectives*
1. To examine dimensions of power and influence.
2. To understand affirmative action.
3. To present examples of oppression, repression, and suppression in our society.
4. To recognize that oppressors are oppressed by the very system they employ to exploit others.
5. To understand the process of victim blaming, self-deception, and overall oppression.
6. To understand the color blind perspective and generalize to similar topics.

# POWER

Power is an elusive and confusing concept. It may be what you think it is or it may not. All people possess some power and can develop it. The power is neither good nor bad in and of itself. The key is how it is used.

According to Janet Hagberg (2003) in Real Power: Stages of Personal Power in Organizations (3$^{rd}$ ed.), there are six stages of power which people may progress through. Each stage has positive and negative dimensions as well as inherent developmental struggles. These are not moved through by age and experience, neither is there a right or wrong way to move through them. There are several other theories of leadership and power as well. Examine them and decide which is most appropriate for you. In the meantime fill out the following organizational power analysis and compare your answers with others. An analysis is provided for both education and industry.

## ORGANIZATIONAL POWER ANALYSIS (Education)
### Part 1
Estimate the amount of influence that people at each level in your organization have over their or your work. Circle a number on the scale below for each of the levels.

| LEVEL | AMOUNT OF INFLUENCE |
|---|---|
|  | (Almost None) ... (Very Much) |
| Superintendent | 1  2  3  4  5 |
| Top Administrators | 1  2  3  4  5 |
| Assistant Administrators | 1  2  3  4  5 |
| Lead Teachers | 1  2  3  4  5 |
| Teachers | 1  2  3  4  5 |
| Students | 1  2  3  4  5 |
| Others | 1  2  3  4  5 |

Connect the circled numbers with a solid line to produce a "Power Profile." The farther to the right the line is, the more "total influence" exists in the organization. Check the slope of the line. Typically, the more the line approaches vertical, the higher the satisfaction of staff members is.

### Part 2
Beginning with the most influential level BELOW list in order, the most powerful people at that level. Continue the list by adding, in rank order, the most powerful people at the second most influential level and so on.

| RANK | LEVEL | NAME | STRATEGIC RESOURCES |
|---|---|---|---|
|  |  |  |  |

In the column STRATEGIC RESOURCES write the most important resource – activity, material, information, etc. – which that person controls. Looking just at the strategic resource column, rank the resources listed in order of importance. Compare your influence ranking of individuals with your strategic resources list. Reconsider individuals' actual organizational influence where appropriate and revise the original ranking if necessary. Now consider how to make changes within your educational setting to assist in the development of a more inclusive environment.

# ORGANIZATIONAL POWER ANALYSIS (Business/Industry)

## Part 1
Estimate the amount of influence that people at each level in your organization have over their or your work. Circle a number on the scale below for each of the levels.

| LEVEL | AMOUNT OF INFLUENCE | | | | |
|---|---|---|---|---|---|
| | (Almost None) | | | (Very Much) | |
| Board of Directors | 1 | 2 | 3 | 4 | 5 |
| President of Company | 1 | 2 | 3 | 4 | 5 |
| Main Supervisor | 1 | 2 | 3 | 4 | 5 |
| Supervisor | 1 | 2 | 3 | 4 | 5 |
| General Laborers | 1 | 2 | 3 | 4 | 5 |
| Stockholders | 1 | 2 | 3 | 4 | 5 |
| Others | 1 | 2 | 3 | 4 | 5 |

Connect the circled numbers with a solid line to produce a "Power Profile." The farther to the right the line is, the more "total influence" exists in the organization. Check the slope of the line. Typically, the more horizontal the line, the less satisfied members are, while the more the line approaches vertical, the higher the satisfaction of staff members is.

## Part 2
Beginning with the most influential level list in order, the most powerful people at that level. Continue the list by adding, in rank order, the most powerful people at the second most influential level and so on. Stop when you have names in the most powerful categories.

| RANK | LEVEL | NAME | STRATEGIC RESOURCES |
|---|---|---|---|
| | | | |

In the column STRATEGIC RESOURCES write the most important resource – activity, material, information, etc. – that the person controls. Looking just at the strategic resource column, rank the resources listed in order of importance. Compare your influence ranking of individuals with your strategic resources list. Reconsider individuals' actual organizational influence where appropriate, and revise the original ranking if necessary. Now consider how to make changes within your setting to assist in the development of a more inclusive environment.

### References
Burns, J. (1982). *Leadership*. New York: HarperCollins.
DePree, M. (1989). *Leadership is an art*. New York: Doubleday.
Ghandi, M. (1951). *Ghandi: An autobiography*. Boston: Beacon Press.
Hagberg, J. (2003). *Real power: Stages of personal power in organizations* (3rd ed.). Salem, WI: Sheffield.
Lips, H. (1981). *Women, men, and the psychology of power*. Englewood Cliffs, NJ: Prentice Hall.

# POWER AND GROUP STRUCTURE

There is power in working within groups. Societies have used groups to successfully accomplish tasks. The structure of the group often determines its success or failure and the participants' feelings about the group and its outcome.

Groups have existed for a long time and fulfill many functions. Many educators overlook the power and significance of groups in the academic realm. Cooperation is working together to accomplish a goal that is shared by other members of a group while competition is seeking to win at the expense of other(s). A state of positive interdependence exits when members of a group believe they can achieve their goal only if the other members also achieve theirs. This is structured through mutual goals, shared rewards, shared resources, and eventually a mutual identity. This also has incidental effects of prejudice reduction and facilitating greater cognitive and emotional perspective taking abilities than either competitive or individualistic goal structures.

Cooperative learning ensures that all students are meaningfully and actively involved in learning. It ensures that students are achieving their potential and are experiencing psychological success so they are motivated to continue to invest energy and effort into the learning process. Cooperative learning groups provide and arena for students to develop interpersonal and small group skills and leads to greater liking. These groups promote a sense of meaning, pride and esteem by helping and assisting of classmates and provide a context for constructive conflict resolution.

There are many types of cooperative learning groups. Each has a place and function. For more information on these see the references at the bottom of the page.

## COMPETITIVE STRATEGY (Win-Lose, or Lose-Lose)
1. Behavior is purposeful in pursuing own goals.
2. There is secrecy or a hidden agenda.
3. There is an accurate personal understanding of own needs, but it is publicly disguised or misrepresented. Don't let them know what you really want to do most, so they don't know how much you are really willing to give up to get it.
4. Strategies often include acting unpredictable, using mixed strategies, and utilizing the element of surprise.
5. Threats and bluffs are seen as useful.
6. Search behavior is devoted to finding ways of appearing to become committed to a position. Logical and irrational arguments may serve this purpose.
7. Success is often enhanced (where teams, committees, or organizations are involved on each side) by forming bad stereotypes of the other, by ignoring the other's logic, and by increasing the level of hostility. These tend to strengthen in-group loyalty and convince others that you mean business. (Formation of a common enemy.)

## COOPERATIVE STRATEGY (Win-Win)
1. Behavior is purposeful in pursuing goals held in common.
2. There is openness and a known agenda.
3. There is an accurate personal understanding of own needs, and an accurate representation of them.
4. Actions are predictable. While flexible behavior is appropriate, it is not designed to take other party by surprise.
5. Open, genuine attempts at negotiation occur.
6. Search behavior is devoted to finding solutions to problems while utilizing logical and innovative processes.
7. Success demands that stereotypes be dropped, that ideas be given consideration on their merit regardless of sources, and that hostility not be induced deliberately. In fact, positive feelings about others are both a cause and effect of other aspects of cooperative strategies.

### References
Johnson, D. & Johnson, R. (1989). *Cooperation and competition: Theory and research.* Edina, MN: Interaction Book Company.

Johnson, D. & Johnson, R. (2002). *Multicultural education and human relations: Valuing diversity.* Boston, MA: Allyn & Bacon.

# AFFIRMATIVE ACTION

**What is Affirmative Action?**
Affirmative action is an umbrella term which refers to a variety of narrowly tailored and highly regulated efforts used by employers and educational institutions to overcome past and continuing discrimination in order to allow qualified women and minorities to compete equally for jobs, education, and promotional opportunities. There has been a great deal of debate about affirmative action since its inception. Most affirmative action programs do not involve quotas. Most programs are based on goals and timelines to achieve those goals. Goals are voluntary, legal, and may even be exceeded. They provide a target in order to evaluate progress.

**Brief History of Affirmative Action**
The origins of affirmative action are intricately linked to discrimination in the United States. The following is a brief outline of this history:

Originally, civil rights programs were enacted to help African Americans become full citizens of the United States. The Thirteenth Amendment to the Constitution made slavery illegal; the Fourteenth Amendment guarantees equal protection under the law; the Fifteenth Amendment forbids racial discrimination in access to voting.

1866: Civil Rights Act guarantees every citizen "the same right to make and enforce contracts ... as is enjoyed by white citizens ... "

1896: The U.S. Supreme Court ruled in Plessy v Ferguson that "separate but equal" facilities on the basis of race was constitutional. This reinforced the "separate but equal" doctrine. This further fortified the separation of schools and led to a continuing decline in the overall quality of public education for students of color.

1941: President Franklin D. Roosevelt signed Executive Order 8802 which outlawed segregationist hiring policies by defense-related industries which held federal contracts. Roosevelt's signing of this order was a direct result of efforts by Black trade union leader, A. Philip Randolph.

1953: President Harry S. Truman's Committee on Government Contract Compliance urged the Bureau of Employment Security "to act positively and affirmatively to implement the policy of nondiscrimination..."

1954: The U.S. Supreme Court ruled in Brown v. Board of Education that "separate but equal" facilities on the basis of race were unconstitutionally discriminatory overturning Plessy v. Ferguson of 1896.

1964: Congress passed the Civil Rights prohibiting discrimination based on race, sex, national origin and religion in employment and education.

1965: President Lyndon Johnson signed an executive order (11246) requiring federal contractors to undertake affirmative action to increase the number of minorities they employed. The Civil Rights Act of 1964 is the most comprehensive statute on civil rights ever enacted in the United States: Among other things, it bans discrimination in voting rights, public accommodations, public education, and all federally assisted programs.

1965: Voting Rights Act adopted after Congress found "that racial discrimination in voting was an insidious and pervasive evil, which had been perpetuated in certain parts of the country through unremitting and ingenious defiance of the Constitution."

1967: President Lyndon B. Johnson expanded the executive order with the inclusion of women.

1969: Department of Labor hearings exposed continued widespread racial discrimination in the construction agency. In response, President Richard Nixon developed the concept of using "goals and timetables" to measure the progress federal construction companies were making in increasing the number of minorities on their payrolls.

1970: President Nixon extended the use of goals and timetables to all federal contractors. Title VII of the 1964 Act deals with employment. As amended and expanded, especially by the Equal Employment Opportunity Act of 1972, it bans discrimination in employment on the basis of race, color, religion, sex or national origin by employers, unions and employment agencies. Employers can't discriminate in hiring, firing, wages or any terms, conditions or privileges of employment, nor can they limit, segregate or classify employees or applicants by race, color, religion, sex or national origin in any way that would adversely affect their employment status. Employment agencies can't discriminate in referring applicants. Unions can't discriminate in membership or in referral for jobs. Apprenticeship and training programs are also covered by the Act of 1972.

1974: President Nixon declared that affirmative action programs should also include women.

1978: The U.S. Supreme Court held in Regents of California vs. Bakke that universities may take race into consideration as a factor in admissions when seeking to accomplish diversity in the student body. The court in Bakke also held that quotas cannot be used in voluntary affirmative action programs in admissions unless absolutely necessary.

1989: The U.S. Supreme Court held in City of Richmond vs. Croson that the standard to be used in evaluating affirmative action programs in contracting was one of "strict scrutiny."

1990: In 1990 Congress passed the Americans with Disabilities Act which prohibits discrimination on the basis of disability in places of public accommodations.

1995: On June 12, 1995 the U.S. Supreme Court held in Adarand Constructors, Inc. v. Pea that the strict judicial scrutiny standard articulated in the Croson case also applied to affirmative action programs mandated by Congress as well as those undertaken by government agencies.

Much of the opposition to affirmative action is framed on the grounds of so-called "reverse discrimination and unwarranted preferences." In fact, less than 2 percent of the 91,000 employment discrimination cases pending before the Equal Employment Opportunities Commission are reverse discrimination cases. Under the law as written in Executive Orders and interpreted by the courts, anyone benefiting from affirmative action must have relevant and valid job or educational qualifications.

These laws have as a basic goal equal opportunity. But in practice patterns of discrimination still exist and that goal can not be reached without affirmative action. This progress is toward a real rather than hypothetical equality of opportunity. Evaluations are very rarely objective and so perceived abilities or the lack of them is often a result in lack of change. The single group that has benefited the most from affirmative action as a class of people is white women.

**Common Myths**
*Myth: If Jewish and Asian Americans can rapidly advance economically, African Americans should be able to do the same.*
This comparison ignores the unique history of discrimination against Black people in America. As historian Roger Wilkins has pointed out, Blacks have a 375-year history on this continent: 245 involving slavery, 100 involving legalized discrimination, and only 30 involving anything else (Wilkins, 1995). Jews and Asians, on the other hand, have immigrated to North America—often as doctors, lawyers, professors, and entrepreneurs, etc. Moreover, European Jews are often able to function as part of the White majority. To expect Blacks to show the same upward mobility as Jews and Asians is to deny the historical and social reality that Black people face.

*Myth: The only way to create a color-blind society is to adopt color-blind policies.*
Although this assertion sounds intuitively plausible, the reality is that color-blind policies often put racial minorities at a disadvantage. For instance, all else being equal, color-blind seniority systems tend to protect White workers against job layoffs, because senior employees are usually White (Ezorsky, 1991). Likewise, color-blind college admissions favor White students because of their earlier educational advantages. Unless pre-existing inequities are corrected or otherwise taken into account, color-blind policies do not correct racial injustice—they reinforce it.

*Myth: Affirmative action may have been necessary 30 years ago, but the playing field is fairly level today.*
Despite the progress that has been made, the playing field is far from level. Women continue to earn 70 cents for every male dollar. Black people continue to have twice the unemployment rate of White people, half the median family income, and half the proportion who attend four years or more of college. In fact, without affirmative action the percentage of Black students on many campuses would drop below 2%. This would effectively choke off Black access to higher education and severely restrict progress toward racial equality.

**Closing Questions**
The issue of preferences is just a smoke screen and is hypocritical. If in fact opponents are against special treatment why aren't they questioning any other programs? Examples are preferential treatment for women, veterans, athletes, financially wealthy, politically influential, students of alumni, or even geographical preference, religious scholarships or others targeted to certain groups or special programs for persons with disabilities?

I am sure we would all like to live in a world where all people are treated fairly and equitably in all facets of their lives. But until then, what options do we have?

**References**
Bureau of National Affairs. (1979). *Uniform guidelines on employee selection procedures.* Washington, DC: Author.
Citizens' Commission on Civil Rights. (1984, June). *Affirmative action to open the doors of job opportunity.* Washington, DC: Author.
Ezorsky, G. (1991) *Racism and justice: The case for affirmative action.* Ithaca, NY: Cornell University Press.
Graves, L. M., & Powell, G. N. (1994). Effects of sex-based preferential selection and discrimination on job attitudes. *Human Relations, 47,* 133-157.
Heilman, M. E., Simon, M. C., & Repper, D. P. (1987). Intentionally favored, unintentionally harmed? Impact of sex-based preferential selection on self-perceptions and self-evaluations. *Journal of Applied Psychology, 72,* 62-68.
Ivins, M. (1995, February 23). Affirmative action is more than black-and-white issue. *Philadelphia Daily News,* p. 28.
Kravitz, D. A., & Platania, J. (1993). Attitudes and beliefs about affirmative action: Effects of target and of respondent sex and ethnicity. *Journal of Personality and Social Psychology, 78,* 928-938.
Plous, S. (1997). Ten myths about affirmative action. *Journal of Social Issues, 52* (4).

---

**Reflection/Discussion Items**

1. What is the current status of affirmative action?

2. What are your perceptions about affirmative action?

3. What is your definition of the term "reverse discrimination"?

4. Is it "reverse discrimination" or is it "aversive discrimination?

5. Define the concept "white privilege".

6. What is the benefit of diversity in and to a society?

# FOUNDATIONS OF OPPRESSION

*Oppression exists when:*

any entity (individual, group, society), intentionally or unintentionally,

1. imposes an ethnocentric mission
2. refuses to share power
3. maintains unresponsive and inflexible structure or
4. inequitably distributes resources

*for it's supposed benefit, and then rationalizes or justifies its actions in the following ways:*

1. by blaming the victim
2. by punishing the victim
3. by ignoring the victim, or
4. by other means.

In order to analyze a problem, identify the issues and at which level they are being addressed.

DIRECTIONS ↓

| | | |
|---|---|---|
| Mission: | That **toward** which an organization moves | |
| Power: | That **by which** an organization moves | |
| Structure: | That **through** which an organization moves | |
| Resources: | That **from** which an organization moves | |

LIMITS ↑

**Reference**
Adapted from workshops by Robert Terry, 1978-94

---

**Reflection/Discussion Items**

1. Differentiate repression and suppression. Cite examples.

2. Who are the ups?

3. Who are the downs?

4. How does this model apply on all levels of analysis?

5. How can change occur, (see next page as well)?

## Levels of Influence and Resistance and the Factors Impacted

When examining issues at any level of analysis it becomes essential to break out the intersecting variables to better visualize how they impact and are impacted. Influence can be exerted in many ways as can resistance. When looking at this model and making applications remember that most often influence flows from the societal level on down to the individual and resistance comes up from individuals back at society to create change.

Influence flows from societal on down to individuals ---------------------------------------->

| LEVELS/FACTORS | SOCIETAL | GROUP | INDIVIDUAL |
|---|---|---|---|
| **HISTORY**<br>  Race<br>    Gender<br>      Class<br>        Etc. | | | |
| **POWER**<br>  Race<br>    Gender<br>      Class<br>        Etc. | | | |
| **PERCEPTIONS**<br>  Race<br>    Gender<br>      Class<br>        Etc. | | | |

←----------------------Resistance most often flows up from individuals to the societal level

History, power, and perceptions have an impact at all three levels.

### Active Passive Grid

|  | ACTIVE | PASSIVE |
|---|---|---|
| **OPPRESSIVE** | | |
| **ANTI-OPPRESSIVE** | | |

### Active Passive Grid
(With outcomes)

|  | ACTIVE | PASSIVE |
|---|---|---|
| **OPPRESSIVE** | Bigots:<br>Racists,<br>Sexists,<br>Etc. | Passive Non-Bias<br><br>Conformists |
| **ANTI-OPPRESSIVE** | New Conscious to color, gender, etc.<br>New Abolitionists<br>Etc. | Who or what fits here? |

**References**
(Based on work and presentations by R. Terry, 1970-1986, and Frank, Frank & Warring, 1998-2003)

# ILLUSTRATIVE MODEL OF DYNAMICS OF RACE RELATIONS
## (Suggestive, Not Definitive)

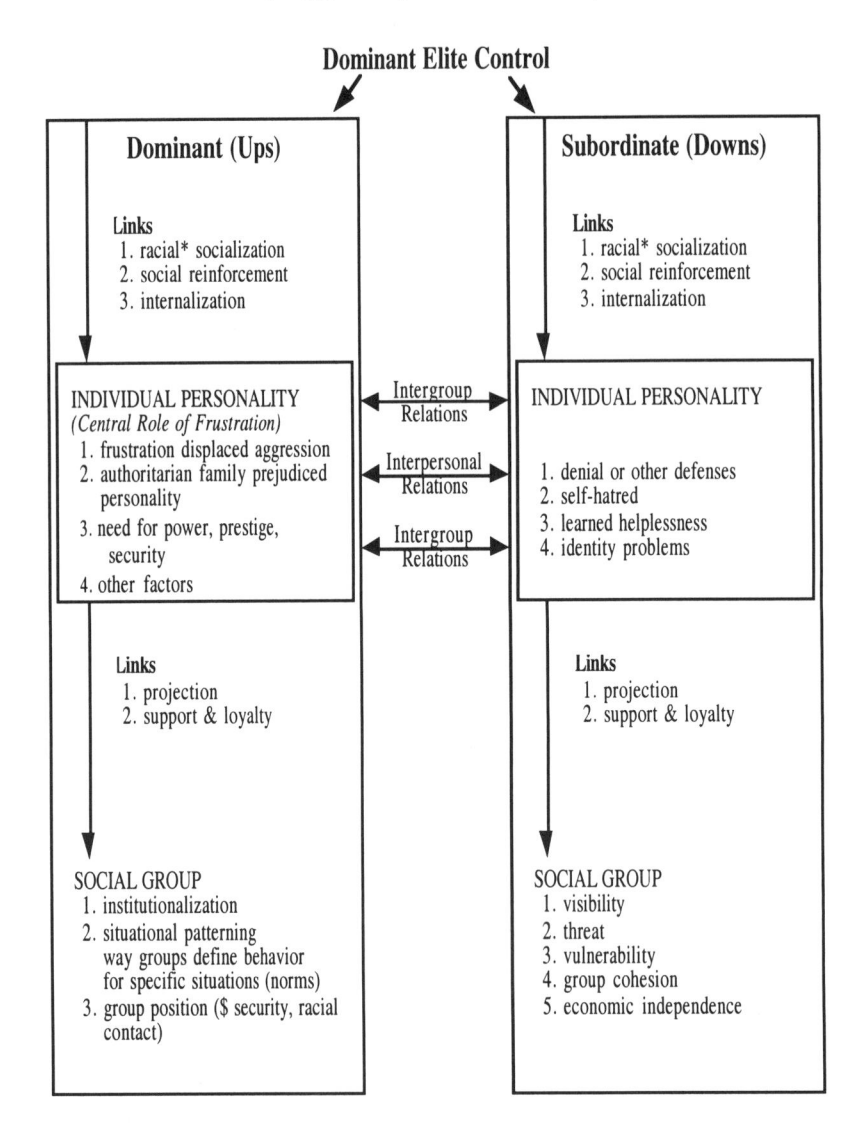

**Dominant Elite Control**

### Dominant (Ups)

**Links**
1. racial* socialization
2. social reinforcement
3. internalization

**INDIVIDUAL PERSONALITY**
*(Central Role of Frustration)*
1. frustration displaced aggression
2. authoritarian family prejudiced personality
3. need for power, prestige, security
4. other factors

**Links**
1. projection
2. support & loyalty

**SOCIAL GROUP**
1. institutionalization
2. situational patterning way groups define behavior for specific situations (norms)
3. group position ($ security, racial contact)

### Subordinate (Downs)

**Links**
1. racial* socialization
2. social reinforcement
3. internalization

**INDIVIDUAL PERSONALITY**
1. denial or other defenses
2. self-hatred
3. learned helplessness
4. identity problems

**Links**
1. projection
2. support & loyalty

**SOCIAL GROUP**
1. visibility
2. threat
3. vulnerability
4. group cohesion
5. economic independence

*Between the two columns:* Intergroup Relations / Interpersonal Relations / Intergroup Relations

Societal, Cultural, Historical, and Economic Context and Characteristics
* Other factors or intersecting variables such as gender may also be applied

## References
Allport, G. (1958). *The nature of prejudice.* Boston, MA: Anchor.
Kinloch, G (1974). *The dynamics of race relations*, McGraw-Hill.
Spring, J. (1997). *Deculturalization and the struggle for equality* (2nd ed.), McGraw-Hill.

### Reflection/Discussion Item
How does this model relate to the previous 5 pages?

# WHAT IS WHITENESS AND THIS SO-CALLED WHITE PRIVILEGE?

This position of white has often been seen as one of privilege in this society. Because of the widespread dominance by members of this group the race or classification is assumed to be white unless otherwise specified. This group has also been called "the meltable ethnics" meaning there is a large amount of perceived conformity by members who self identify as part of this group.

Various terms are used to describe members of this group, as is the case with members of other groups. Terms used in the United States to describe members of this group are Whites, Caucasians, European Americans, and occasionally Anglos. Many members of this group self-identify as American. What does this term really mean and does it apply to members of this group? If it applies only to this group what happens to other Americans?

When the US became a colony of Britain the British Common Law became a reality. It stated that to be considered a person for purposes of full taxation and rights one must be a free, white, male, landowner, twenty-one years old, and a member of the Church of England. In 1790 the United States enacted The Naturalization Law which declared that only "free, white immigrants could qualify to be American citizens (Omi & Winant, 1994). The class and ethnic differentials that existed then became symbols which carried into the socioeconomic status differences that exist today (Roeddiger, 1999).

According to Hacker (1992) two groups that were discriminated against despite being European were the Irish and Italians. They had very low status and in order to survive accepted the most hazardous and low paying jobs upon emigration to the U.S. Many of the specific European sub-groups settled in enclaves to avoid interaction with others. This phenomenon changed with second generation Europeans as they moved into mainstream society. A succession of world wars and economic booms facilitated this transition. As this trend continued ethnicity for them diminished in importance.

The term mainstream is often used to refer to a population that sees itself as interrelated and supportive of a particular set of values and a worldview. A sense of rugged individualism and competition coupled with the bootstrap ideology highlight this worldview. Obviously there are individuals whose values and view differ however the socialization process emphasizes these basic elements. Much diversity exists within the white category as within all other categories, nonetheless whiteness emerged as a category, which reflects a fundamental belief in the inherent genetic superiority of the white race.

In 1988 Peggy McIntosh published an article which was her autobiographical account of white-skin privilege. She defined white skin privilege as "an invisible package of unearned assets which white people can count on cashing in each day, but about which they were meant to remain oblivious" (p1). She then developed a list of 46 conditions of white privilege pertaining specifically to law, crime, and the courts. This was the impetus for many lengthy and protracted conversations on the topic of white privilege even though DuBois raised the issue in the 1920's. So why does it take a person who is white to bring the issue out front?

The concept of whites actually having a culture and DuBois discussed racial identity again in 1935 as an opportunity structure whereby European immigrants could easily assimilate into society. This was brought forward into the educational discourse more recently by Fine, Powell, Weiss & Wong (1997) who assisted in understanding some of the racial markers of society. When examined at either an individual or systems level it sheds light into the areas of preference and preferential treatment. This as well as work by Delgado & Stefancic (1998) examined whiteness, white culture, how whites define race, and how they view racism and white privilege. Whiteness is difficult to define for many whites due to an ingrained denial of privilege fostered by the rugged individualism inherent in the culture of the United States of America.

Whiteness is a global phenomenon that can be understood by examining colonization around the world by some of the European nations. Racial identity is a lived experience within a specific social context. According to Allen (2001) this social context is constructed and lived each and every day of life through a system that differentiates individuals into territories on the basis of skin color. This has the net result of producing different experiences for whites and people of color.

Most of the manifestations of whiteness in mainstream culture carry no explicit identification of specific association to white people. This gives the illusion of inclusion for all people and allows whites to be invisible and assume characteristics of normalcy. This further creates the dimension of focus on other groups. Consequently, most whites are oblivious to it presence and impact which appears to them to be normal and appropriate.

Tatum (1994) views the issue of race as critical to a socially just and equitable education as well as educational practice and policy. Whiteness must be identified and examined for what it is. Once it is isolated it must be examined in light and relation to intersecting variables such as gender, sexual orientation, class, age, and others. These all have an impact on individuals and must be examined and understood as social contexts. Sleeter (1996). Examines power and privilege in feminist discussions in gender and education as way to clarify and examine how white women benefit from the system as well.

The social contexts of the intersecting variables, and specifically that of whiteness must examine the issues of power and exploitation as a fundamental element (Roediger, 1999). What are the social contexts and how do they differentiate the fundamental elements? These must be examined to better understand their impact. Karenga (1999) states that whiteness studies can actually cultivate misunderstandings by confusing racial prejudice with racism. Racism is really about privilege and power, and the resulting benefits received by select individuals. Refer back to the discussions and definitions of these items for a clarification.

The different stage theories have applications to this phenomenon as well because stages of progression have generally been similar and are following patterns of awareness much the same as identity development. Think about the following progressions as you read this.

---

**Stages of possible progression**

Stages prior to understanding
1. Indifference or obliviousness-not aware of whiteness
2. Denial-whiteness has not bearing on anything
3. Individualized identity awareness-looking as aspects of self as individual and not as part of white culture
4. Beginning to understand-acknowledging whiteness and starting to examine its impact and importance

Stages that whites who are coming to understand whiteness and white privilege often go through are:
5. White savior-I am here to help and save all people of color.
6. Multicultural intellectualist-I understand and can explain all of these concepts without taking action.
7. White as ally-I understand and I am working to change the system for the betterment of all.

---

**Summary**
The entire process of racism is rooted in struggles over group membership, interests, and identity. Racialization has created a socially recognizable system of codes that situates people in one racial group or another. Part of this process is the socially constructed grouping of people and the beliefs, values, language, and privilege that accompany it.
When analyzing this be sure to separate the terms racism and prejudice. Any individual can be prejudice but only those who benefit from the system and consciously or unconsciously maintain it. The form of racism that has been institutionalized globally through European imperial colonization is called whiteness. It is a system of advantage that privileges those who become identified as white while disprivileging those who are non-white.

Once whites learn how whiteness constructs a very different world of experience for them they have a choice to make. Then can choose to continue operating with business as usual or they can choose to take action and work for social change as anti-racists. Examine your identity development process and ask how yours incorporates issues of social justice and anti-racism. Listening and attempting to understand are steps in the right direction, then analyze and take action. It is only when whites move into the third stage of the second level that they are able to take positive action.

**References**

Allen, R. (2001). Wake up, Neo.: White consciousness, hegemony, and identity in The Matrix. In J. Slater, S. Fein, & C. Rossatto (Eds.) The Freirean legacy. New York: Peter Lang Publishers.

Delgado, R., & Stefancic, J. (1998). *Critical white studies: Looking behind the mirror.* Temple University Press.

DuBois, W.E.B. (1935). *Black reconstruction in America.* New York: Simon & Schuster.

Fine, M., Powell, L., Weiss, L. & Wong, L. (Eds.). (1997). *Off white: Readings on race, power, and society* (preface vii-xii). New York: Routledge.

Hacker, A. (1992). *Two nations: Black and White, separate, hostile, unequal.* New York, NY: Scribner.

Karenga, M. (1999). Whiteness studies: Deceptive or welcome discourse? *Black Issues in Higher Education, 16(6),* 26-28.

Kincheloe, J., Steinberg, S., Rodgiruez, N., Chennault, R. (Eds.). (1998). *White reign: Deploying whiteness in America.* New York: St. Martin's Press.

McIntosh, P. (1988). *White privilege, color and crime: A personal account.* Wellesley: MA: Author.

Omi, M. & Winant, H. (1994). *Racial formation in the U.S.* (2$^{nd}$ ed.). New York, NY: Routledge.

Roedigger, D. (1999). *Wages of whiteness: Race and the making of the American working class.* New York: Verso.

Sleeter, C. (1996). *Power and privilege in with middle-class feminist discussions of gender and education.* In C. Sleeter, Multicultural education as social activism, 1996. Albany: State University of New York Press.

Tatum, B. (1994). Teaching white students about racism: The search for white allies and the restoration of hope. *Teachers College Record 95(4), 462-476.*

---

**Reflection/Discussion Items**
**(Be sure to allow equal time for all group members to discuss these items.)**

1. In a group of four name and describe some effects of one unearned privilege you have had in life.

2. In a group of four discuss a way in which you have seen white privilege at work in school.

3. Name at least one way in which you can use your power to share power or use privilege to weaken systems of unearned privilege.

4. Discuss some frustrations, difficulties, or payoffs you have seen in the use of time.

5. What questions do you have concerning this issue and its application to you? (Are these true questions or statements of denial?)

# SECTION VII

# SOCIOECONOMIC STATUS AND POVERTY

***Rationale*:** It is necessary to develop a deeper understanding of socioeconomic status and poverty as it impacts and students in schools. This will assist in understanding personal actions and contextual orientations of self and others and can lead to improvements in academic success.

***Objectives:***
1. To examine poverty and socioeconomic status.
2. To understand how poverty is defined.
3. To understand the impact of poverty and status on teachers' and students' behavior and interactions.
4. To understand expectations and the element of socioeconomic status in school and society.

# POVERTY

**What is Poverty?**
Poverty is the condition of being poor. When it is manifested for two or more generations it is called generational poverty. If it exists for a shorter time and is caused by circumstances such as death or illness it is labeled situational poverty. These need to be taken into account when examining the income inequality in the United States. Income inequality has increased in the United States during the last twenty years which has led to an increasing divide in the school experiences and consequently in those leaving school.

In order to assist in understanding economic bias and resulting pressures the following pages are designed to provide information that may not be known or applied. A specific socioeconomic group reflects assets, prestige, privileges, and power. It very strongly impacts the choices one has or often as in the case of schools, the choices one is given.

Education in the United States is not uniformly the same for everyone. Children of different social classes are likely to attend vastly different types of schools, to encounter different types of instruction, to study different curricula, to have different types of co-curricular activities, and to leave school at different times.

**The Nature of Poverty**
Increases in the prevalence of poverty have been accompanied by changes in the nature of poverty. Poor individuals living in high poverty communities have a lower access to jobs, to quality public and private services, transportation systems, and informal social support systems. They are also subjected to increased exposure to life threatening environmental stressors such as street violence, illegal drugs, homelessness, and negative role models. These all contribute to disadvantages for children and adults. This poverty status often called socioeconomic status (SES) creates overwhelming odds against those who are in poverty (McLoyd, 1998).

When the basic infrastructure is missing numerous problems result for the individuals and ultimately for society. When you think of leaving school remember to examine dropout compared to graduation rates. Regardless of ethnicity or race, poor children are much ore likely than non-poor children to suffer developmental delay and damage, drop out of high school, and to give birth during the teen years. College attendance is also heavily dependent on access to financial resources, and if you do not graduate from high school it is almost impossible to go to college. So as you can see the variables once again intersect (race, gender, SES, education, etc.).

**Teachers and Schools**
Classrooms and schools are significant sources of variation in the achievement of students. They also appear to contribute to the income gap between economic groups through academic and interpersonal processes. Even in kindergarten and lower elementary grade teachers tend to perceive poor and low SES students as less capable. They have also been shown to provide to the academic achievement gap in a number of ways. If the teachers grew up in a middle class environment they are more likely to hold differential expectations and more likely to hold social class biases. If teachers are aware of these biases and behaviors changes can be made to help to eliminate them which will consequently lead to narrowing of the achievement gap.

Integrated programs for youth in poverty require interdisciplinary collaboration among community residents, schools, churches, business, law enforcement officials, politicians, and others. Programs that are the most effective are those that extend beyond the individual youth to modify the school environment (Durlak & Wells, 1997).

On the next page is a chart that show poverty guidelines developed by the Department of Health and Human Services. As you read through it please consider options you have in comparison with others. Options are a sign or symbol of power and choice. People in poverty have extremely limited options.

**Poverty Measures**

| The following information is based on 2003 Department of Health and Human Services Poverty Guidelines* |||| 
|---|---|---|---|
| Size of Family Unit | 48 Contiguous States and Washington, D.C. | Alaska | Hawaii |
| 1 | $8,980 | $11,210 | $10,330 |
| 2 | 12,120 | 15,140 | 13,940 |
| 3 | 15,260 | 19,070 | 17,550 |
| 4 | 18,400 | 23,000 | 11,160 |
| 5 | 21.540 | 26,930 | 24,770 |
| 6 | 24,680 | 30,860 | 28,380 |
| 7 | 27,820 | 34,790 | 31,990 |
| 8 | 30,960 | 38,720 | 35,600 |
| For each additional person | 3,140 | 3,930 | 3,610 |

*Programs using the guidelines to determine eligibility include the national school lunch program, Head Start, the Food Stamp program, the Low-Income Home Energy Assistance program, and the Children's Health Insurance Program. The US Census Bureau also has a slight difference based on the number of adults living in the home and if they are over or under age 65. The poverty guidelines are not defined for Puerto Rico, The U.S. Virgin Islands, American Samoa, Guam, the Republic of the Marshall Islands, the Federated States of Micronesia, the Commonwealth of the Northern Mariana Islands, and Palau.*

**Poverty Measures**

There are two slightly different versions of the federal poverty measure. The poverty thresholds are the original version of the poverty measure and are updated each year by the Census Bureau. These are used for statistical purposes to determine estimates of the number of people living in the United States in poverty each year.

The second version is the poverty guidelines, which are issued each year by the Department of Health and Human Services. These are used to determine financial eligibility for certain federal programs such as the school lunch program. Both versions are updated annually using the Consumer Price Index. Do not be confused if you see slightly different versions. This stems from different decisions made by different agencies at different times.

Suppose a family consists of five people: two children, their mother, father, and a great aunt. Their poverty level in 2003 was $21,540 so if their total income from all five people is $21,540 or higher they are not considered "poor" according to the official government level. As you can see from this, they are not rich and will have to do without a lot of items in order to survive. So the real issues becomes one of survival and quality of life.

The U.S. Census reports that in 1999, 20.8 percent of children in the U. S. under 18 lived in poverty. This occurs not only in urban areas but also in rural and suburban ones. However, urban areas often receive the most press due to population density. In industrialized or post-industrialized countries such as the United States and Canada, approximately three quarters of the population live in urban centers (Marsella, 1991). In developing countries the number of cities has been increasing at such a rapid rate that there are twice as many cities in developing countries as in industrialized or post-industrialized countries (United Nations Children's Fund, 2000).

The center estimates that between 1979 and 1999, the number of children under age six living in poverty in the United States grew from 3.5 million to 9.1 million, and the percentage of such children living in families with incomes below the poverty line rose from 18% to 25%. The United States ranks lowest in caring for children in poverty and is the only "industrialized" or "post-industrialized" nation in the world that does not provide a direct subsidy to families with children.

**Understanding Elements of Economics**
Understanding and working with students (and their families) from poverty is contingent upon examining some of the perspectives they may operate from. Regardless of race or ethnicity, children who are in poverty are much more likely than to suffer developmental delays and damage, drop out of high school, and to give birth during their teen years.

After you complete and discuss the poverty exercise there is a brief description of how people in that particular category most often view the item and often behave in school. Remember that not all people who are or who appear to be in a certain category will operate in the same manner.

**Reference**
Department of Health and Human Services (2003). *The 2003 Health and Human Services poverty guidelines,* http://www.gov/hhes/poverty.htm.

---

**Reflection/Discussion Items and Activity**

1. What does this information indicate to you?

2. How will this be beneficial in developing a contextual understanding for others with whom you work?

3. On the following page is an activity to help you learn more about economics. Be sure so spend no more than you are allocated and keep track of all assumptions. You will be asked to explain your budget, justify your spending, and all assumptions you have made.

# POVERTY EXERCISE

Consider yourself as the sole support of your family of four. You may define the ages, sex, and living arrangements for your family. They must live within 50 miles of the metropolitan area. You must have 2 or 3 children under 17 years old. Make careful note of all the assumptions you are making. You will be given an amount of money by the professor. This is your monthly income after taxes. You have no other income! Please budget your money in the following categories.

| ITEM | BUDGET | GROUP BUDGET |
|---|---|---|
| Rent or Mortgage (insurance?) | | |
| Utilities (heat, electric, phone, etc) | | |
| Food (eat out?) | | |
| Clothing (jewelry?) | | |
| Transportation (insurance?) | | |
| Medical/Dental Expenses | | |
| Insurance (all) | | |
| Recreation/Entertainment | | |
| Savings or Investments | | |
| Other | | |
| TOTAL | | |

List all of your assumptions for this budget:

---

**Reflection/Discussion Items**

1. Keep track of all your expenditures and assumptions for each. After you have completed your budget you will be assigned to a group for budget comparison and discussion of all assumptions and implications.

2. When your group has discussed its basic assumptions you will be asked to share them with the class.

3. How do economic assumptions impact students in schools today?

4. What else have you learned from this activity?

# PERCEPTIONS, SOCIOECONOMIC STATUS, AND SCHOOL BEHAVIOR

Socioeconomic status is a social class identity group that has a strong impact on the lives of individuals. It has bee estimated that 80% of the individuals in the United States will remain in the same socioeconomic class income bracket in which they were born. It is extremely important for educators to consider how our own class structure, class values, and class behavior constantly impact all of our thoughts and decisions. The following information comes from work by Payne (1999) and Slocum and Payne (2000) and is designed to provide assistance in attempting to understand the values and behavior of students.

| SES | Value/Ideology | School Behavior |
|---|---|---|
| | **Possessions** | |
| POVERTY | People | Sticks up for friends |
| MIDDLE CLASS | Things | Give gifts in appreciation |
| WEALTH | One of a kind objects, legacies, pedigrees | Give expensive gifts (origin is important) |
| | **Time** | |
| POVERTY | Present most important-decisions made for the moment based on feelings or survival | Tardy-decisions based on survival |
| MIDDLE CLASS | Future most important-decisions made against future ramifications | Punctual, plans for homework, prioritizes |
| WEALTH | Traditions and past history most important decisions partially made on basis of tradition | Follows schedules and traditions |
| | **Money** | |
| POVERTY | To be used spent | Spends money, shares with friends |
| MIDDLE CLASS | To be managed | Saves money and plans for its use, does not share |
| WEALTH | To be conserved invested | Never talks about money |
| | **Personality** | |
| POVERTY | Is for entertainment - a sense of humor is highly valued | Class clown, jokes a lot, loud and uses colorful language |
| MIDDLE CLASS | Is for acquisition and stability achievement is highly valued | Displays social graces, uses please and thank you |
| WEALTH | Is for connections - financial, political, and social connections are highly valued | People acknowledged and valued for their titles and families |
| | **Food** | |
| POVERTY | Key question: Did you have enough? Quantity is important | Will take food from others, wants more |
| MIDDLE CLASS | Key question: Did you like it? Quality is important | Won't eat what is not liked |
| WEALTH | Key question: Was it presented well? | Won't eat cafeteria food, prefers gourmet |

| SES | Value/Ideology | School Behavior |
|---|---|---|
| | Appearance is important | meals |
| | **Destiny** | |
| POVERTY | Believes in fate - can not do much to mitigate chance | Not my fault, no sense of choice, they don't like me |
| MIDDLE CLASS | Believes in choice - can change the future with good choices now | Makes choices to receive payoffs |
| WEALTH | Nobility obligates, rights and obligations | Follow in footsteps of family, obligation to social and family status |
| | **Education** | |
| POVERTY | Valued and revered as an abstract but not as a reality | Can't see relevance of school to world, not practical, won't use it |
| MIDDLE CLASS | Crucial for climbing success ladder and making money | Motivated, crucial for success rite of passage |
| WEALTH | Necessary tradition for making and maintaining connections | Follows in footsteps of family, obligation to social class and status of family |
| | **Language** | |
| POVERTY | Casual register language is about survival | May use profanity, verbally reacts quickly without thinking of consequences |
| MIDDLE CLASS | Formal register language is about negotiation | Able to verbalize thoughts and feelings, uses language to manipulate |
| WEALTH | Formal register language is about connections | Name dropping and subtle inferences |
| | **World View** | |
| POVERTY | Sees the world in terms of local setting | Reference point is immediate neighborhood |
| MIDDLE CLASS | Sees the world in terms of national setting | Reference point reflects national perspective, travels and takes weekend retreats |
| WEALTH | Sees the world in terms of international setting | Reference point is international, vacations in foreign countries and has multiple homes |
| | **Family Structure** | |
| POVERTY | Tends to be matriarchal | Don't call my momma/auntie no phone |
| MIDDLE CLASS | Tends to be patriarchal | Don't call or tell my dad |
| WEALTH | Depends on who has the money | Don't embarrass my family name |

| SES | Value/Ideology | School Behavior |
|---|---|---|
| | **Clothing** | |
| POVERTY | Clothing valued for the individual style and expression of personality | Makes a personal statement with hair and clothing, may look like entertainers |
| MIDDLE CLASS | Clothing valued for its quality and acceptance into the norm, label important | Wears what is fashionable |
| WEALTH | Clothing valued for its artistic sense and the expression, designer is important | Wears designer clothes, makes artistic statement |
| | **Driving Force** | |
| POVERTY | Survival, relationships, and entertainment | School is to be with friends and to entertain |
| MIDDLE CLASS | Work and achievement | School is for achievement, good grades |
| WEALTH | Financial, political, and social connections are the most important | The school attended and persons attending with make a statement |

## Personal Application

What is your personal perception and description of each item? Has it changed over time? How will you relate to and work with students whose perceptions may differ from your own? These are some of the questions you will need to answer to deal more effectively with socioeconomic status bias and how it impacts a person. Remember to compare your salary with that of the average person in the community in which you are working to better understand some of their perceptions, attitudes, and behaviors.

## Conclusions

It is important to understand how unconscious attitudes may be formed relating to class bias. Being in poverty is rarely about a lack of intelligence or ability. Students who come from poverty situations need to have at least two sets of behaviors from which to choose so they can understand and differentiate street behavior from school behavior. In order to better understand and deal with these expectations it helps to know where people have been and how they perceive situations. This will help to meet their needs and provide successful learning environments. There are many strategies for helping students from poverty.

Some of the key elements to keep in mind are listed here.
Poverty is relative.
Generational and situational poverty is very different.
Develop healthy and supportive relationships.
Establish comprehensive support systems that provide academic, emotional, and social support.
Structure, choice, and skill building need to be part of the discipline approach.
Use a variety of teaching modalities. As an example, academically challenged students are often most effective with kinesthetic learning.
Teach and empower behavior choice and understand that home and school behaviors may be vastly different.
Students will respond to appropriate techniques when applied in a fair and consistent manner.
Work to ensure that opportunities to participate are provided for all students.
To mover from poverty to middle class or middle class to wealth an individual must give up relationships for achievement.

Apply this information to develop a broader contextual basis for the values and behavior of the individuals with whom you interact. With this contextual base understanding and more appropriate actions can follow.

**References**

Durlak, J. & Wells, A. (1997). Primary prevention mental health programs for children and adolescents: A meta-analytic review. *American Journal of Community Psychology,* 25, pp. 115-152.

Federal Register. (2000). Vol. 65, No. 31, February 15, pp. 7555-7557.

Marsella, A. (1991). *Urbanization and Mental Disorder: An overview of conceptual and methodological research issues and findings.* Report prepared for the Urbanization panel of the World Health Organization Commissions on Health and the Environment. Geneva, Switzerland: World Health Organization.

McLoyd, V. (1998). Socioeconomic disadvantage and child development. *American Psychologist,* Vol. 53, no. 2, pp. 185-204.

National Center for Children in Poverty (1999). http://cpmcnet.columbia.edu/dept/nccp/

Payne, R. (1998). *A framework for understanding poverty.* Baytown, TX: RTF Publishing.

Slocum, P. & Payne, R. (2000). *Removing the mask: Giftedness in poverty.* Baytown, TX: RTF Publishing

United Nations Children's Fund (2000). *The progress of nations.* New York: Oxford University Press.

U.S. Census Bureau (2003). *Poverty,* Washington, DC: Author. http://www.census.gov/

U.S. Department of Health and Human Services (2003). *The 2003 Health and Human Services poverty Guidelines,* http://www.gov/hhes/poverty.htm.

---

**Reflection/Discussion Items**

1. What have you learned from this section?

2. What will you do differently in interactions with students in schools?

3. How will you attempt to relate differently (if need be) with students and their families whose economic situation differs from yours and/or your previous level?

# THE TRUTH ABOUT WELFARE

In a recent memo from COPE, a publication of the Committee on Political Education of the AFL-CIO, 10 key facts were printed to dispel the myths that have grown up in this country concerning welfare.

The following facts are from COPE the fact sheet on "Welfare: Everybody's Whipping Boy":

**Fact No. 1** People wind up on welfare not because they are cheats, loafers or malingerers, but because they are poor. They are not just poor in money, but in everything. They've had poor education, poor health care, poor chances at decent employment and poor prospects for anything better.

**Fact No. 2** But even most of the poor are not on welfare. Some 58 million Americans receive some form of welfare benefits. There are more than 35 million officially below the poverty level of $18,400 a year for a family of four. Another 30-50 million are just barely above it. Any $18,400 a year, as everyone knows, does not afford extravagance.

**Fact No. 3** Of the 58 million receiving welfare, about 30 million are children under 18 years of age.

**Fact No. 4** Less than one percent – about 550,000 – of the welfare participants are able-bodied males. Many of these are in their late-middle years. Most are uneducated or undereducated. All are required by law to sign up for work, and among the fathers in this group one in three is enrolled in work training.

**Fact No. 5** Apart from children and the relative handful of potential employables, on welfare are more than 15 million aged, more than one million totally and permanently disabled or blind. All of these are in programs roughly supported 50-50 by state and local couples, most of whom work full time but are paid less than they would be on welfare. These are the working poor.

**Fact No. 6** No one is getting rich on welfare. It allows, at best, barebones living. In no state does the average welfare payment bring a family up to poverty level. Maximum payments for a family of four range from $1,100 a year in Mississippi to $12,600+ in New York, New Jersey, Massachusetts, Minnesota and Connecticut. Thirty-nine states pay less than their own established standard of need.

**Fact No. 7** Cheating and fraud in welfare are minimal. There is, of course, some cheating and dishonesty among welfare clients. Try to imagine any program involving 58 million persons that is entirely free of fraud. But the U.S. Department of Health, Education and Welfare estimates there is cheating among less than one percent of welfare cases. Add to this another two to three percent on the rolls due to misunderstanding or technical-bureaucratic error, and there is an upper range of four to five percent receiving benefits that are either completely or partially ineligible. It is likely that this range of cheating, plus error, exists in income tax payments of citizens and in many other areas of activity.

**Fact No. 8** Welfare mothers are not churning out illegitimate children. Nearly 70 percent of all children in welfare families are legitimate, according to the Social and Rehabilitation Services of Heath and Human Services. Thirty percent of welfare families with any children have only one child; 25 percent have two; 18 percent have three. The remaining families have four or more children.

**Fact No. 9** More than 48 percent of welfare families are white; about 43 are black. Most of the remaining are American Indians, Asians and other racialized population. Many are immigrants who recently arrived in the U.S.

**Fact No. 10** There is no evidence to sustain the belief that welfare is necessarily habit-forming, that is that "once on welfare, always on welfare." Half the families on welfare have been on the rolls 20 months or less; two-thirds have been on the rolls less than three years. Fewer than one in five has received welfare for five years or more. About 65 percent of welfare cases at any given time are on for the first time; about one-third are repeaters.

# SECTION VIII

# SEXISM, HETEROSEXISM, GENDER FAIR ISSUES, SEXUAL HARASSMENT, HOMOPHOBIA AND RELATED ISSUES

***Rationale*:** The last few decades have seen an increased push for equality in employment and other rights (credit, ownership of property, parental leave, etc.) across sexual lines. Proponents of social, educational, and legal change have pointed to patterns of socialization that, they say, lead to a loss of academic potential, of self-esteem, and loss of occupational potential. Gender roles have been and will likely continue to be challenged and changed with more flexible patterns developing. Schools and social service institutions can expect increasing pressure to change biased practices, both those that pertain to learning environments and the process by which women and men, gays, lesbians, bisexuals and persons who are transgendered (GLBT) are treated.

## ***Objectives***

1. To identify and compare examples of personal and cultural biases related to institutional and instructional bias.
2. To define some of the words currently in use such as sexism, heterosexism, homophobia, feminism, sexual harassment, and other related terms.
3. To raise awareness of the pervasiveness of harassment, heterosexism, homophobia, and institutional sexism.
4. To examine the power aspects of gender related bias and to examine one's own power to keep or change sexist practices.
5. To identify sources of prejudice and sexual harassment.
6. To examine ways in which to move from sexist to nonsexist practices in classrooms, schools, and the community.
7. To examine one's own attitudes, feelings, and behavior with respect to conventional and unconventional sex-role and gender stereotyped behaviors.
8. To recognize structural biases against the recognition of female and GLBT competence.
9. To recognize individual and structural biases surrounding homophobia.
10. To identify and understand elements of bias against persons who are GLBT.
11. To examine ways to eliminate sexual harassment, heterosexism, and homophobia.

# GENDER

Popular beliefs concerning the differences between females and males offer differ from scientific reality. People do not chose to be born a boy or girl, this is determined before birth and is often one of the first element discussed about them. Although described by their gender and discussed prior to and after birth, the only real difference in sex is reproductive organs. Despite this fact they are discussed differently creating the construction of gender for the child.

The net result of the early discussions that carries over for a lifetime is the creation of socially constructed beliefs called gender. In differentiating then, gender is socially constructed while sex is biological. "Sex refers to the biological differences between men and women; gender relates to the normative expectations attached to each sex" (Walsh, 1997, p.7). Western societies see two separate and discrete sexes and two distinguishable genders because society is built on two classes of people. Once this category of gender is given, people and their attributes become "gendered" and gender often operates on a continuum from masculine at one end to feminine at the other. This is sometimes described in a linear fashion and other time in a circular one. An example of the linear continuum is shown here.

| Gender Continuum |
|---|
| Masculine <--------------------------------------------------------------------------------------------→ Feminine |

### Role Socialization

One of the most important learning experiences in any society is the knowledge that one is separate from other members of the family. This leads to a development of crucial elements in self-identity of which gender is a significant part. The gender group, according to Cushner, McClelland, and Safford (2003) is more important to your sense of self than almost anything else. In all cultural groups the identity based on gender includes sets of rules and expectations for how girls and boys should act and speak, what clothing to wear, and their sense of place in family and community. Although few differences separate men and women, the two are often symbolically segregated. Many of these symbolic issues lead to specific social behaviors tied to status.

When children are young they are programmed to operate in one manner or the other. The reality is that most of us slide or move back and forth on the gender continuum and that we all possesses capabilities in both areas. The actions, of course, may be forbidden unless we are allowed to experiment or move away from our cultural groups' expectations. In order to better conceptualize this you can think of gender as a cultural group with its own values, symbols, and behaviors (Banks, 2001). A child is taught and learns to distinguish women from men and boys from girls. The child also learns to express appropriate types of behavior and demonstrate gender appropriate preferences for self and others.

Gender creates its own lived reality and the following definitions are often used to clarify this. Gender identity is the psychological sense of being male or female. Gender role behavior is conformity to culturally defined norms of masculinity or femininity. Sexual orientation is the feeling of attraction to males, females, or both.

### Gender Bias

Neither sex nor gender are pure categories. This is why the continuum is helpful in understanding this phenomenon. Gender bias is having an unfair expectation and/or treating girls and boys much differently. This is quite prevalent when comparing boys and girls from low-income families. Girls from low-income families have been found to be less likely to attend college than those from more affluent ones due to family finances according to Sadker and Sadker (1994). Their choices are limited although it appears that a slight impact has been made on occupational choice for girls of high socioeconomic status because they are now more likely to choose careers once held only be males.

Work on the culture of women in the last three decades has focused on a construction of knowledge. In this construction ways in which knowledge is grounded in the personality of the researcher are seen as crucial. The basic culture of the person impacts their production and construction of a knowledge base (Code, 1991). The sex (gender identity) of the person doing the interpretation, the knower, is truly a significant component of the entire process. According to Belenky (1986), Harding (1991), and Goldberger et al. (1996) women's ways of knowing differ from men's in the U.S. There is a unique structure created by social, economic, and cultural position, which impacts the knowledge base and knowledge structure.

Although gender and social class have both been found to have an interactive effect on achievement, gender and social class, they have more often than not been treated in isolation in the research. The research has also most often been standardized on middle class populations and it reflects the predominant view of researchers themselves. The significant components in socialization that are further intertwined with social class are parents/family, television, children's books, toys, and play activities. Even equity research has failed to treat social class, race, and gender as intersecting issues according to Flanagan (1993). There are compounding effects of each that lead to specific outcomes dealing with self-image, achievement, and behaviors.

Studies of gender or class in relation to achievement also show a bias in discipline. Many psychologists have adopted a passive role due to beliefs in rugged individualism and only look at motivation. They fail to account for the intersection of the variables and their overall impact. The fields of vocational education are even more pronounced in their biased treatment of individuals along class, race, and gender lines according to Wirt, et al. (1989).

**Intersecting Variables**
Gender, ethnic group, economics (SES), and other variables intersect to provide different outcomes. Schools are one component in the process along with mass media, significant adults, economic constraints and opportunities, community values, religion, and larger cultural value systems. Socioeconomic status or social class refers to access to economic, political, and cultural power in a society.

Over 70% of all women between the ages of 20 and 64 are working outside the home. According to the U. S. Census Bureau (2000) in two parent families, the working women account for 50% or African American family income, 40% or Hispanic/Latino American family income, and over 35% of European American family income. They all play an essential role in economic survival.

A multicultural curriculum that includes information that helps students examine and clarify their gender stereotypes and misconceptions will help both boys and girls to attain educational equity. Content about people of color, women, and persons with exceptionalities should be included in the curriculum. These assist in giving everyone an accurate view of U.S. society and culture. A pluralistic democracy functions best when all citizens fully participate.

Girls and boys as individuals are very diverse and they are far more alike in their skills, competencies, and educational outcomes than they are different according to Banks (2001). The strengths and deficits often associated with each sex as separate are in reality not innate to either group. These can not be attributed to biological differences; they are socially conditioned responses. Regardless of the sources of the gender gap, schools have a mission to educate all students to levels of competency and broaden skill opportunities rather than enforce stereotypes. Even though it is clear that women and men have similar intelligence, there are some differences in the ways they are treated in society.

**The Best and Worst States for Women in 2002: Politics, Economics, Reproductive Rights, Health**
Many women in the U.S. are seeing important changes in their lives and access to political, economic, and social rights. Not all women, however, have full access to the country's political and economic resources, nor are they sharing equally in the fruits of progress. Women do not enjoy equality with men and lack many of the legal guarantees that would allow them to achieve it. The rankings and grades for each of the composite indices presented below were calculated by combining data on several indicators of women's status in each of the five areas. The Institute for Women's Policy Research (2002) examined the indicators of women's status and based on their data developed the following figures as they compared women in each of the 50 states and the District of Columbia.

**Political Participation**

| Best States | Worst States |
|---|---|
| 1. Washington | 50. Pennsylvania |
| 2. Maine | 49. New Jersey |
| 3. Minnesota | 48. Kentucky |
| 4. California | 47. Pennsylvania |
| 5. Missouri | 46. West Virginia |

(excludes the District of Columbia)

**Employment and Earnings**

| Best States | Worst States |
|---|---|
| 1. District of Columbia | 51. West Virginia |
| 2. Maryland | 50. Louisiana |
| 3. Alaska | 49. Mississippi |
| 4. Minnesota | 48. Wyoming |
| 5. Colorado | 47. Arkansas |

**Social and Economic Autonomy**

| Best States | Worst States |
|---|---|
| 1. District of Columbia | 51. Arkansas |
| 2. Maryland | 50. Louisiana |
| 3. Colorado | 49. Mississippi |
| 4. Connecticut | 48. West Virginia |
| 5. Massachusetts | 47. Kentucky |

**Reproductive Rights**

| Best States | Worst States |
|---|---|
| 1. Hawaii | 51. Mississippi |
| 2. Vermont | 50. North Dakota |
| 3. Maryland | 49. South Dakota |
| 4. Connecticut | 48. Wisconsin |
| 5. California | 47. Nebraska |

**Health and Well Being**

| Best States | Worst States |
|---|---|
| 1. Utah | 51. District of Columbia |
| 2. Hawaii | 50. Kentucky |
| 3. North Dakota | 49. Mississippi |
| 4. Minnesota | 48. West Virginia |
| 5. South Dakota | 47. Louisiana |

Based on these and other related factors a composite rating was completed which indicated which are the best and worst states for women according to the Institute for Women's Policy Research (2002).

**Overall Rank**

| Best States | Worst States |
|---|---|
| 1. Massachusetts | 51. Mississippi |
| 2. Minnesota | 50. Tennessee |
| 3. Vermont (all tied) | 49. Kentucky |
| 4. Connecticut | 48. Oklahoma |
| 5. Washington (tied) | 47. Arkansas |
| 6. Alaska | 46. Alabama |
| 7. Maine | 45. Pennsylvania |
| 8. New Hampshire (tied) | 44. Florida |

### Women in the United States: What's Promising

Between the fall of 1996 and fall of 2002, the number of women governors jumped from one to five, the number of women in the U.S. Senate grew from nine to 13, and the number of women in the U.S. House increased from 49 to 60. In all but four states, the wage ratio between women's and men's earnings rose between 1989 and 1999. Between 1995 and 1999, women's poverty fell in all but eight states and nationally it dropped from 13.7 percent to 12.0 percent. Between 1996 and 2002, 19 states adopted laws mandating comprehensive coverage for contraceptives by health insurance companies. Some of these are in danger of being repealed. Women's average annual incidence rate of AIDS decreased from 9.4 per 100,000 in 1997 to 8.7 per 100,000 in 2000. Between 1998 and 2002, 20 states introduced legislation that would expand unemployment insurance coverage to cover parental leave (although none passed it).

### Women in the United States: What's Disappointing

The proportion of women state legislators grew only slightly, from 20.8 percent to 22.6 percent, between 1996 and 2002, and in a third of all states women's political representation dropped. In 25 states where the ratio of women's to men's earnings increased between 1989 and 1999, it did so in part because men's earnings fell (in constant dollars).

In eight states, women's poverty actually increased between 1995 and 1999, and in another nine states, it fell by less than 1.0 percentage point (compared with 1.7 percentage points nationally). In 1996, 14 states had waiting periods for women seeking abortions; by 2002, 22 states did. Between 1997 and 2000, rates of chlamydia grew from 336 to 404 per 100,000 women. Since 1996, additional nine states have implemented family caps, denying benefits to children conceived or born while a mother is receiving welfare. Women are more likely to vote than men in all but seven states: Hawaii, Kentucky, New Jersey, North Dakota, Oklahoma, Pennsylvania, and South Dakota. However, the number of women holding legislative seats has increased only slightly and is nowhere near the 50% mark.

### Women in Minnesota

Women in Minnesota and the United States as a whole are seeing important changes in their lives and in their access to political, economic, and social rights. However, they by no means enjoy equality with men, and they still lack many of the legal guarantees that would allow them to achieve that equality. Women in Minnesota and the nation would benefit from stronger enforcement of equal opportunity laws, better political representation, adequate and affordable childcare, and other policies that would help improve their status. The rankings and grades for each of the composite indices in the chart below were calculated by combining data on several indicators of women's status in each of five areas. These data were used to compare women in Minnesota with women in each of the 50 states and the District of Columbia. In addition, they were used to evaluate women's status in Minnesota in comparison with women's ideal status, as reflected in the state's grades

**How Minnesota Ranks on Key Indicators**

| Indicator | National Rank | Regional Rank | Grade |
|---|---|---|---|
| Composite Political Participation | 3 | 1 | B |
| Employment and Earnings | 4 | 1 | B |
| Social and Economic Autonomy | 8 | 1 | B- |
| Reproductive Rights | 15 | 1 | B- |
| Health and Well Being | 4 | 2 | B+ |

Although more women are entering traditional male fields of employment many barriers still exist. Such discrimination greatly affects the quality of life for women and families. As you can tell from these readings and tables the status of women has greatly improved across the United States however it still has a long way to go to become closer to equal with that of men.

Conscious and unconscious separation and gender discrimination of girls and boys in school on the basis of perceived sex happens on a regular basis in schools today. This behavior emphasizes differences much the same way sorting students by race or religion would. Differential treatment also occurs in schools, which impacts academic achievement. Boys are often called upon more frequently, asked more difficult questions, given longer wait time, and if they give an incorrect answer are told to keep trying. The net effect of this behavior is to convey messages to girls that they are not as worthy of an education. Think about your school experiences and reflect on process and outcomes. Think about how you will operate in your profession.

**References**

Banks, J. (2001). *Cultural diversity in education: Foundations, curriculum, and teaching,* (4th ed.). Needham Heights, MA: Allyn & Bacon.

Belenky, M. Clinchy, B., Goldberger, N., & Tarule, J. (1986). *Women's ways of knowing: The development of self, voice, and mind.* New York: Basic Books.

Code, L. (1991). What can she know? *Feminist theory and the construction of knowledge.* Ithaca, NY: Cornell University Press.

Flanagan, C. (1993). Gender and social class: Intersecting issues in women's achievement. *Educational Psychologist* 28(4), 357-378.

Goldberger, N., Tarule, J. Clinchy, G. & Belenky, M. (Eds.). (1996). *Knowledge, difference, and power,* New York: Basic Books.

Massey, D., and Denton, N. (1993). *American apartheid: Segregation and the making of the underclass.* Harvard University Press.

Cushner, K., McClelland, A., and Safford, P., (2003). *Human diversity in education: An integrative approach* (4th ed.). New York, NY: McGraw-Hill.

Nelson, J. (1995). *Post-industrial capitalism: Exploring economic inequality in America.* Thousand Oaks, CA: Sage.

Sadker, M. & Sadker, D. (1994). *Failing at fairness: How America's schools cheat girls.* New York: Scribners.

The Institute for Women's Policy Research (2002). *The status of women in the states. Author.* 1707 L. Street NW, Suite 750 Washington, DC 20036

U. S. Census Bureau (2000). Statistical Abstract. Washington, DC: Author. http://www.census.gov/

Walsh, M. R. (Ed.), (1997). *Women, men, and gender: Ongoing debates.* New Haven, CT: Yale University Press.

Wirt, J., Murasicin, L., Goodwin, D., & Meyer, R. (1989). National assessment of vocational education: Summary of findings and recommendations. Washington, DC: U.S. Department of Education Institute for Women's Policy.

---

**Reflection/Discussion Items**
1. Have you ever felt you were a victim of gender bias?
2. What is the overall impact of sexism in your school?
3. What can you do as a professional to minimize sexism?

# SEMANTIC DEROGATION:
## An Exercise In Logical Thinking

Directions: Describe the situation and find the parallel word for each of the ones listed below. When you have finished break into a small group of 3 or 4 and discuss the questions on the bottom of the page.

*Female*                                            *Male*

nymphomaniac
whore

spinster
old maid

DFL ladies

chick
broad
babe

bitch
castrating bitch

the little woman

little old ladies

girl (to describe females
regardless of age) as in "going out
with the girls"
or
"How are you girls?"

### Reflection/Discussion Items

1. Does the parallel word mean the same as the word used for females?

2. Is the parallel word negative or a put-down?

3. Does it imply status?

4. If you couldn't find a parallel word, why not?

5. What assumptions are reflected in the words in the "female" column?

6. Why is language so laden with assumptions?

NOTE: In the above exercise, the bias of the Emma Willard Task Force on Education is that there really are no parallel words that have the same connotation as the "female" word. For example, to be a "bachelor" carries status; to be a "spinster" or "old maid" doesn't. "Stud" does not have the same connotation and lack of status as "nymphomaniac" or "whore" does. Our language reflects our society and looking at language is a good way to start to analyze how people are perceived and treated.

# MYTHS AND REALITIES: AN INQUIRY

**Myth or Reality: A Woman's Place is in the Home.**

1. From 1960 through 2000, the rate of entry of women in Minnesota into the labor force increased by (40%, 60%, 90%). For men, the rate of entry from 1960 through 2000 increased (6%, 14%, 20%).

2. According to the U.S. Department of Labor, Minnesota women make up (40%, 50%, 55%) of the labor force.

3. In 1999, the Department of Labor estimated the basic income needed for a family of four as follows:
    a low standard ($11,181; $17,050; $19,460)
    an intermediate standard ($16,266; $23,621; $28,434)
    a high standard ($23,621; $32,240; $38,323)

4. In 2001, white women age 25-34 with a bachelor's degree earned ($26,800; $29,300, $44,400).

5. In 2001, Black women age 25-34 with a bachelor's degree earned ($19,200, $22,300, $28,400).

6. In 2001, Hispanic/Latina women ages 25-34 with a bachelor's degree earned ($20,800, $25,400, $27,600).

7. In 2001, Asian women age 25-34 with a bachelor's degree earned ($24,300, $29,300, $44,700).

**Myth or Reality: Women Will Be Taken Care of by Their Husbands.**

8. There are (24, 34, 49) million unmarried women over the age of 25 in the United States.

9. The divorce rate in 1990's was (1:4, 1:5, 1:3, 1:2).

10. Of the women who are granted child support payments by court adjudication, only (80%, 50%, 20%) are still receiving payments after three years.

11. In the decade of the 1990s, the rate of increase in single parent families was (2%, 20%, 60%).

12. Of the 48 million people over retirement age in the U.S., (18; 24, 32) million are women.

13. The percentage of women workers covered by pension plans is (23%, 45%, 52%). Of men workers: (36%, 46%, 52%).

**Myth or Reality: Women Can Be Anything They Want To Be.**

14. Half of all women workers are employed in (7, 34, 58) different kinds of occupations. Half of all men workers are employed in (24, 55, 63) different kinds of occupations.

15. According to U.S. Department of Labor statistics, women make up
    (65, 89, 98)        percent of all private household workers.
    (57, 76, 85)        percent of all clerical workers.
    (73, 85, 90)        percent of all elementary school teachers.
    (61, 80, 91)        percent of all librarians.
    (73, 85, 95)        percent of all nurses.
    (1.3, 4.5, 7.8)     percent of all carpenters.
    (1.1, 4.5, 6.5)     percent of all plumbers.
    (1.9, 2.5, 5.3)     percent of all sheet metal workers.

**Myth or Reality: College and Civil Service System Gives Women a Chance.**

16. At 35, a married woman who has completed her family has a work life expectancy of (21, 27, 34) years.

17. Of the 42 million adults 35 and over enrolled in school in 2002 (16, 36, 58) percent were women.

18. The proportion of college and university degrees earned by women:

    B.A.   1990's   (42, 51, 57).
           1980's   (13, 34, 51).
           1940's   (6, 23, 41).
    M.A.   1990's   (38, 49, 54).
           1980's   (12, 24, 39).
           1930's   (6, 15, 40).
    Ph.D.  1990's   (5, 16, 22).
           1980's   (6, 13, 19).
           1920's   (.8, 3, 15)

19. Percent of women in senior management positions in the nation's largest corporations is (0.05%, 3.0%, 8%, 14%).

**Myth or Reality: But Things Are Improving for Women . . .**

20. The average woman's earnings are (56%, 65%, 74%, 81%) of a man's earnings when both work full-time at year-round jobs.

21. In 1999, male heads of household with full-time jobs averaged (median figure, U.S.) ($414, $543, $668) per week. Female heads of household averaged ($296, $398, $492).

**References**

U. S. Census Bureau (2000). Statistical Abstract and March 2002 Survey. Washington, DC: Author.
    http://www.census.gov/
(Based on the 2000 Census Bureau & 2003 Department of Labor Statistics)

---

**Discussion/Reflection Activity**
Fill out what you think are the correct answers and then form groups of 3 or 4 persons and compare your responses.

# Education and Average Income

What impact does an education have on earnings? Is there still a gender and racial bias in the income structure?

Average Income for persons with a bachelor's degree, 2002

|  | Men | Women |
| --- | --- | --- |
| All Races | $63,354 | $36,913 |
| White | $65,046 | $36,698 |
| Black | $46,511 | $35,448 |
| Hispanic | $45,446 | $35,142 |
| Asian | $59,882 | $41,484 |

*Information is based on full time employees.
Source: Census Bureau March 2002

Income gaps over the last decade have increased rather than decreased and even though almost twice as many Asians as whites have bachelor's degrees there is still a disparity in average incomes.

According to the census bureau high school graduation rates have increased from 32.6% for men 36% for women in 1950 to 83.8% for men and 84.4% for women in 2002. The rates for men were slightly higher in 2000 for men with 84.2% earning high school diplomas.

The percent of people who completed four or more years of college (ages 25-29) increased from 10% in 1950 to a high of 26.7% in 2000. Even with this increase people of color and women lag behind white men.

Among the 25 most populous states, Minnesota led the field in the percentage of people who graduated with 91.7% of the men and 92.7% of the women ages 18 or older with high school completion. The overall graduation data showed Minnesota tied with Alaska for the nation's lead with a 92.2% graduation rate. Of those who graduated in 2001, 82% of the women and 75% of the men completed high school in four years.

**Reference**
U. S. Census Bureau (2002). Statistical Abstract and March 2002 Survey. Washington, DC: Author.
http://http://www.census.gov/

## FACTS REGARDING THE STATUS OF WOMEN

1. There were 66 million working women in 2001, a significant increase from 5.3 million in 1900 and 18.4 million in 1950.
2. Today, about 60% of all women are in the labor force, compared with nearly 75% of all men. By 2005, the percentage of women in the labor force is projected to rise to 62%, while the number of men in the workforce will decline from 75% to 73%.
3. 70% of part-time workers are women. Further, over one million women earn wages below the Federal minimum wage.
4. Nearly three-quarters of all mothers are in the labor force. Even among mothers with young children, 70% work for pay.
5. Over the course of her career, the average woman loses approximately $250,000 to the wage gap.
6. In 1999, America's working families lost $200 billion of annual income to the wage gap, an average of $4,000 per family, even after accounting for differences in education, age, location an the number of hours worked.
7. According to the Center for Women's Business Research, currently one in 18 (6%) U.S. women are business owners.
8. There were over 6 million women-owned businesses in 2002. Women of color owned 1.2 million of these firms.

9. Women-owned firms represent 28% of all U.S. businesses, generating $1.15 trillion in sales, and 20% of these firms are owned by women of color.
10. Women-owned firms in the U.S. are more likely than all firms to offer flex-time, tuition reimbursement, and profit sharing to their employees.
11. According to a 2002 Catalyst study of the Fortune 500 companies, women held 15.7% of the corporate officer positions. It is estimated that women will hold 27.4% of all corporate officer positions by 2020.
12. In 2002, women held 7.9% of the highest corporate officer positions.
13. In the 107th Congress, women held 13 (13%) of the 100 seats in the U.S. Senate and 60 (13.8%) of the 435 seats in the U.S House of Representatives. In addition, two women serve as Delegates to the House representing the District of Columbia and the Virgin Islands.
14. Of the 60 women serving in the 107th Congress, 13 are African-American, six are Hispanic, and one is Asian-American. In addition, there are two women delegates, a Caribbean-American representing the Virgin Islands and an African-American from the District of Columbia.
15. Currently, five women serve as governors of their state and 17 serve as lieutenant governors.
16. Women with pensions receive less than half the amount that men receive. In 2000, the median benefit amount was $4,200 annually for women compared to $7,800 for men, representing a retirement wage gap of 53%.
17. The percentage of women receiving benefits based solely on their own earnings history is expected to rise from 37% in 1997 to 60% in 2060.
18. Widowhood can severely jeopardize a woman's economic prospects. Elderly widows receive, on average, only $5,964 a year in Social Security benefits as compared to an average of $14,580 for the joint Social Security benefit received by a married couple.
19. Currently there are more than 6.5 million older persons living alone and 77% are women. By 2020, this total will be 13.3 million--85% of whom will be women. 45% of older women living alone are poor or near-poor.
20. The economic prospects for single elderly women of color are drastically affected during retirement. In 2000, 43% of elderly single African-American women and 37.7 % of elderly single Hispanic women lived in poverty.
21. The U.S. has the highest poverty rate of older women of all post-industrial nations.
22. The median family income in married-couple households was $60,471 in 2001. In female headed households, the median family income was $28,142, which is over 40% less than male headed (with no wife present) household median income of $40,715.
23. In 2000, African-American women accounted for 30% of all female-headed households and had a median income of $18,244 and Hispanic female-headed householders earned a median income of $20,765.
24. More than one in four American women over the age of 18 have experienced domestic violence.
25. Every year in the American workplace, approximately 120,000 employees are victims of violence committed by an intimate: current or former spouse, lover, partner, or boyfriend/girlfriend.

Business and Professional Women/USA and the BPW Foundation (January 2003). Facts for women.
Author: 1900 M Street, NW, Suite 310 Washington, DC, 20036

---

**Discussion/Reflection Items**

1. Did you find any surprises with these facts?

2. What causes these to occur?

3. How do these factors impact schools?

# HOW TO TELL A BUSINESSMAN FROM A BUSINESSWOMAN

He's aggressive . . . she's pushy.

He's good on details . . . she's picky.

He loses his temper because he's so involved in his job . . . she's bitchy.

When he's depressed (or hung over), everyone tiptoes past his office . . . she's moody, so it must be her time of the month.

He follows through . . . she doesn't know when to quit.

He's confident . . . she's conceited.

He stands firm . . . she's hard.

His judgments are her prejudices.

He's a man of the world . . . she's been around.

He drinks because of the excessive job pressure . . . she's a lush.

He isn't afraid to say what he thinks . . . she's mouthy.

He exercises authority diligently . . . she's power mad.

He's close-mouthed . . . she's secretive.

He climbed the ladder of success . . . she slept her way to the top.

He's a stern taskmaster . . . she's hard to work for.

*Source: Unknown*

---

**Discussion/Reflection Items**

1. Describe each situation listed above.

2. How and why are these differentially defined?

3. What is the net effect of a biased language system?

4. What can be done to change this (discuss all three levels of analysis)?

# A GRATEFUL WIFE HAS SECOND THOUGHTS

*By Ellen Goodman*

I know a woman who is a grateful wife. She has been one for years. In fact, her gratitude has been as deep and constant as her affection. And together they have traveled a long, complicated road.

In the beginning, this young wife was grateful to find herself married to a man who let her work. That was in 1964, when even her college professor said without a hint of irony that the young wife was "lucky to be married to a man who let her work." People talked like that then.

Later, the wife looked around her at the men her classmates and friends had married and was grateful that her husband wasn't threatened, hurt, neglected, insulted – the multiple choice of the mid '60s – by her job.

He was proud. And her cup overran with gratitude. That was the way it was.

In the late 60s, when other, younger women were having consciousness-raising groups, she was having babies and more gratitude.

You see, she discovered that she had a Helpful Husband. Nothing in her experience had led her to expect this. Her mother was not married to one; her sister was not married to one; her brother was not one.

But at 4 o'clock in the morning, when the baby cried and she was exhausted, sometimes she would nudge her husband awake (wondering only vaguely how he could sleep) and ask him to feed the boy. He would say *sure*. And she would say *thank you*.

The Grateful Wife and the Helpful Husband danced this same pas de deux for a decade. When the children were small and she was sick, he would take charge. When it was their turn to carpool and she had to be at work early, he would drive. If she was coming home late, he would make dinner.

All you have to do is ask, he would say with a smile.

And so she asked. The woman who had minded her *Ps* and *Qs* as a child minded her *pleases* and *thank yous* as a wife. Would you please put the baby on the potty? Would you please stop at the store tonight for milk? Would you please pick up Joel at soccer practice? Thank you. Thank you. Thank you.

It is hard to know when gratitude first began to grate on my friend. Or when she began saying *please* and *thank you* dutifully rather than genuinely.

But it probably began when she was tired one day or night. In any case, during the car-time between one job and the other, when she would run lists through her head, she began feeling less thankful for her moonlighting job as household manager.

She began to realize that all the items of their shared life were stored in her exclusive computer. She began to realize that her queue was so full of minutiae that she had no room for anything else.

The Grateful Wife began to wonder why she should say *thank you* when a father took care of his children and why she should say *please* when a husband took care of his house.

She began to realize that being grateful meant being responsible. Being grateful meant assuming that you were in charge of children and laundry and running out of toilet paper. Being grateful meant having to ask. And ask. And ask.

Her husband was not an oppressive or even thoughtless man. He was helpful. But helpful doesn't have to remember vacuum cleaner bags. And helpful doesn't keep track of early dismissal days.

Helpful doesn't keep a Christmas present list in his mind. Helpful doesn't have to know who wears what size and colors. Helpful is reminded; helpful is asked. Anything you ask. *Please* and *thank you.*

The wife feels, she says, vaguely frightened to find herself angry at saying *please* and *thank you*. She wonders whether she is, indeed, an ingrate. But her wondering doesn't change how she feels or what she wants.

The wife would like to take just half the details that clog her mind like grit in a pore and hand them over to another manager. The wife would like someone who would be grateful when she volunteered to take his turn at the market, or his week at the laundry.

The truth is that after all those years when she danced her part perfectly, she wanted something else. She doesn't want a helpful husband. She wants one who will share. For that, she would be truly grateful.

---

**Discussion/Reflection Items**

1. How do you interpret this story?

2. Why did the outcome occur?

3. What other options were available?

# I READ A STORY ABOUT A YOUNG WOMAN . . .

*By Ellen Goodman*

I have been pondering this perplexing situation I have been placed in. I was educated at fine schools. I learned to play good enough field hockey to be entrusted with the position of center half, third string, in high school. (I could have made first string, but I bruise easily.) I was taught a proper game of tennis, how to entertain, how to run a household, and how to act and dress properly.

I went to an acceptable junior college (two years was plenty for grooming . . . for marriage). I made the Dean's List. I even made first-string center half on the college field hockey team.

After graduating second in my class I returned to my parents' home to live. I commuted daily on the Penn Central to my new job as assistant in one of the top interior design firms in the country. I was working for $90 a week (I was supposed to feel privileged to work with such "great people"). I wasn't paying for food or rent, so I still could afford the symbol of every New York working girl, a pair of black patent leather Guccis. There we stood, every morning on the platform, waiting for the train, all wearing identical shoes. And feeling very smug.

I was dating a local fellow who also had returned to his hometown after college and commuted daily to his job as a clerk in a prestigious company on Wall Street.

We married in grand style; my mother made my write-up in the paper sound quite impressive. After a honeymoon, we settled into a one-bedroom co-op overlooking a wooded field. I continued working in the city for a year, but the 45-minute commute was tiring. And I still had to cook and grocery shop when I got home.

I gave notice to my prestigious employer and took a part-time job in a gift shop in the suburban sanctuary we called home. I opened a decorating studio and, with the help of Mother, obtained clients who were pleased with my work, and brought in some extra income.

I became editor of our local monthly literary publication: *The Villager*. I joined the Junior League and volunteered my time to help those less fortunate. My marriage was familiar, secure, and routine.

Several years later we bought a small carriage house. I decorated it and produced a baby. I resigned from *The Villager* to give more time to motherhood.

By this time my bank clerk was wearing Brooks Brothers suits and wingtip shoes, and was riding to and from Wall Street in a used Lincoln Continental limousine, bought collectively by six of the suburb's young executives.

A headhunter became interested in "my man" and coaxed him to Minneapolis. He was offered a prestigious job at a prestigious company.

We moved 1,200 miles. We bought a house in a local suburb, which I decorated on an executive's budget.

Our house, paint barely dry, was put on the market after a year. We had separated.

I trusted this man I had been married to for close to seven years. He was also the only adult within 1,200 miles whom I knew well. We wrote an "agreement in a spirit of friendship and compromise." This was my husband's second divorce, my first.

I have gone back to work out of necessity. I moved into the city to be closer to my job and the day-care center. I bought a "handyman's special" that eats up my meager income. I resigned from the Junior League. Now I am one of the less fortunate.

I don't have a meal waiting for me when I come home at night; I have a load of dirty laundry. On weekends I work on my house and clean it and grocery shop.

This was the first year since the divorce in which I did my taxes myself. After taxes and paying $2,500 for child care there was not much left over. With all my experience and maturity, I had to start at the bottom.

Suddenly, at age 32, I felt as if I had been plunged into a cold ocean. The current is strong and the competition stiff. And I'm not bringing up my child the way I'd planned.

I was talking to a friend in St. Paul the other day. A housewife, married, mother, Junior Leaguer, carbon copy of my former self. I realized that where she is – and where I once was – and where I am now are miles apart.

I'm back to where I was nine years ago. I lost the social status, the Saturday night dinners at expensive restaurants, the vacations, the companionship . . . and the income.

I have survived on my own. I have even encountered a new individual I rather like . . . me. I think I'm going to make it.

---

**Discussion/Reflection Items**

1. How do you interpret this story?

2. If your interpretation is different from others discuss why.

# SEXUAL HARASSMENT

## An Overview
Title VII of the Civil Rights Act of 1964 protects workers from discrimination based upon race, sex, national origin, color, or religion. Various federal laws have expanded these protections to include age, disability, and citizenship status. Many state and local laws go farther by extending protection to areas such as marital status and sexual orientation.

The Federal courts showed a concern for the working environment as early as 1971, when they ruled that workers had a right to an environment free of ethnic, religious or racial discrimination. They ruled that workers' rights were violated by the pervasive use of derogatory terms and by abusive treatment.

Several more years passed before sexual harassment was recognized as a form of prohibited discrimination.

## The Civil Rights Act of 1991
More recent events have ensured that sexual harassment will receive increased attention in the 1990's. Spurred in part by the public fervor surrounding the 1991 Senate confirmation hearings of Judge Clarence Thomas, Congress enacted the Civil Rights Act of 1991 for the express purpose of providing "additional remedies under federal law . . . to deter unlawful harassment." The Act facilitates bringing actions against employers and encourages litigation by providing for compensatory and punitive damages and trial by jury. More specifically, the Act authorizes as much as $300,000 in compensatory damages in addition to the back pay, front pay, reinstatement, and attorneys' fees provisions previously available under Title VII.

## Types of Sexual Harassment
According to the EEOC there are basically two types of sexual harassment. These are quid pro quo and hostile work environment.

## Quid Pro Quo Sexual Harassment
Early cases focused on situations where female employees were victims of adverse employment actions for refusing their superiors' sexual advances. This type of sexual harassment is called "quid pro quo" harassment, which literally means "something for something."

"Quid pro quo" harassment occurs when getting or keeping a job is conditioned upon acceptance of sexual advances, requests for sexual favors, or other verbal or physical conduct of a sexual nature. An example of this type of sexual harassment is a supervisor threatening to terminate an employee for refusing to have sexual relations (or a date, etc.) with the supervisor or a powerful co-worker. This is the most obvious form of sexual harassment.

There are also more subtle forms of harassment that would go uncorrected if sexual harassment claims were limited to pure "quid pro quo" incidents.

## Hostile Work Environment Sexual Harassment
In 1980, the EEOC published guidelines recognizing a second type of sexual harassment, "hostile work environment." These guidelines recognize that a worker's emotional and psychological well being may be injured by harassment even though the worker's job is not impacted directly.

A "hostile work environment" which is the most common occurs where harassing behavior is so severe or pervasive that it can be said to alter the conditions of employment and has the effect of interfering with an individual's work performance or creating an intimidation, hostile, or offensive work environment. This more subtle form of harassment can exist even where there is no actual or threatened economic injury to the individual claiming to be harassed.

**Examples of Sexual Harassment**
There are five common types of sexual harassment.
1. Physical assaults of a sexual nature, which include rape, sexual battery, molestation, or intentional physical conduct, which is sexual in nature.
2. Sexual advances, propositions, or other sexual comments such as gestures, jokes, or remarks of a sexual nature. Other sub-types include preferential treatment or promises in exchange for submitting to sexual conduct, and sexual attention or conduct making job more difficult.
3. Display of publications in the workplace that are revealing, suggestive, demeaning, or pornographic in nature are another type. Other items such as signs that segregate employee by sex, except for restrooms, can be construed as sexual harassment.
4. A fourth type is sexual favoritism where employment benefits and opportunities are granted due to an employee's submission to an employer's or supervisor's sexual advances or requests for sexual favors.
5. Retaliation for making a sexual harassment complaint such as arbitrary discipline, unwarranted change in work assignment, poor work performance review, of failure to cooperate to discuss work related matters with an employee also constitute sexual harassment.

If you are wondering how this applies to students in schools think of their work as academic or athletic or some other type of performance.

Title VII does not require asexuality nor androgyny in the work or school environment. It forbids only behavior that is objectively offensive.

**Definition**
*Harassment on the basis of sex is unlawful under local, state, and federal laws. Unwelcome sexual advances or requests of a sexual nature constitute sexual harassment when (1) submission to such conduct is made explicitly or implicitly a term or condition of an individual's employment, (2) submission to or rejection of such conduct by an individual is used as the basis for employment decisions affecting such individual, or (3) such conduct has the purpose or effect of unreasonably interfering with an individual's work performance or creating an intimidating, hostile, or offensive working environment.*

In determining whether alleged conduct constitutes sexual harassment, the courts will look at the record as a whole and at the totality of circumstances, such as the nature of the sexual advances and the context in which the alleged incidents occurred.

An employer is responsible for the acts of its supervisory employees with respect to sexual harassment regardless of whether the specific acts complained of were authorized or even forbidden, and regardless of whether the employer knew or should have known of their occurrence.

An employer is responsible for co-workers in the workplace when the employer knows or should have known of the conduct, unless the employer can show that it took immediate and appropriate corrective action.

An employer may be responsible for the acts of non-employees with respect to sexual harassment where the employer knows or should have known of the conduct and fails to take immediate and appropriate corrective action.

Prevention is the best tool for the elimination of sexual harassment.

Where employment opportunities or benefits are granted because of an individual's submission to the employer's sexual advances or requests for sexual favors, the employer may be held liable for unlawful sex discrimination against other persons who were qualified for but denied that employment opportunity or benefit.

All employers are required to have a policy prohibiting sexual harassment and a specific reporting procedure. If you do not feel that you can work within your organization you may contact your city or state human and/or civil rights department.

In educational settings such as schools, teachers and other personnel are considered supervisory employees, and co-workers may apply to students.

    <u>In St. Paul call or write</u>:
    City of St. Paul Human Rights Department      Telephone:    651-298-4288
    Room 515
    St. Paul, MN 55102

    <u>In Minneapolis call or write</u>:
    City of Minneapolis Civil Rights Department      Telephone:    612-348-7736
    Room 239 City Hall
    Minneapolis, MN 55415

    <u>Others in Minnesota call or write</u>:
    State of Minnesota Human Rights Department      Telephone:    651-297-2786
    5th Floor Bremer Tower                                                 1-800-652-9747
    7th Place and Minnesota Street
    St. Paul, MN 55101

Since 1980, there have been numerous court decisions resolving sexual harassment issues, but none has been as significant as the Supreme Court's decision in *Meritor Savings Bank v. Vinson,* 477 U.S. 57 (1986). This decision defined the parameters of sexual harassment and reaffirmed the obligation of employers to put into place preventative measures as well as to respond effectively to complaints. The guidelines laid down by this decision have become the foundation for prevention programs established by employers.

**Unlimited Tort Damages**
Since sexual harassment often involves unsolicited, offensive, physical touching and psychological and emotional harm, victims can bring additional state law claims known as "torts" (civil wrongs). These torts, which most often include assault. Battery, and intentional infliction of emotional distress, are particularly attractive to plaintiffs because they allow for the enormous judgments which are too often returned by juries.

These concepts and how they apply to you are explained in greater detail with a variety of examples and exercises.

Remember, sexual harassment comes in many forms from people directed at people.

**Sexual Harassment is:**

1. Male directed at female

2. Male directed at male.

3. Female directed at male.

4. Female directed at female.

The issue is one of Power!

> **Discussion/Reflection Items**
> 1. What are the rules and regulations for school personnel in Minnesota?
>
> 2. Other items follow the section on Legal Implications

On the following pages are legal implications and a short history of court decisions regarding sexual harassment. For more information you can consult with specialists in your school. All schools are required to have at least two lines of reporting and Minnesota follows a Mandatory Reporting Procedure.

# LEGAL IMPLICATION

**Is It Sexual Harassment?**

OCCURRENCE OF SEXUAL HARASSMENT is determined only after the situation is examined and the facts are reviewed.

**Laws Prohibiting Sexual Harassment**

SEXUAL HARASSMENT is discriminatory behavior prohibited by –

- Title VII of the Civil Rights Act of 1964
- Title IX, Educational Amendments of 1972
- Minnesota Human Rights Act, Chapter 363, 1992
- Civil Rights Act 1991
- U.S. Supreme Court, 1993
- 1998 upheld that same sex harassment is actionable

Many other rulings have upheld the illegality of sexual harassment.

The courts have consistently ruled that Title VII applies to educational institutions through Title IX of the education amendments of 1972. This states in part, "No person in the United States shall, on the basis of sex, be excluded from participation in, be denied the benefits of, or be subjected to discrimination under any educational program or activity receiving federal financial assistance." This law includes relationships between teachers and students and between students and their peers in much more than just athletics. Think about drama productions or other situations in which issues may occur.

**Causes of Sexual Harassment**
Common causes include communication problems, social norms, and/or abuses of power. These can occur in any situation or work environment.

Harassment must be subjectively and objectively hostile and abusive. Some of the keys are examining the frequency of the conduct, the severity of the conduct, whether it is physically threatening or humiliating, and/or whether or not it interferes with a person's work performance.

# SEXUAL HARASSMENT COURT DECISIONS

The following court cases were selected to show trends of the employer's and employee's expanding legal and financial liabilities for sexual harassment that occurs in their workplaces.

## 1974

**Monge v. Beebe Rubber Co.**, 316 A. 2d 549, 114 **N.H. 130, 25 E.P.D. 31,** 643 (N.H. S.Ct. 1974)
An employer's termination at will of an employment contract, which was indefinite in its term, was a breach of contract when it was motivated by malice because a female employee refused the sexual advances of her foreman.

## 1979

**Miller v. Bank of America**, 600 F. 2d 211 (9th Cir. 1959)
Final determination was made in 1981 by the 9th Circuit Court of Appeals. Bank of America *was* liable for a supervisor's sexual harassment even though his behavior violated company policy and the Bank was unaware of his sexual harassment. This liability is based on the legal concept of *respondeat superior* under Title VII of the 1964 Civil Rights Act.

## 1980

**Clark v. World Airways, Inc.** 24 E.P.D. 18, 287 (1980)
Plaintiff lost her Title VII claim because she could not prove that the sexual harassment by her supervisor was a term or condition of employment. However a $52,000 punitive damage award was upheld on a claim of sexual assault.

## 1981

**Bundy v. Jackson**, 641 F. 2d 934 (C.A.D.C. 1981)
Sexually stereotyped insults and demeaning propositions constitutes sexual harassment and is a form of sex discrimination, regardless of whether the plaintiff lost any tangible job benefits as a result.

**Rogers v. Loews L'Enfant Plaza Hotel**, 526 F. Supp. 523, 28 E.P.D. 32, 553 (D.D.C. 1981)
Plaintiff, who was sexually harassed by her immediate supervisor while working at a hotel-restaurant, was entitled to general and punitive damages under state tort law theories of intrusion, assault and battery, and intentional infliction of emotional duress.

**Wright v. Methodist Youth Services**, 511 F. Supp. 307 (N.D. 111,1981)
Termination of a man because he rejected sexual advances made by his male supervisor was a violation of Title VII. The theory was that a similarly situated woman would not have had sexual demands made of her.

## 1982

**NLRB v. Downslope Industries, Inc.**, 676 F. 2d 1114 (6th Cir. 1982)
Freedom from sexual harassment is a "working condition" for which employees may organize to protect themselves from under the National Labor Relations Act.

## 1985

**Davis v. United States Steel Corp.**, 779 F. 2d 209 (4th Cir. 1985)
The observation and inaction of a supervisor of an employee engaging in sexual harassment is sufficient to make the company liable under the doctrine of *respondeat superior.* Supervisor has responsibility to take necessary corrective action.

## 1986

**Meritor Savings Bank v. Michelle Vinson**, U.S. Court of Appeals for the District of Columbia, Circuit, 84-1979, Decided June 19, 1986.
Sexual harassment is a form of sex discrimination under Title VII of the 1964 Civil Rights Act. A claim of "hostile environment" sexual harassment is actionable under Title VII. Employers cannot always be held liable for sexual harassment by management personnel. A grievance procedure and policy against discrimination, coupled with the employee's failure to use that procedure does not immunize the employer from liability.

## 1987

**Boyd v. James S. Hayes Living Health Care Agency, Inc., et al.**, No. 84-2233 GB, May 13,1987

Her employer's administrator sexually harassed a female employee during a business trip. He insisted that she come to his hotel room, touched her, tried to get her to look at a sexually explicit movie and magazine, and attempted to restrain her departure. Upon returning to work she was disciplined for poor work performance and then terminated. The female employee was able to establish that her employer's reasons for disciplining and terminating her were pretextual and that the real reason was her rejection of the administrator's sexual advances.

**O'Dell v. Basabe**, Idaho 4th District, No. 88547

O'Dell was the Personnel Director of the Land and Livestock Division of the J.R. Simplot Co., a large agricultural firm. When an assistant complained to him of sexual harassment from the company's president he conducted an investigation and provided support to the woman. The president fired O'Dell after O'Dell's 18-month investigation and O'Dell's continued support of the woman. The jury found in favor of O'Dell under both common law and Idaho's Human Rights Act. They awarded O'Dell $1 million in punitive damages. He also received $420,500 mostly for the loss of past and future wages and benefits.

**Ross v. Double Diamond, Inc.**, USDC, N. Tex, 1987, 45 FEP Cases 313

A female employee sued her employer for hostile work environment sexual harassment after working only two days and won. The court concluded that the woman was degraded and that her psychological well-being was 'seriously impaired'. And the court found that if harassment is frequent and/or intensely offensive, a pattern can be established in a short time.

## 1988

**In re Peters**, 428 N.W.2d 375 (Minn. 1988)

The Minnesota Supreme Court held that a hostile environment exists "when employment is conditioned, either explicitly or implicitly, on adapting to a workplace in which the employee is the target of repeated, unwelcome, sexually derogatory remarks or physical contact of a sexual nature; and the hostility of that environment must be judged from the perspective of the victim."

## 1989

**Sanchez v. City of Miami Beach** Florida courts held that city is liable for hostile work environment created by sexual harassment based on conduct of other police officers.

## 1991

**Jensen v. Eveleth Mines**, 57 F.E.P. Cases 873 (D. Minn. 1991)

A Minnesota federal judge held that the standard to be applied in a case involving sexual harassment was "whether a reasonable woman would find the work environment hostile."

**Robinson v. Jacksonville Shipyards, Inc.**, 760 F.Supp. 1486 (M.D. Fla. 1991)

In **Robinson**, a Florida federal court held that harassing behavior directed toward women created a hostile environment. The plaintiff was one of a few female workers employed at a shipyard. At the shipyard, calendars, pictures of nude women and advertisements were displayed throughout the workplace. In addition, comments were made such as "honey," "dear," "baby," "sugar," "sugar booger," and "mama" and "there's nothing worse than having to work around women." The court, in looking at the totality of the circumstances, concluded that the perspective of a reasonable woman must be considered and determined that a hostile environment had been created.

**Radtke v. Everett**, 471 N.W.2d 660 (Mich. Ct. App. 1991)

In **Radtke**, a Michigan court applied the reasonable woman standard. A female employee had been on break with her coworker when he touched her, made sexual comments and kept her from leaving the couch on which they were sitting and attempted to kiss her. When she complained, she was told that women like her had to be careful with men because of their "cute, bubbly" personalities. The court, in applying the reasonable woman standard, held that the female employee's reaction was not idiosyncratic or hypersensitive, particularly because she was scheduled to work with the harasser the following day and was often scheduled to work alone with him.

**Ellison v. Brady**, 924 F.2d 872 (9th Cir. 1991)
In **Ellison**, the Ninth Circuit Court of Appeals articulated the reasonable woman standard in a case involving sexual harassment. A female revenue agent for the IRS claimed that she was sexually harassed by a male co-worker. The co-worker had asked her to lunch and she had accepted his offer. It was a practice within the office for agents to go out for lunch in groups. No one else was in the office when the two had their original lunch. After the lunch, the male co-worker began spending time around the agent's desk and pestered her with unnecessary questions. Four months after their lunch, the co-worker asked the female agent to have a drink with him after work. The agent declined and suggested instead that they have lunch the next week. She avoided her male co-worker during lunch times until he again asked her for lunch, which she declined. The co-worker, a few days later, handed the female agent a note indicating that he had cried over her last night. The note shocked the female agent. The note was followed by a card and letter, which also frightened the female agent. The trial court dismissed the female agent's complaint, indicating that the male co-worker's conduct was isolated and trivial. The appellate court reversed, holding that the perspective of the victim, the female agent, should be applied, rather than stereotyped notions of acceptable behavior.

## 1993
### U. S. Supreme Court (November, 1993)
Justice Sandra Day O'Connor issued a ruling stating that one must look at all the circumstances to determine whether the work environment is a hostile one. The factors to be considered include:

1. the frequency of the conduct;

2. the severity of the conduct;

3. whether or not the conduct was physically threatening and/or humiliating;

4. whether or not the conduct unreasonably interfered with work performance; and,

5. whether or not the conduct caused any psychological harm.

## 1997
**Cummings** The Minnesota Supreme Court upheld that same sex harassment and that one gender need not be affected differently than the other.

**Costilla v. State of Minnesota** Minnesota Supreme Court ruled that an employer's liability for sexual harassment by a third party (members of the public, contractors, non-employees) is based on the employer's response to an employee's complaints.

## 1998
**Faragher v. City of Boca Raton** U.S. Supreme Court upheld that even if an employer was unaware of harassment they can be help liable for the harassment of a supervisor.

**Burlington Industries v. Ellereth** U.S. Supreme Court upheld that the employer is responsible for the actions of a supervisor

**Oncale** U.S. Supreme Court held that same sex harassment is actionable
**Oncale Case** – The US Supreme Court held that same sex harassment is actionable. Title VII requires neither a sexuality nor androgyny and forbids offensive behavior that is pervasive enough to create an objectively hostile or abusive environment

**Hall v. Gus Construction Co., Inc.** 8th Circuit Court of Appeals ruled that harassment does not have to be "sexual" but can be based on gender and includes items such as teasing, hazing, belittling, taunting, and/or favoritism.

**1999**
   **Davis v. Monroe County Board of Education** (US Supreme Court 1999).
   Any school receiving federal money can face a sex-discrimination suit for failing to intervene energetically when a student complains of sexual harassment by another student. Justice Sandra Day O'Connor writing for the majority said "student-on-student sex harassment" could be a deeply serious matter, affecting a child's ability to learn and school officials who ignored protracted and serious harassment could be sued under Title IX.

Between 1993 and 2003 there were numerous court decisions rendered dealing with all aspects of harassment including third party harassment.

Sexual harassment in schools in not a simple matter of teasing or name-calling but rather behavior that is severe and pervasive and objectively offensive. When it reaches this level it denies victims an equal access to education and participation in school activities. Schools are to have clear and specific guidelines that are well known. They are also required to have specific lines of reporting.

In Minnesota all schools are required to have specific policies condemning sexual harassment, a procedure that is available to complainants, and procedures providing for prompt and equitable resolution of complaints. Title IX protects all children in schools regardless of their grade or age.

---

**Discussion/Reflection Items**

1. How do you personally define sexual harassment?

2. What are some of the causes of sexual harassment?

3. How do you decide if something is sexual harassment or not?

---

On the following pages are case studies based on actual situations from the workplace and from schools. Read these and decide if you think that it is sexual harassment and/or if any actions should be taken. After you have done that, discuss it with a small group or 3 or 4 persons.

# SEXUAL HARASSMENT CASE STUDIES

Read the examples. Decide whether each situation falls into one of the categories described, and if any actions should be taken.

1. Jerry James is an outgoing teacher with a cheery greeting for everyone. He often greets one of the female students with a remark such as:

    • Hey, today you're looking great!

    • That is a good-looking outfit you're wearing.

    • Has anyone ever told you how good you look in blue?

    A. Is this sexual harassment?   Inappropriate school behavior?

    _____ YES   _____ YES

    _____ NO   _____ NO

    B. Are any actions advisable? If so, what?

    _____

    _____

2. Tom Turtle enjoys his role as the clown and storyteller in the school. Usually his stories are enjoyed by everyone. Lately, several of his stories have concerned sexual activities. Marty Lawhorn does not like the stories. She laughs along with everyone else. (Both Tom and Marty are students)

    A. Is this sexual harassment?   Inappropriate school behavior?

    _____ YES   _____ YES

    _____ NO   _____ NO

    B. Are any actions advisable? If so, what?

    _____

    _____

3. In the situation described in No. 2, Marty tells Tom that she finds his jokes about sexual activities embarrassing and that she wishes he would not tell them. Tom and others in the school continue to tell this type of story.

    A. Is this sexual harassment?   Inappropriate school behavior?

    _____ YES   _____ YES

    _____ NO   _____ NO

    B. Are any actions advisable? If so, what?

    _____

    _____

Read the examples. Decide whether each situation falls into one of the categories described, and if any actions should be taken.

4. Georgia Jones is a new secretary for the principal at the Bright High School. Her duties require her to go out in the building frequently. She wears flimsy, revealing dresses without a slip on hot, summer days. She walks with a pronounced hip swing. In her conversations with the male students, she bats her eyes and makes frequent remarks with double meanings. For example, when she asked Fred Smith to bring a large package up to the front office, she said: "I always need a big, strong man to take care of me. I don't understand these women who seem to get along without a man."

    A. Is this sexual harassment?     Inappropriate school behavior?

        _____ YES                 _____ YES

        _____ NO                 _____ NO

    B. Are any actions advisable? If so, what?

    _____

    _____

5. Mr. Cool always calls every female student in his class "Baby" or "Honey." He refers to his female teachers and staff this way. When women attend staff meetings or briefings, he addresses them as "Baby" or "Honey." It is a small town. He is a very friendly, folksy person.

    A. Is this sexual harassment?     Inappropriate school behavior?

        _____ YES                 _____ YES

        _____ NO                 _____ NO

    B. Are any actions advisable? If so, what?

    _____

    _____

6. Bev Slate is a good student and athlete in school. She looks upon herself as "one of the boys" and frequently initiates a round of sexual jokes between classes and at lunch. She makes frequent comments about the fact that she is glad she wasn't born twenty years earlier when there was a dual standard for men and women. She has even "goosed" one of the male students when she walked by him as he bent over a desk reading.

    A. Is this sexual harassment?     Inappropriate school behavior?

        _____ YES                 _____ YES

        _____ NO                 _____ NO

    B. Are any actions advisable? If so, what?

    _____

    _____

Read the examples. Decide whether each situation falls into one of the categories described, and if any actions should be taken.

7. Lisa is 6 years old and rides the bus to school. Other children on the bus have been taunting her about the parts of her body and made explicit suggestions that she have oral sex with her father. You are her teacher and she mentioned it to you.

    A.  Is this sexual harassment?        Inappropriate behavior?

    _____ YES                            _____ YES

    _____ NO                             _____ NO

    B.  Are any actions advisable? If so, what?

    _____
    _____

8. Angelina is a sophomore and found out at the beginning of the year that there were obscene remarks about her scrawled on the walls of the boys' restroom: "Angelina sucked my _____ after she sucked my dog's _____. Angelina is a slut." You are one of her teachers and on different occasions have overheard boys brag about it and Angelina complaining to her girlfriends.

    A.  Is this sexual harassment?        Inappropriate behavior?

    _____ YES                            _____ YES

    _____ NO                             _____ NO

    B.  Are any actions advisable? If so, what?

    _____
    _____

9. You are a new teacher to the school. On one occasion the students put on a skit as a fundraiser during which a male character had a mirror on his shoe for the express purpose of looking up the dress of a female character who said, "Oh, don't look up my dress. I don't have any panties on." On another occasion the students conduct a "mistletoe madness" lip-synch contest during which some "teen gals" were dressed in lingerie and sang a song titled "Sex Shooter" while making undulating movements with their bodies in response to the male students in the audience making catcalls and sexual comments. You attend both fundraisers.

    A.  Is this sexual harassment?        Inappropriate behavior?

    _____ YES                            _____ YES

    _____ NO                             _____ NO

    B.  Are any actions advisable? If so, what?

    _____
    _____

Read the examples. Decide whether each situation falls into one of the categories described, and if any actions should be taken.

10. You find out that a list is circulated by the boys listing the "25 most f _ _ _ able girls" in your school. This list also contains paragraphs describing the girls' bodies and what they were particularly adept at sexually. While one of the girls, Kaileen complains about it, others find it complimentary.

    A.  Is this sexual harassment?        Inappropriate behavior?

        _____ YES                       _____ YES

        _____ NO                        _____ NO

    B.  Are any actions advisable? If so, what?

        _____

        _____

11. While at a youth hockey tournament with a friend and her friend's family Patty is sexually assaulted by three teenage boys she knew. After returning home Patty, who is 15 years old, and her family press charges against the boys, ignoring the pleas both of the boys' families and the youth Hockey Association. Eventually the boys were found guilty of fourth-degree sexual assault. You are a teacher at her school and over hear students calling her "slut," "whore," and "bitch," and saw threats scrawled on her locker, such as "kill the bitch, she took our friends to court."

    A.  Is this sexual harassment?        Inappropriate behavior?

        _____ YES                       _____ YES

        _____ NO                        _____ NO

    B.  Are any actions advisable? If so, what?

        _____

        _____

12. You teach Family Consumer Science. Rodney is the only boy in this section. On more than one occasion most of the girls have refused to work with him and he has reported his work destroyed by classmates.

    A.  Is this sexual harassment?        Inappropriate behavior?

        _____ YES                       _____ YES

        _____ NO                        _____ NO

    B.  Are any actions advisable? If so, what?

        _____

        _____

# Some Examples of Sexual Harassment

## Verbal

- Referring to an adult as a girl, hunk, doll, babe, or honey
- Whistling at someone, cat calls
- Making sexual comments about a person's body
- Making sexual comments or innuendoes
- Turning work discussions to sexual topics
- Telling sexual jokes or stories
- Asking about sexual fantasies, preferences, or history
- Asking personal questions about social or sexual life
- Making sexual comments about a person's clothing, anatomy, or looks
- Repeatedly asking out a person who is not interested
- Making kissing sounds, howling, and smacking lips
- Telling lies or spreading rumors about a person's personal sex life

## Non-verbal

- Looking a person up and down (elevator eyes)
- Staring at someone
- Blocking a person's path
- Following the person
- Giving personal gifts
- Displaying sexually suggestive visuals
- Making facial expressions such as winking, throwing kisses, or licking lips
- Making sexual gestures with hands or through body movements

## Physical

- Giving a massage around the neck or shoulders
- Touching the person's clothing, hair, or body

Differentiate flirting from harassment.

# THE EFFECTS OF SEXUAL HARASSMENT
## Chart on Economic/Educational and or Psychological Effects

|  | **Effects on the Victim** | **Effects on the Harasser** | **Effects on the Work Unit** |
|---|---|---|---|
| **Potential Psychological Effects** |  |  |  |
| **Potential Economic/ Educational Effects** |  |  |  |

# Rights And Responsibilities

### Student Rights

1. A school environment free of harassment

2. Information about rights and responsibilities

3. A complaint procedure

### Student Responsibilities

1. Tell the person that the behavior is offensive.

2. If the behavior continues, advise school personnel.

### School Liability

*A SCHOOL IS LIABLE* for sexual harassment in the school or at school related functions:

Supervisor to Student: Even if the employer is unaware of the supervisor's conduct.

Student to Student: If he/she knows or reasonably should have known that acts of sexual harassment are taking place; and/or if he/she does not take prompt, appropriate corrective action.

### Formulating A Policy

1. Define sexual harassment
    ~ Give specific examples

2. Establish a complaint procedure
    ~ Refer to EEOC guidelines, consult local counsel or your state education department

3. Set a time frame for response
    ~ When will the investigation be completed and a report issued

4. Establish disciplinary actions
    ~ Inform everyone of potential liability for criminal and civil penalties

5. Ensure confidentiality
    ~ Protect privacy rights and prevent any unnecessary disclosure

6. Protect against retaliation
    ~ Protect all parties involved including witnesses

# Stopping Unwanted Sexual Attention

If you are receiving unwanted sexual attention, tell the person that such behavior is unwelcome. If that person does not take you seriously, the following methods are suggested for stopping the behavior.

**Say It again.** Like a broken record, you may have to repeat your objections until the unwelcome behavior stops. Restate your objections. "I understand what you are saying but I don't want you to...." Repeat that statement until the person stops the behavior and takes your request seriously. And you don't have to explain or justify why you want the person to stop.

Keep notes with times, dates, places, and any witnesses.

**Talk to your supervisor.** (If it is your supervisor doing the sexual harassment, talk with his or her supervisor.)

**Write a letter** to the sexual harasser and include the following:

- a description of the unwelcome behavior

- the time the behavior occurred

- the fact that you want it stopped

- the warning that if the behavior does not stop, you will take further action

- your signature and the date

Make a copy and give the letter to the harasser in front of a witness.

**Contact your organization's personnel or resource people** to assist you in informally or formally stopping the unwanted sexual attention.

Contact the City or State Human Rights offices.

# Sexual Harassment Complaint Procedure

**If You Are Making the Complaint**

- Inform harasser that behavior is unwelcome.

- Ask someone to witness your statement if harasser may be antagonistic.

- Write a letter informing the harasser that described behavior is unwelcome. Sign, date, and present in front of witnesses. ***Keep a copy***.

- Keep a detailed list of actions including time, date, place(s), witnesses, etc.

- Act to prove allegations, not destroy alleged harasser.

- If behavior does not stop, advise management: document.

- Use the complaint procedure in your school's plan.

- Clearly identify behaviors surrounding complaint.

**If the Complaint Is Made Against You**

- Clearly identify the behaviors surrounding the complaint.

- Seek assistance in the affirmative action office or your personnel office.

- Gather supporting data and witnesses: document.

- Be cooperative with the investigator.

- Be informative: tell all facts relevant to complaint.

- Do not treat the complainant differently from others.

- Be sure you know your rights during each phase of informal/formal investigation procedures.

- Work with investigator to reach a resolution.

(You may seek the advice of the state department of human rights or your own legal counsel at any time during the complaint process.)

---

**Reflection/Discussion Items**

1. What does this mean to you and your classroom?

2. How can you insure that harassment does not occur in your school and classroom or work area?

3. On the following page is a Test on Sexual Harassment and Facts and Myths about Sexual Harassment. Read these over and discuss the items in a small group of 3 or 4 persons.

# A Test On Sexual Harassment

**TRUE or FALSE**

1. Men in male dominated workplaces usually have to change their behavior when a woman begins working there.
2. An employer is not liable for the sexual harassment of one of its employees unless that employee lost specific job benefits or was fired.
3. A court can require a sexual harasser to pay part of the judgment to the employee he or she sexually harassed.
4. A supervisor can be liable for sexual harassment done by one of his or her employees to another.
5. An employer can be liable for the sexually harassing behavior of management personnel even if it is unaware of that behavior and has a policy forbidding it.
6. It is appropriate for a supervisor, when initially receiving a sexual harassment complaint, to determine if the alleged recipient overreacted or misunderstood the alleged harasser.
7. When a supervisor is talking with an employee about an allegation of sexual harassment against him or her, it is best to ease into the allegation instead of being direct.
8. Sexually suggestive visuals or objects in a workplace don't create a liability unless an employee complains about them and management allows them to remain.
9. The lack of sexual harassment complaints is a good indication that sexual harassment is not occurring.
10. It is appropriate for a supervisor to tell an employee to handle unwelcome sexual behavior if he or she thinks that the employee is misunderstanding the behavior.
11. The **intent** behind employee A's sexual behavior is more important than the **impact** of that behavior on employee B when determining if sexual harassment occurred.

## Facts And Myths About Sexual Harassment

Each teacher, coach, manager or supervisor must be able to separate the facts from the myths about this complex and sensitive issue. When management personnel use objective, factual information, they are able to recognize, prevent, and take appropriate corrective action to informally resolve sexual harassment situations.

**FACT:** People are sexually harassed because they are perceived as vulnerable and/or a threat to members in their work group.

**FACT:** Sexual harassment is no more of a problem in blue-collar workplaces than in white-collar workplaces.

**FACT:** Most management personnel and employees don't understand what subtle sexual harassment behaviors are.

**FACT:** Men and women usually agree that if a supervisor tells an employee to "put out or get out," such behavior is sexual harassment. However, in most workplaces, men and women generally **don't** agree on how much sexual harassment exists or what types of behavior constitute sexual harassment.

**MYTH:** If an employer trains employees about sexual harassment, it will polarize males and females, create problems where no problems exist, and encourage employees to file false charges.

**MYTH:** Professional people do not engage in sexually harassing behaviors.

**MYTH:** Sexual harassment is usually caused by the victim's clothing or behavior.

**MYTH:** An employer who does not receive sexual harassment complaints does not have sexual harassment incidents.

# GAY, LESBIAN, BISEXUAL, AND TRANSGENDERED

In most groups within Western society the general public as well as scientists usually presume that two categories of sexual orientation exist: "heterosexual" and "homosexual" (Bohan, 1996). If these do exist, inclusion and exclusion criteria are far from clear and they differ between communities. Language and terms change over time and people need to be sensitive to these changes.

The term gay is used to refer to males while the term lesbian is used to refer to females. The term bisexual refers to an attraction to both males and females. Not all cultures define sexual orientation, as does the European American Community. In Native spirituality two-spirit is a term often used. This term represents more of a spiritual/social identity that encompasses alternative sexuality, alternative gender, and an integration of Native spirituality (Tafoya, 1996, 1997).

Gender identity is the psychological sense of being male or female. Gender role behavior is conformity to culturally defined norms of masculinity or femininity. Sexual orientation is the feeling of attraction to males, females, or both. Sexual orientation is not bipolar and many components are involved other than sexual behavior. Sexual orientation is one component of a person's identity, which also includes culture, ethnicity, gender, and personality traits to name a few of the other intersecting variables.

Transgender or transgendered is a term often applied to a person who is one biological sex and feels that they should be the other. They speak of being trapped in the body of the wrong sex. Often the person will act and dress the societal stereotypical way of the sex they feel they really should be.

Often the term homophobia is used to describe the rejecting attitudes toward lesbians and gay persons, and bi-phobia toward bisexual persons. Herek (1995) recommended using al alternative term, heterosexism. This is often defined as the ideological system that denies and stigmatizes any non-heterosexual form of behavior, identity, relationship, or community. Heterosexism captures more of the oppression directed at persons who are gay, lesbian, and bisexual.

Heterosexism is a unique form of prejudice, discrimination, and other rejecting actions. In all areas of life the basic rights of persons who are gay, lesbian, and bi-sexual are either denied or violated. There is also an increase in the incidence and severity of violence perpetrated against these persons. The consequences of these actions or threats of such action can be very severe in terms of mental health, education, and occupations.

Sexual minority youth often feel unsafe in their schools, homes, and communities because they are targets of anti-gay attitudes (PFLAG, 1997). Society's negative attitudes about homosexuality can be internalized leading to feelings of lack of self worth. This often leads to higher risk of suicide, drop out rates, and drug and alcohol abuse. Stereotypes about lesbian and gay people need to be unlearned to fundamental resources can be made available to assist in the creation of safe spaces where people can learn and grow.

## References
Bohan, J. (1996). *Psychological and sexual orientation: Coming to terms.* New York: Routledge.
Herek, G. (1995). *Psychological heterosexism in the United States.* In A. D'Augelli & C. Patterson (Eds.) Lesbian, gay, and bisexual identities over the lifespan: Psychological perspectives (p. 321-346). New York: Oxford University Press.
PFLAG Parents, Families, and Friends of Lesbians and Gays (1997). *Fact sheet: Sexual minority youth.* PFLAG 1101 14th Street NW Suite 1030, Washington, DC 20036. http://www.pflag.org.
Tafoya, T. (1996). Native two-spirit people. In R. Cabaj & T. Stein (Eds.) *Textbook of homosexuality and mental health (pp. 603-617).* Washington, DC: American Psychiatric Press.
Tafoya, T. (1997). *Native gay and lesbian issues: The two-spirited.* In B. Greene (Ed.) Ethnic and cultural diversity among lesbians and gay men (pp. 1-10). Thousand Oaks, CA: Sage.

# DEALING WITH HOMOPHOBIA

Phobia is defined in Webster's (1999) dictionary as "an irrational, excessive, and persistent fear…(p1082)". "Homophobia" is not yet found in many dictionaries, but the meaning is quite clear. It is a real fear of homosexuals or persons perceived to be gay, lesbian, bisexual, or transgendered (GLBT).

To even raise the subject of homosexuality in discussions is certain to elicit some outrage. Some people feel that any consideration of or discussions regarding homosexuality without condemning it outright as being "unnatural" is wrong. These discussions can and often do evoke fear and strong emotion. But if we are to deal with discrimination, racism, and other "ism's", we must consider all other issues involving discrimination including discriminating against persons who are or are perceived to be GLBT.

We do not intend to take a moral position regarding the "rightness" or "wrongness" of any sexual orientation issue. Nor do we intend to try to justify the legitimate existence and right of any one sexual orientation over another, but it is extremely important to discuss some possibilities of misinformation that we all have been exposed to throughout our lives in an attempt to understand some of the issues.

We must be wary of justifying oppression or discrimination in any way through the use of religion. Various religious groups have tried and those that continue to try to justify and legitimize slavery, racial segregation, anti-Semitism, and male domination have used similar arguments. It is also important to note that many religious groups strongly advocate the civil rights of lesbians and gay men, and various caucuses of differing faiths are working toward increasing rights for gays and lesbians within religious communities.

We all have personal opinions and deeply held beliefs. Our perceptions of what is "natural", however, are often the product of socialization. What has long been proscribed, legislated, and condemned can come to be seen as "unnatural". It is instructive to note, for example, that homosexuality was considered "natural" for some in most European societies until the 13th century when religious groups who controlled governments, began an attempt to declare it "unnatural" on religious grounds. It is also significant to understand that many American Indians believed it to be "natural" and a gift.

We also need to discuss the question of "proselytizing", since this is usually raised when efforts are made to discuss homosexuality in an open forum. Many people fear that such discussions will somehow "lure" youngsters into homosexuality from heterosexuality. People do not want to be accused of influencing people to become gay so they usually try to avoid discussing the subject altogether. This, of course, makes the assumption that being a gay male or lesbian is a matter of free choice. People erroneously imagine or assume they really have the power to guide children to the "right" choice.

Though the direction of one's sexuality may be a matter of choice for a small percentage of adults, the majority of gay men and lesbians become aware that they are somehow "different" from the heterosexual norm when quite young. This awareness generally occurs in a profoundly anti-gay social setting and in spite of a heterosexual society that continually reinforces the superiority of heterosexuality over homosexuality. Given the issue that gay men and lesbians succeed in discovering their sexual identity in the pervasiveness of heterosexual influences provides a strong argument that sexual orientation is not influenced by "proselytizing".

To date, science has not positively determined how sexual orientation develops, however recent research has begun to point to genetic factors other than free choice. We only know that homosexuality, like heterosexuality, has existed in all types of families, in all societies, throughout history. According to current research, approximately ten-fifteen percent of individuals in the population are either gay men or lesbians. They face discrimination daily, particularly in education, jobs and housing. They also face name calling, taunting, hatred and violence.

The critical issue is that persons who are or are perceived to be gay, lesbian, bisexual, or transgendered are legitimate and productive citizens of our communities and are entitled to the same rights as the other citizens of our communities; and that is to be free from harassment and discrimination.

The term sexual orientation is preferred over sexual preference. It refers to sexual and affectional relationships of all types. When referring to specific women or men and groups, the adjectives lesbian and gay male are preferred to the adjective homosexual, and the nouns lesbians and gay men to the noun homosexuals. When reference is made to people who relate sexually and affectionately to both men and women, the terms bisexual women and men and bisexual persons, or bisexual as an adjective are preferred.

On the next page you will find a glossary of terms to assist in understanding language. Remember that language is a powerful tool that communicates specific messages and respect is communicated through language use.

**Reference**
Webster (1999). New World Collegiate Dictionary p1082 (4th ed.). Cleveland, OH: Macmillan.

---

**Discussion/Reflection Item**
1. Refer to the terminology on the next page.

2. Do these terms clarify questions for you?

# GLOSSARY OF TERMS

**Bisexual:** A woman or man who forms primary loving and sexual relationships with members of both sexes; someone who has a continuing affection, emotional, romantic and/or erotic attraction to persons of both sexes.

**Gay Male:** A man who forms his primary loving and sexual relationships with other men; a man who has a continuing affectional, emotional, romantic and/or erotic attraction to someone of the same sex.

**Heterosexism:** The societal assumption and norm that the practice of heterosexuality is the only acceptable, sanctioned expression of human sexuality, and that homosexuality and bisexuality are wrong.

**Heterosexual:** Someone who forms primary loving and sexual relationships with persons of the opposite sex, and who has a continuing affectional, emotional, romantic and/or erotic attraction to someone of the opposite sex.

**Homophobia:** Consists of those negative feelings, attitudes, actions or behaviors against Lesbians, Gays and bisexuals. It is likewise a fear of one's own same-sex sexual or affectional feelings as well as being perceived as Gay or Lesbian.

**Homosexual:** A clinical and technical term that is not generally used by Lesbians and Gays to refer to themselves or their community. For example, Congressman Barney Frank refers to himself as gay or openly gay, not admittedly homosexual or a practicing homosexual.

**Lesbian:** A woman who forms her primary loving and sexual relationships with other women; a woman who has a continuing affectional, emotional, romantic and/or erotic attraction to someone of the same sex. Some Lesbians prefer to call themselves Lesbian and use the term Gay to refer to Gay men; others use the term Gay to refer to both men and women.

**Lover, Partner and Significant Other:** Terms that Lesbians, Gays and bisexual people use to identify those people with whom they have romantic or sexual relationships.

**Out or Out of the Closet:** A term, which means being open and public about being Lesbian, Gay or bisexual. A closeted person hides the fact that they are Lesbian, Gay or bisexual. Some people are out in some settings (e.g., with friends) but not out in other settings (e.g., at work or with family)

**Transgendered:** A term, which often means a person who is one biological sex and feels that they should be the opposite.

**Inappropriate terms often associated with persons who are or are perceived to be gay, lesbian, bisexual, and transgendered.** *Fag, Dyke, Faggot, Lezzie, Homo, Queer, Fairy, Fruit, Pansy and Sissy:* All insulting terms to people who are Lesbians, Gays bisexual, and transgendered. They are the equivalent to insulting terms for Italians, Asians, African Americans, women or people withexceptionalities, etc.

# Statistics on GLBT Youth

**Suicide:** Gay youth are two to three times more likely to attempt suicide than other young people are. It is estimated that 30% of completed youth suicides are related to issues of sexual orientation. Suicide is the leading cause of death among gay male, lesbian, bisexual, and transgender youth.
 ~ U.S. Department of Health and Human Services, 1999

**Violence:** 45% of gay males and 20% of lesbian females experience verbal or physical assault in high school. 28% of these youth are forced to drop out of school because of harassment based on their sexual orientation.
 ~ National Gay and Lesbian Task Force, "Anti-Gay/Lesbian Victimization", 1984

**Runaway / Homelessness:** 50% of gay and lesbian youth interviewed report that their parents rejected them due to their sexual orientation.
 ~ Remafedi, "Male Homosexuality: The Adolescent's Perspective," *Pediatrics*, 1987

26% of gay youth are forced to leave home because of conflicts with their families over issues of sexual orientation.
 ~ National Gay and Lesbian Task Force, "Anti-Gay / Lesbian Victimization", 1984

Up to half of the gay or bisexual males forced out of their homes engage in prostitution to support themselves, greatly increasing their risk for HIV.
 ~ National Gay and Lesbian Task Force, "Anti-Gay / Lesbian Victimization", 1984

On any given night, there are between 82 and 219 gay, lesbian, bisexual and transgender youth (ages 18-21) living on the streets in Minnesota.
 ~ Wilder Research Center, "Gay, Lesbian, Bisexual and Transgender Homeless Youth Host Home Feasibility Study," 1997

**HIV / AIDS:** 63 % of gay and bisexual males (ages 13-21) in a recent Minnesota study were found to be at "extreme risk" for HIV due to unprotected intercourse or intravenous drug use.
 ~ Remafedi, "Predictors of Unprotected Intercourse Among Gay and Bisexual Youth," Pediatrics, 1994

From 1987 to 1991, one in every four newly infected individuals in the U.S. was age 22 or under.
 ~ Rosenberg, Biggar, Goedert, "Declining Age at HIV Infection in the United States," *New England Journal of Medicine,* 1994

**Substance Abuse:** 28% of gay males (ages 13-21) in a recent Minnesota study were found to have an alcohol or drug problem, based on the Substance Abuse Inventory. This was directly related to identity image issues and harassment.
 ~ Remafedi, Youth and AIDS Projects, 1996

**Isolation:** 80% of lesbian, gay, and bisexual youth report severe isolation problems.
*Social isolation:* having no one to talk to
*Emotional isolation:* feeling distanced from family and peers because of their sexual identity
*Cognitive isolation:* lack of access to accurate information about sexual orientation
 ~ Hetrick and Martin, "Developmental Issues and Their Resolution for Gay and Lesbian Adolescents" 1987

# PREVENTING HOMOPHOBIA IN SCHOOL
## Suggestions for Ways to Include Lesbian, Gay and Bisexual Issues in School

[Based on work by Women's Educational Media as part of the *Respect for All* video series for elementary children, educators, and parents.]

### Why Discuss Lesbian and Gay Issues with Children?

All children need to feel safe in schools and to have their personal experience validated. Teachers do not necessarily know which children in their classes have a gay or lesbian parent, aunt, uncle, cousin, grandparent, or other significant person in their lives; which children have friends whose parents are gay; or *which children will grow up to be gay themselves*. All children need to have the existence of gay people recognized, and to be taught that all people, regardless of sexual orientation, are entitled to respect.

Addressing homophobia lies at the heart of promoting gender equity in the classroom and preventing violence among young people. Fear of being labeled gay scares many children - boys and girls - from exploring activities and behaviors that branch out beyond those which are typically associated with their own gender. Girls may shy away from playing sports, boys may shy away from dance, music, or art. All children may receive negative messages about the natural affection they feel for friends of their same sex. When children are not taught WHY it is wrong to hurl anti-gay epithets at each other ("faggot," "lezbo," "you're so gay"), they may fell justified in participating in or condoning anti-gay violence when they grow older. All children need to understand that homophobia, like racism and sexism, hurts everyone, and that each of them can be an ally in standing up to it.

### How Much Do You Have to Say?

Combating homophobia and the invisibility of lesbians and gay men in the educational system, and standing up to anti-gay name-calling does not mean teaching about sexual acts. There are age-appropriate ways to talk with children about gay people in our society. Listen to what the children want to know and answer their questions. Let the other children in the class share information. You don't have to have all the answers; the important thing is to convey that it is okay to discuss these issues; it is okay for kids to have questions about them; and that you believe in respect for everyone.

### What if You Personally Don't Believe that Homosexuality is Okay or Aren't Sure What You Think?

Acknowledging that gay, lesbian, and bisexual people exist is not the same as saying that you personally believe that homosexuality is okay. Not acknowledging that gays exist is like not acknowledging that people of color or people with disabilities or different religions exist. They are part of our world. You can create a safe space for children to discuss lesbian and gay issues without making judgments or engaging in dialogue about your own personal beliefs or concerns.

### How Can Teachers Include Lesbian and Gay Issues in the Classroom?

*Introduce the vocabulary*

At minimum, find some time in your classroom to use the words lesbian, gay, and bisexual and make sure the children understand what those words mean. No one is too young to hear or say those words. They are not bad words. In fact, most children have heard and use those words, or negative references to them, without knowing what they mean. They are descriptions of people that exist in their world. If you are not comfortable saying those words, practice saying and explaining them with another teacher or sympathetic parent.

*Look for the teachable moment.*

You do not necessarily have to plan a whole lesson around lesbian and gay issues. But you can use moments when the children bring the issue up to create a safe space for dialogue around these issues. If you hear kids calling each other faggot, take time not just to say "we don't allow name-calling her," but to have a discussion about why and how that particular name is hurtful. Have the children role-play what they could say if someone says that to them or to their friends.

*Use current events.*

If you discuss the news in your classroom, bring in an article about some issue connected to lesbian and gay rights. Have the children debate the issue, or explore both sides. Ask them what they think.

Acknowledge that authors, historical figures, and other famous people who come up in class discussions are gay, lesbian, and bisexual.

Do you ever use literature by Walt Whitman, James Baldwin, or Willa Cather or discuss sports and mention tennis players like Martina Navratalova or Olympic diver Greg Louganis? Do people talk about popular culture and bring up shows like "Married with Children" (that stars a woman who is a lesbian) or performers (like Elton John or K.D. Lang)? You can counter gay invisibility by simply mentioning that these people are gay or bisexual.

If there are openly gay and lesbian teachers, staff, or parents at your school or individuals in your community, you can refer to them in a respectful way and mention some information that lets the children know that that individual is gay and that you respect them.

Change the sexual orientation of some of the characters in books you read to the class or in written assignments. Ninety-nine percent of the couples in children's books are heterosexual. While sex is never discussed, the characters are male and female - either married or in love. Try reading the book or making the assignment with a male or female couple. If the children raise objections, use that discussion as a jumping off point to discuss why it seems unusual or "wrong" to them.

When discussing families, talk about all different kinds of families, whether or not they are represented in your classroom. Remember that some parents may not be "out" and may not be visible to you. Read a book to your class in which there is a child that has two moms or dads. When discussing that book give the name "lesbian" or "gay" to the relationship between those two adults.

If there is a gay family in your classroom, ask the parents if they would like to come in and talk about being a gay family. Ask other parents in non-traditional family structures if they would like to come and talk about their families. If there is not and openly gay family, invite one from another class, or from a community organization that provides speakers from gay families.

When you have a unit that touches on any <u>social justice issue</u> (the civil rights movement, for example) adds a part to it that talks about other social justice concerns and include the lesbian and gay rights movement. If you don't feel comfortable talking about it, invite a speaker who does.

If you do any units that involve <u>media literacy</u> (having the children monitor TV shows for violence, or the way women and men or people of color are portrayed), ask them to watch TV for a week and write down any time there is a mention of gay people or a gay character is portrayed. Have a class discussion about the implications of those results.

If you are doing <u>a unit on the different communities</u> that make up your city, include the lesbian and gay community. Refer to local gay history, landmarks, or culture; invite lesbian and gay parents or others from the community to speak to your class. Remember to convey that the lesbian and gay population is comprised of individuals from all the other communities you are studying (e.g. the Chinese or African-American community).

Do a unit on name-calling. Talk about how different kinds of taunting hurt children in different ways (teasing about language differences, color, size, for example) and include anti-gay name-calling. Ask the children to talk about why it's hard to tell their friends to stop using those names, and role-play ways that kids can intervene. Talk about why it's important to you not to use anti-gay language (it might be a time to acknowledge that you have lesbian and gay friends or colleagues or relatives).

Celebrate Holidays. In October, celebrate National Coming Out Day (usually on October 11). Invite and openly gay and lesbian individual to your class and encourage the children to ask questions. Have them write a letter to someone they know (either personally or who is famous) about Coming Out Day. In June, acknowledge that there will be a lesbian and gay pride celebration in their area or in other parts of the country. Talk about the history of that event and have a discussion of why gay people would want to have such a celebration.

Support Groups. Some schools have support groups for students of all ages who wish to participate on a voluntary basis. Provide information on these to all students.

Continue these efforts and contact local, state, and national organizations for more specific information and ideas.

---

**Reflecftion/Discussion Items**
1. What is your initial response to the information presented in this section?

2. How can you address homophobia in your school/classroom?

3. How can you be more proactive in assisting others in their understanding and support for students of all ages?

4. On the next page are 25 statements about working or associating with persons who are LGBT. Read and rank each statement according to the scoring key provided. On the page following the statements you will find a scoring key. Compute your score and work on the questions on that specific page.

# INDEX OF HOMOPHOBIA

This questionnaire (Hudson & Ricketts, 1988) is designed to measure the way you feel about working or associating with persons who are LGBT. It is not a test, so there are no right or wrong answers. It is designed to provide useful information for you to assess your attitudes and beliefs. It is only effective if you are honest with yourself. Answer each item as carefully and as accurately as you can by placing a number beside each one as follows:

| | |
|---|---|
| 1 | strongly agree |
| 2 | agree |
| 3 | neither agree nor disagree |
| 4 | disagree |
| 5 | strongly disagree |

1. I would feel comfortable working with a male homosexual. _____
2. I would enjoy attending social functions at which homosexuals were present. _____
3. I would feel uncomfortable if I learned that my neighbor was homosexual. _____
4. If a member of my sex made a sexual advance toward me I would feel angry. _____
5. I would feel comfortable knowing that I was attractive to members of my sex. _____
6. I would feel uncomfortable being seen in a gay bar. _____
7. I would feel comfortable if a member of my sex made an advance toward me. _____
8. I would be comfortable if I found myself attracted to a member of my sex. _____
9. I would feel disappointed if I learned that my child was homosexual. _____
10. I would feel nervous being in a group of homosexuals. _____
11. I would feel comfortable knowing that the leader of my religious group was homosexual. _____
12. I would be upset if I learned that my brother or sister was homosexual. _____
13. I would feel that I had failed as a parent if I learned that my child was gay. _____
14. If I saw two men holding hands in public I would feel disgusted. _____
15. If a member of my sex made an advance toward me I would be offended. _____
16. I would feel comfortable if I learned that my daughter's teacher was a homosexual. _____
17. I would feel uncomfortable if I learned that my spouse or partner was attracted to a member of his or her sex. _____
18. I would feel at ease talking with homosexual person at a party. _____
19. I would feel uncomfortable if I learned that my boss was homosexual. _____
20. It would not bother me to walk through a predominantly gay section of town. _____
21. It would disturb me to find out that my doctor was homosexual. _____
22. It would feel comfortable if I learned that my best friend of my sex was homosexual. _____
23. If a member of my sex made an advance toward me I would feel flattered. _____
24. I would feel uncomfortable knowing that my son's male teacher was homosexual. _____
25. I would feel comfortable working closely with a female homosexual. _____

The scoring for this index is on the next page.

# Index of Homophobia Scoring

Items 3, 4, 6, 9, 10, 12, 13, 14, 15, 17, 19, 21, and 24 must be reversed scored. After reverse scoring these items, the total score is obtained by summing the 25 item responses and subtracting 25 from the sum.

You should have a score somewhere between 0 and 100

    0-25 = Nonhomophobic

    25-50 = Moderate nonhomophobic

    50-75 = Moderate homophobic

    75-100 = Strongly homophobic

After reviewing your score and the previous statements think about how you will work effectively with students, families, and colleagues who are gay, lesbian, bisexual, or transgendered.

**Reference**
Hudson, W. & Ricketts, W. (1988). Index of homophobia. In C.M. Davis, W.L. Yarber, & S.L. Davis (Eds.), *Sexually-related measures: A compendium.* (pp. 155-156). Lake Mills, IA: Graphic Publishing Company.

---

**Reflection/Discussion Items**

1. How do you interpret your score?

2. Do you think this is an accurate reflection of your honest feelings? Why or Why not?

3. If we assume that a lower score is more appropriate, how could you lower your score?

4. What questions or concerns do you have?

5. On the next page is the Riddle Scale. Read it over and assess your attitudes toward difference.

# ATTITUDES SCALE

## Attitudes Toward Differences: The Riddle Scale*

| Attitude | Characteristics |
|---|---|
| Repulsion | People who are different are strange, sick, crazy and aversive. |
| Pity | People who are different are somehow born that way and it is pitiful. |
| Tolerance | Being different is just a phase of development that...most people 'grow out of'. |
| Acceptance | This implies that one needs to make accommodations for another's differences and does not acknowledge that another's identity may be of the same value as their own. |
| Support | Supportive persons work to safeguard the fights of those who are different from themselves. |
| Admiration | This acknowledges that being different in our society takes strength. |
| Appreciation | This attitude values the diversity of people and is willing to confront insensitive attitudes. |
| Nurturance | Nurturance assumes the differences in people are indispensable in and to society. |

**Reference**
Riddle, D. (1994). *Alone no more: Developing a school support system for gay, lesbian and bisexual youth.*

*Attitudes Scale developed by Dorothy Riddle, Ph.D., a psychologist from Tucson, AZ.

---

**Reflection/Discussion Items**
1. On the next page are 20 general knowledge review questions. Respond to each on with True or False based on you understanding.

2. After you have scored each item form a small group of 3 or 4 persons and compare your responses.

3. Identify statements you disagree upon and discuss why.

# GENERAL KNOWLEDGE REVIEW

The following twenty statements are provided for a review of the information and your general knowledge.

(Please mark each one either TRUE or FALSE)

_____ 1. The words "homosexual" and "heterosexual" are adjectives to describe experiential behavior.

_____ 2. People should not be described as adjectives.

_____ 3. Most people during their lifetime experience both psychic and physical homosexual and heterosexual responses.

_____ 4. Because a person has a number of homosexual or heterosexual experiences doesn't necessarily make them such.

_____ 5. The terms "gay" and "straight" includes the ability to respond physically, psycho-emotionally, and spiritually to someone of the same or opposite gender.

_____ 6. Being male, masculine, and straight means the same.

_____ 7. Everybody is either predominantly gay or straight.

_____ 8. Women and men are exactly opposite in genetics, hormonal balance, anatomical, physiological, psycho-emotional make-up.

_____ 9. All men and women are alike in the above qualities.

_____ 10. Someone's sex and gender are the same thing.

_____ 11. Gender means more than someone's biological sex.

_____ 12. There are a lot of gray zones on the continuum of gender diversity.

_____ 13. Most people have varying degrees of maleness-femaleness, masculinity/femininity, and gayness-straightness, for example.

_____ 14. Most gays look straight.

_____ 15. Gay men and lesbian women are generally content with their sex and gender.

_____ 16. Someone who wants to change sex is transsexual.

_____ 17. Gays and lesbians are usually as moral, healthy, normal, religious, masculine, etc. as "straight" men and women.

_____ 18. Most child molesters (pedophiles) are straight men who prefer children of the opposite sex.

_____ 19. Gays and lesbians have the ability to be as competent as parents, teachers, and spouses as anyone else does.

_____ 20. Gay males don't necessarily make good ballet dancers, creative artists, sensitive counselors, and interior decorators, and Lesbians don't necessarily make good mechanics, police officers and truck drivers.

# HETEROSEXUAL PRIVILEGE

After reading the preceding section do you still find yourself confused? Ok, then if you are heterosexual answer the following questions

1. What caused your heterosexuality?

2. When and how did you first decide you were a heterosexual?

3. Is it possible our heterosexuality is just a phase you may outgrow?

4. Is it possible your heterosexuality stems from a neurotic fear of others of the same sex?

5. Isn't it possible that all you need is a good gay or lesbian lover?

6. Heterosexuals have histories of failures in gay relationships. Do you think you may have turned to heterosexuality out of a fear of rejection?

7. If you've never slept with a person of the same sex, how do you know that you wouldn't prefer that?

8. To whom have you disclosed your heterosexuality?

9. Why do heterosexuals feel compelled to seduce others into their sexual orientation?

10. Why do you insist on making a public spectacle of your heterosexuality? Can't you just be what you are and keep it quiet?

Did you find any surprises when you read these questions? When you remove the word heterosexual and replace it with the word homosexual it becomes a series of questions that are often asked of gays and lesbians. Hopefully this has helped you to understand more of what this section is attempting to illustrate.

What if you don't believe homosexuality or bisexuality are ok?
Acknowledging that GLBT people exist is not the same as saying that you personally believe that homosexuality is ok. You can still create a safe space for GLBT people and discuss issues without engaging in a dialogue about your own personal beliefs or concerns. Respect, support, and safety are primary concerns. How does your school rate?

| Reflection/Discussion Items |
| --- |
| 1. How does this apply to you and your classroom? |
| 2. How can you help to create a safe zone in your school? |
| 3. What will you do when the teachable moment occurs? |

# Section IX

# AGE AND AGE BIAS

*Rationale:* Age and age bias (ageism) impact all individuals in society.

*Objectives:*
1. To understand the general field of aging and perceptions related to it.
2. To develop an increased awareness of one's definition and perceptions about aging.
3. To understand how age is often related to ethnicity and socioeconomic status.
4. To develop strategies for dealing with ageism in schools and society.

# AGE AND AGE BIAS

Every person will pass through the various stages in life and eventually join the ranks of the aged. Like all other microcultures thinking, perceiving, and behaving is a function of the age group to which one belongs. It is helpful to understand various aspects of age and the age bias present in order to avoid stereotyping or categorizing individuals. With life expectancy increasing each year, those in the aged cohort increase in numbers daily.

Like the cultural and ethnic groups the aged category of individuals face prejudice and discrimination on a daily basis. Are those pictures and jokes about elderly as harmless as they appear on the surface? Remember, those who discriminate will one day be in this group themselves and face the treatment they have imposed on others.

## OBJECTIVES FOR THE REDUCTION OF AGE PREJUDICE

|  | AGE RESTRICTIVENESS | AGE DISTORTION | COUNTERING AGE-ISM |
|---|---|---|---|
| **COGNITIVE OBJECTIVES** | 1. Knowledge of age restrictive attitudes, norms, and laws. | 1. Knowledge of the general field of perception with special emphasis on the pygmalion and halo effects. | 1. Knowledge of the aging process. |
|  | 2. Knowledge of how people restrict feelings and behavior because of age-restrictive attitudes, norms, and laws. | 2. Knowledge of research studies that have found age distortion. | 2. Knowledge of the strengths, uses, and limitations of work that depicts developmental tasks and phases. |
|  | 3. Knowledge of strategies to reduce age restrictiveness. | 3. Knowledge of how people stereotypically view themselves and others at different ages. | 3. Knowledge of how age-ism affects people over 65. |
|  |  |  | 4. Knowledge of career and life-planning skills. |
|  |  |  | 5. Knowledge of how the media contributes to age-ism. |

|  | **AGE RESTRICTIVENESS** | **AGE DISTORTION** | **COUNTERING AGEISM** |
|---|---|---|---|
| **AFFECTIVE OBJECTIVES** | 1. Increased awareness of one's feelings about age restrictiveness.<br><br>2. Increased appreciation for the extent to which age restrictiveness influences human growth and development.<br><br>3. Increased desire to take action to reduce age restrictiveness. | 1. Increased sensitivity for detecting age distortion in oneself and others.<br><br>2. Increased aversion to age distortion in oneself and others.<br><br>3. Increased desire to take action to reduce age distortion. | 1. Increased awareness of one's personal definition of old age.<br><br>2. Increased awareness of personal fears about aging.<br><br>3. Increased acceptance of oneself and others throughout the age spectrum.<br><br>4. Increased appreciation of life planning.<br><br>5. Increased desire to reduce and eliminate age-ism in oneself and others. |

|  | AGE RESTRICTIVENESS | AGE DISTORTION | AGE-ISM |
|---|---|---|---|
| **BEHAVIORAL OBJECTIVES** | 1. Individuals will write letters to public and private sector officials demanding that age restrictive practices and policies end. | 1. Individuals will write letters of objection to the producers of media presentations that support age stereotypes and letters of support to producers who counter age stereotypes. | 1. Individuals will organize to develop and promote programs which will reduce and eliminate age bias. |
|  | 2. Individuals will in some way not act their age and encourage others to do the same. | 2. Individuals will significantly increase the amount of time they spend in one-to-one interaction with people in different age brackets. | 2. Individuals will write positive scenarios of their life 10 to 50 years in the future. |
|  | 3. Individuals will interview and educate others about age restrictiveness. | 3. Individuals will take part in functions of groups whose membership is largely composed of persons in a significantly different age bracket (e.g., a young adult attending a senior citizen picnic). | 3. Individuals who have been reluctant to give their correct age will do so with pride. |

## Conclusion

Age prejudice is an affliction of all ages. Acting our age might put us in accordance with social expectations, but at the cost of being in discordance with our own being. An old proverb says it well by asking: "Which is better – the dandelion or the oak?" The answer: The one that actualizes itself. At any age individuals have the opportunity to grow towards this, but age impedes the passage and places barriers between people of all ages.

---

**Reflection/Discussion Items**

1. On the following pages are comparisons of age biased and non-age biased thoughts and behaviors. Consider these and your personal position as you read them.

2. How can you apply countering ageism elements in your school/classroom?

# COUNTERING AGE-ISM

## The Health of the Elderly

| *Ageist* | *Non-Ageist/Recommended* |
|---|---|
| I hate the thought of getting older because old means physical complaints and illness . . . I don't want to be an invalid. | Getting older is natural . . . most old people aren't invalids . . . I'll take care of myself now so I'll feel good later. |
| At 72, she is confused, apathetic, withdrawn, taking no interest in anything. | All her life she has been confused, apathetic, withdrawn, taking no interest in anything. No wonder she's that way at 72. |
| The old are always sick, they end up in nursing homes. | Some old people get sick, but few are in nursing homes. |

## Economics and Aging

| *Ageist* | *Non-Ageist/Recommended* |
|---|---|
| Old people belong on the shelf. They shouldn't take a younger person's job. | No one belongs on the shelf . . . We each have something to contribute. |
| What do they have to look forward to? Food stamps and old age relief! | Some older people are poor . . . food stamps and SSI help, but sometimes it's not enough. |
| Old people should retire. They've lost their skills. They can't do a decent job. | Older people shouldn't be forced to retire . . . they should have the choice. Many have skills that can only be acquired over many years. |

## Families, Love, and Relationships

| *Ageist* | *Non-Ageist/Recommended* |
|---|---|
| Most old people are socially isolated and lonely. | Few people are socially isolate just because they are older. |
| Most older people are neglected by their families. | Most older people are close to their families. |
| It's silly for people over 65 to marry. | You're never too old to fall in love and get married. |

Reprinted by permission from *Truth About Aging*, American Association of Retired Persons, 1984 (updated 2003).

### Leisure Activities

*Ageist*

Retired people just sit and
watch life pass them by.

Tennis is a game for the young.
As with most sports, a thirty-five –
year-old is over-the-hill.

A smart politician goes after
the youth vote.

*Non-Ageist/Recommended*

In retirement, many people become
involved in activities they didn't have
time for when they were working.

Tennis is a sport for a lifetime. You
may slow down as you get older but
if you change your strategy to
compensate, you can continue to play
a very competitive game.

A smart politician does not overlook
the power of any segment of voters.

### Age Norms and Social Roles

*Ageist*

What does an old man like that
want with a sports car?

That man she's with must be half
her age!

Ask my grandmother. I'm sure she'll
do it. She always has plenty of time!

*Non-Ageist/Recommended*

Now that his children are on their
own, he can have that sports car he's
always wanted.

Men of all ages find her attractive.

Ask my grandmother. She always
tries to make time to help others.

### Generational Characteristics

*Ageist*

Most old people are pretty
much alike.

When people get old, they become
more faultfinding, irritable, and
demanding.

Old people are unable to adjust to
change.

*Non-Ageist/Recommended*

All people are individuals who
become more unique with age and
a lifetime of experiences.

Some people are more faultfinding,
irritable, and demanding than others.

Some people are slow to adjust to
change.

**Vocabulary Considerations**

Avoid the following:

- patronizing adjectives such as *cute*, *sweet*, *dear*, and *little*

- negative physical descriptors such as *crippled, deaf, dentured, emaciated, feeble, fragile, frail, frowning, gray, inactive, wrinkled, withered, dirty,* and *doddering*

- negative personality descriptors such as *cheerless, dull, eccentric, foolish, morose, meek, obstinate, queer, sad,* and *senile*

- demeaning labels and expressions such as *old maid, old codger, old biddy, fuddy-duddy, lecher, old fool, Geritol generation, golden agers, has been, over the hill, out of date,* and *fading fast*

- the stereotypes of older women such as *passive, dependent, frivolous, shrewish,* and *nagging*


**Recommendations**
The following guidelines are offered as ways in which the older population can be fairly and accurately depicted.

1. The proportion of older people should be equal to their distribution in the general population.
2. The older woman should appear more often than the older man.
3. A balanced view of the physical process of aging should be sought, emphasizing both the continuing strengths and abilities as well as the physical difficulties of the old age.
4. Since focusing on the nursing home population gives a distorted view of the elderly and only serves to reinforce negative stereotypes of aging, such over-representation should be avoided.
5. Older people should be represented in all economic levels: affluent, middleclass, and poor.
6. The older person should frequently be accorded an occupational identity and shown in a diversity of employment settings.
7. Older people should be shown in a number of different living arrangements: =living with spouse, residing with children, living with non-relatives, or living alone.
8. Older persons should be portrayed as having normal human needs, including the desire for sexual expression.
9. Older people often should be shown as active, creative, and dynamic individuals who engage in worthwhile activities.
10. The potential in old age of attaining an enriched emotional, spiritual, social, and intellectual life should be recognized.
11. The individuality of older people should be affirmed by showing them in alternative life styles that are commensurate with individual needs and abilities.
12. Older women should often be shown pursuing interests that extend beyond the family setting.
13. Specific personality traits or social values should not be attributed to old age alone but rather should be viewed as part of a complex societal environment.
14. Older people should be depicted as complex, three-dimensional individuals who demonstrate a range of realistic emotions and behaviors.

# Considerations for Composition of Illustrations, Photographs, Etc.

**Avoid more than occasional depiction of persons who are older:**

- in rocking chairs, knitting, napping, watching television

- baking cookies, babysitting

- in ill-fitting, dark colored, out-of-style clothing; "orthopedic" shoes; hats

- with canes, wheelchairs, in nursing homes

- only with other old people or very young children

- with gray hair, dentures, no teeth, bald, stoop-shouldered, bow-legged, excessively overweight or underweight

- who are engaged in passive/slow-moving sports such as walking, golfing, playing cards, playing chess, "in the park", fishing, swimming, jogging, sailing

- alone; only with peers/same sex

- idle

**Positive alternatives show people who are older:**

- dancing, shopping, in restaurants, at theatre, gardening, traveling, doing volunteer work

- as lawyers, teachers, doctors, business people

- dressed in stylish clothing but not juvenile fads, well-fitted, in tasteful colors

- with few orthopedic devices; living independently

- with people of all ages

- with hair of various colors, including gray and white; with classic and popular styles; with teeth

- playing tennis, handball, skiing

- with persons of various ages, in groups and couples

- in a variety of business, hobby, and civic activity situations

**In everyday life, older people can be seen in a variety of situations. Show them that way.**

---

**Reflection/Discussion Items**

1. How does this apply to you and your classroom/school?

2. What can you do to foster acceptance in your community?

# SECTION X

# APPLYING EDUCATION THAT IS MULTICULTURAL AND ANTI-BIASED

***Rationale*:** Application to individual situations is necessary in order to continue the process of becoming multicultural. Becoming multicultural implies understanding and promoting the acceptance of intersecting variables and diverse perspective taking strategies. The shift from multicultural education to education that is multicultural is in emphasizing education as a multicultural process and integrating this into all standards of effective performance and practice throughout the entire educational endeavor.

## *Objectives*
1. To understand and apply major concepts and issues in multiple intelligence and ways of teaching.
2. To discuss and incorporate the meaning of multicultural education.
3. To analyze the ways in which variables such as race, class, gender, exceptionality, affectional orientation, and other factors influence our curriculum, attitudes, and behavior.
4. To understand and apply major intersecting variables in schools and society.
5. To understand and apply multicultural education as an idea or concept, an educational reform movement, and an ongoing process.
6. To examine classrooms and rethink curriculum and pedagogy.
7. To increase critical and appreciative abilities.
8. To understand the roles of parents, guardians, and others in the community.
9. To know how to aid in the process and implementation of multicultural gender fair education.
10. To integrate all course topics into actual personal and professional practice.
11. To develop and maintain an inclusive environment for all.
12. To make social action decisions that are anti-biased.

Remember: Change is inevitable while personal and professional growth are both optional.

# LEARNING STYLES, MULTIPLE INTELLIGENCE, AND WAYS OF TEACHING

The schools in the U.S. have maintained a heavy reliance on reading, writing, and mathematical skills. In the vernacular of multiple intelligence, these are categorized as linguistic and logical-mathematical. The emphasis in these two areas has had a significant impact on students who have any difficulty in these areas and perform better in other ones according to Gardner (1997). There is no other way to account for the variable rates of success in schools among certain populations, claims Kunjufu (1984) than the teaching styles of the educators. When these do not match those of the students or the students are not rewarded for using other learning styles their progress suffers.

Students differ in the way they approach the learning process. Researchers have been studying these learning styles for decades. The results of these studies are now being applied to the educational process. A learning style is a pattern of behavior and performance by which a person approaches an educational experience. Knowledge about this process provides insights that move beyond individual differences to the realm of overall learning. It also offers a value neutral approach for the understanding of individual differences among ethnically diverse students and within any one group (Bennett, 2003).

Numerous instruments now exist for the diagnosis and analysis of these learning styles. Learning style is related to a worldview and that certain learning styles tend to be predominant in certain cultures (Ramirez & Castaneda, 1974). Students differ in their need for structure and their need for an explanation of instructions as well as other areas such as perception and type of task.

Ways of teaching can be enhanced through and awareness and use of learning styles and theories of intelligence or multiple intelligences. These have been identified and explored as ways to include all students in the learning process. Using the experiences and intelligences of students can create an emerging multicultural curriculum. This will benefit all students and encourage them to become more involved in the educational process.

Multiple Intelligences emphasizes the concept of intelligence not as one fixed cognitive ability but as a collection of capacities. These are not really learning styles but are potential capacities highly correlated to the diversity of people and their environments.

Huber (2002) has developed a planning grid that includes outcomes, intelligences, instruction, interaction patterns, esteem focus, and diversity as key components of any culturally responsible curriculum. Thematic units developed and taught using this grid and focusing on the eight intelligences provide an opportunity for all students to succeed.

**Intelligences, Ways of teaching, Materials, and Possible Occupations**
Armstrong (1994) discusses ways of teaching and outlines some of the key components within each intelligence and what teachers can do to facilitate learning by students who operate in that arena. The following information contains some of the work by Armstrong (1994) on multiple intelligences as well as other ideas for each arena. The theory of multiple intelligence is based on work by Gardner (1983) who is a cognitive and developmental psychologist. He defined intelligence as the human ability to solve problems or to make something that is valued in one or more cultures (p 11). Initially he identified seven intelligences but later added an eighth, the naturalist.

**Eight Intelligences**
1. *Verbal/Linguistic*
   *The understanding of the phonology, syntax, and semantics of language, and its pragmatic uses to convince others of a course of action, help one to remember information, explain or communicate knowledge, or reflect upon language itself.* (Armstrong p13)

Sensitivity to the sounds rhythms and meanings of words, sensitivity different functions of language
Interesting occupations: poet or journalist, playwright, orator, novelist, comedian, salesperson, lawyer

Ways of teaching: lecture, word games, discussions, storytelling, choral reading, journal writing, independent reading in man genres
Teaching materials: books, tape recorders, stamp sets keyboard, books on tape

2. *Logical/Mathematical*
   *The understanding and use of logical structures, including patterns and relationships, and statements and propositions, through experimentation, quantification, conceptualization, and classification, sensitivity to and capacity to discern logical or numerical patterns, ability to handle long chains of reasoning. (Armstrong p13)*

Interesting occupations: scientist or mathematician, accountant, inventor

Ways of teaching: brain teasers, problem solving, science experiments, mental calculation, number games, critical thinking
Teaching materials: calculators, math manipulatives, science equipment, and math games

3. *Visual/Spatial*
   *The ability to perceive the visual world accurately, to perform transformations and modifications upon one's initial perceptions, and to be able to re-create aspects of one's visual experience (even in the absence of relevant physical stimuli). (Armstrong p13)*

Capacities to perceive the visual–spatial world accurately and to perform transformations on one's initial perceptions
Interesting occupations: navigator or sculptor, painter, topologist, choreographer

Ways of teaching: visual presentations, metaphor, art activities, mapping, imagination games, mind visualization
Teaching materials: graphs, maps, videos, LEGO sets, art materials, optical illusions, cameras, picture library

4. *Bodily/Kinesthetic*
   *The ability to control one's bodily motions and the capacity to handle objects skillfully. (Armstrong p13)*

Abilities to control one's body movements and to handle objects skillfully
Interesting occupations: dancer, athlete, actor, surgeon, and choreographer

Ways of teaching: hands-on learning, drama, dance, sports that teach tactile activities, relaxation exercises
Teaching materials: building tools, clay, sport equipment, manipulatives, tactile learning resources

5. *Musical/Rhythmic*
   *The ability to understand and express components of music, including melodic or rhythmic patterns, through figural or intuitive means (the natural musician) or through formal analytic means (the professional musician). (Armstrong p13)*

Abilities to produce and appreciate rhythm, pitch, and timbre and an appreciation of the forms of musical expressiveness
Interesting occupations: composer or performer, singer, conductor

Ways of teaching: songs, rap, CDs, songs that teach
Teaching materials: tape recorders, rape collection, musical instruments

6. *Interpersonal*
   *The ability to notice and make he distinctions among other individuals with respect to moods, temperaments, motivations, intentions, and to use this information in pragmatic ways, such as to persuade, influence, manipulate, mediate, or counsel individuals or groups of individuals toward some purpose. (Armstrong p14)*

Capabilities to discern and respond appropriately to the moods, temperaments, motivations, and desires of other people
Interesting occupations: educator, salesperson, doctor, politician, sociologist, and leader

Ways of teaching: cooperative learning, peer tutoring, community involvement, social gatherings, and simulations
Teaching materials: board games, party supplies, props for role-plays

7. *Intrapersonal*
   *The ability to access one's own emotional life through awareness of inner moods, intentions, motivations, potentials, temperaments, and desires, and the capacity to symbolize these inner experiences, and to apply these understanding to help one live one's life. (Armstrong p13-14)*

Capabilities to access one's own feelings and the ability to discriminate among them and draw upon them to guide behavior, knowledge of one's own strengths, weaknesses, desires, and intelligence
Ways of teaching: individualized instruction, independent study, options in course of study, self-esteem building
Teaching materials: self-checking materials, journal, and materials for projects

8. *Naturalistic*
   *The capacity to recognize and classify the numerous species of flora and fauna in one's environment (as well as natural phenomena such as mountains and clouds), and the ability to care for, tame, or interact subtly with living creatures, or with whole ecosystems. (Armstrong p14)*

Capabilities to understand nature and the natural phenomena, ability to gather data or impressions about it
Interesting occupations: forester or environmental explorer, veterinarian, biologist, oceanographer, farmer

Ways of teaching: outdoor exploration, observations, experiments, tours of particular environments, study and care of plants and animals
Teaching materials: notebooks, binoculars, tape recorders, books about nature and environments, photographs and films, gardens

**Criteria**
Gardner has set four basic criteria for what counts as a human intelligence. First, it must be connected with a portion of the brain. Second and third it must exist in special populations that excel or are impaired in the ability. Fourth, it must have an identifiable developmental history.

Gardner argues that culture is integral to this theory and that all of the world's cultures value the eight intelligences he has identified. In every culture the elders pass on to their younger members the systems, stories, art, music, social mores, political institutions, and number systems of the society. Thus, the importance of culturally relevant teaching to student success is important.

**Culturally Relevant Teaching**
Culturally relevant teaching has been described by some as just good teaching. According to Bennett (2003) it embodies the principles of students experiencing academic success, students developing or maintaining cultural competence, and students developing a critical consciousness through which they may challenge social injustice.

Ferguson and Womack (1993) studied 200 teachers and found that the more courses they took in instructional techniques termed pedagogy, the more successful they and their students were. While subject matter knowledge itself is important, pedagogy and appropriate instructional design with multiple strategies accounts for more success for students and teachers.

Closely related to these is Goleman's (1995) concept of emotional intelligence. This is defined as the ability to manage emotions, empathize, and handle relationships. By utilizing emotional intelligence teachers can assist students in developing multiple skills for success.

**References**

Armstrong, T. (1994). Multiple intelligence in the classroom. Alexandria, VA: ASCD.

Armstrong, T. (2003). The multiple intelligences of reading and writing: Making the words come alive 13-14. Alexandria, VA: ASCD.

Bennett, C. (2003). Comprehensive multicultural education: Theory and practice. (5th ed.). New York, NY: Allyn and Bacon.

Ferguson. P. & Womack, S. (1993). The impact of subject matter and education coursework on teaching performance. Journal of Teacher Education 44 (1) 55-63.

Gardner, H. (1983). Frames of mind: The theory of multiple intelligences. New York: Basic Books,

Gardner, H (1993). Multiple intelligences: The theory into practice. New York: Basic Books.

Gardner, H. (1997). Beyond multiple intelligences. Keynote speech at the annual meeting of the Association for Supervision and Curriculum Development, San Antonio, Mar 22-25.

Goleman, D. (1995). Emotional intelligence: Why it can matter more than IQ for character, health, and lifelong achievement. New York: Bantam.

Haggarty, B. (1995). Nurturing multiple intelligences: A guide to multiple intelligences theory and teaching. New York: Addison Wesley.

Huber, T. (2002). Quality learning experiences for all students. San Francisco, CA: Caddo Gap Press.

Kunjufu, K. (1984). Developing positive self-images and discipline in Black children. Chicago: African American Images.

Ramirez, M. & Castaneda, A. (1974). Cultural democracy: Bicognitive development, and education. New York, NY: Academic Press.

---

**Reflection/Discussion Items**

1. Which of the multiple intelligences do you prefer?

2. Which of the multiple intelligences do you utilize most frequently?

3. How will you work with students who prefer other ones?

4. How can you incorporate all eight multiple intelligences into your classroom?

5. How does this apply to the concept of culturally relevant teaching?

# MODELS OF CURRICULUM AND ORGANIZATIONAL LEVELS

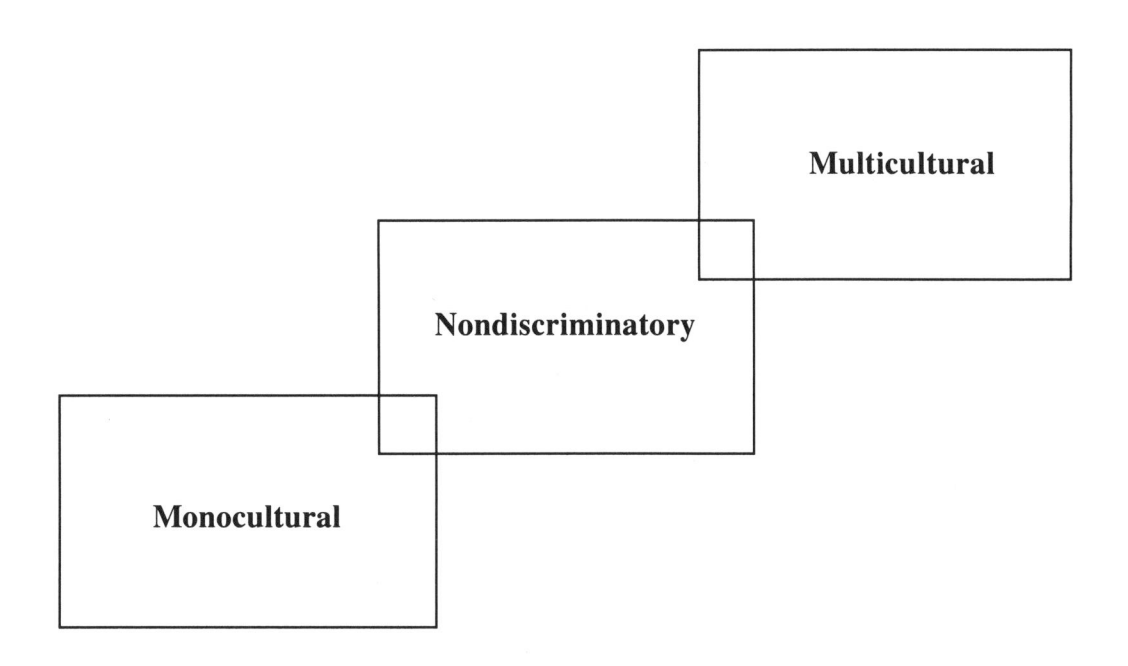

```
                                    ┌──────────────────┐
                                    │                  │
                                    │   Multicultural  │
                          ┌─────────┼──┐               │
                          │         │  │               │
                          │  Nondiscriminatory         │
                ┌─────────┼──┐      │  │               │
                │         │  │      └──┼───────────────┘
                │         │  │         │
                │ Monocultural         │
                │         │  └─────────┘
                │         │
                └─────────┘
```

According to James Banks amd Cherry McGee Banks in Multicultural Education: Issues and Perspectives (4th Ed.), (2001, p. 229) schools move through levels of curriculum integration as they evolve. The four levels are:

1. The Contributions Approach
    ~ focus on some heroes, holidays and cultural events

2. The Additive Approach
    ~ some content, concepts, and themes are added to the curriculum without changing its structure

3. The Transformation Approach
    ~ the structure of the curriculum is changed to enable students to view concepts, themes, issues, and events from diverse perspectives

4. The Social Action Approach
    ~ students make decisions on important social issues and take action to help solve them

The next stage in the process would be acting in a manner that is consistently anti-biased to make social actions.

---

**Reflection/Discussion Item**
If you utilize the graphic above, how do you apply the 4 levels of Banks and Banks.

---

On the following pages are forms to use in evaluating media and materials for bias.

# PRELIMINARY SCREENING FORM

This preliminary screening form is to be used in determining whether an item of curriculum material (guide, lesson plan, book, film, video, CD, tape, or other medium) seems, on brief examination, to justify full analysis or whether it should be rejected at the outset. Only a sampling of contents and format is required. No item will be accepted for final analysis that does not meet all of the four criteria given in this screening form.

| Title | Date of publication |
|---|---|
| Author | Preliminary reviewer (print name) |
| Author | Preliminary reviewer (print name) |

1. **Relevance** (check [✓] yes or no):

   The item should appear relevant to the teaching of the ethnic heritage of one or more minority groups of color (e.g., American Indians, Black Americans, Asian Americans/Pacific Islanders, Hispanic/Latino(a) Americans, other Latin Americans or Spanish Americans, Portuguese Americans, Jewish Americans) and/or to teaching about cultural diversity and pluralism in America.

   |   |   | Yes | No |
   |---|---|---|---|
   | a. | Does the content include a discussion of one or more diverse groups within the United States? | | |
   | b. | Do the pictures or illustrations clearly portray persons of color, places, or cultures? | | |
   | c. | Are persons (or animals representing persons) of clearly different ethnicity portrayed in close, beneficial interpersonal relationships (e.g., as husband and wife, as friends, as work partners)? | | |
   | d. | Are characteristics portrayed in a way likely to counteract stereotyping (e.g., dark skin color shown as desirable, poor people shown as worthy and contributing)? | | |
   | e. | Does the content portray clearly the advantages of diversity among individuals or groups? | | |
   | f. | Is there other specific evidence of appropriateness to ethnic heritage education? If so, specify under "Remarks." | | |

2. **Appropriateness** (check [✓] yes or no):

The item should be appropriate to one or more grade levels from kindergarten through grade twelve.

|   |   | Yes | No |
|---|---|---|---|
| a. | Is the vocabulary level appropriate for the intended grade level(s)? | | |
| b. | Is size of print and/or format appropriate for the intended grade level(s)? | | |

3. **Standards of Quality** (check [✓] yes or no):

The text, illustrations, format, and general style should meet standards high enough that the use of the item can be recommended.

|   |   | Yes | No |
|---|---|---|---|
| a. | Are those features clearly appropriate to the intended purpose? | | |
| b. | Is the presentation clear? | | |
| c. | Is the item durable and not too expensive? | | |
| d. | Is the aesthetic quality good? | | |

4. **Nondiscriminatory Content** (check [✓] yes or no):

The author(s) should avoid any reference that may be construed as grossly hostile, prejudiced, discriminatory, or adverse to any ethnic group.

|   |   | Yes | No |
|---|---|---|---|
| a. | Do pictures or illustrations portray people of color group in non-demeaning ways (unless a mitigating explanation is given; e.g., slaves presented as human, not faceless and subservient)? | | |
| b. | Does the textual matter avoid negative allusions to persons of color (including demeaning terms) without mitigating explanation? | | |

**Reviewer's Recommendation:**

Recommended for full review _____    Not recommended for full review _____
(Give reasons under "Remarks.")

*Remarks*

_____

_____

_____

_____

_____

_____

_____

# CURRICULUM ANALYSIS QUESTIONNAIRE

**Instructional Purpose and Design:**

1. Describe the general content and format of the material:

2. What is the instructional purpose of the work (e.g., to improve communication skills, to facilitate understanding of diverse groups, and so forth) as stated by the author or publisher?

3. What is its recommended role in the curriculum (e.g., basic textbook, supplementary unit, and so forth) as stated by the author or publisher?

4. What is its target (e.g., grade level, ability level and so forth) as stated by the author or publisher?

5. What organization(s) or group(s) sponsored the development of the material?

6. What specialists were consulted in the development of the material (e.g., representatives of ethnic groups, representatives from different geographic areas, experts in different disciplines)?

**Physical Characteristics of the Material:**

7. Describe in detail the quality of the physical characteristics of the material (e.g., paper, binding, print, pictures or illustrations, recordings, labeling, manageability of parts, auxiliary materials needed but not supplied, and so forth):

| **Ethnic Perspective**<br>(Use spaces to check [✓] or comment.) | Native American/ American Indian | Blacks or African American | Asian American/ Pacific Islander | Hispanic/ Latino(a) American | Other Latin or Spanish American | Jewish American | Please Add Others |
|---|---|---|---|---|---|---|---|
| 8. Are these racial and ethnic groups included in the material? | | | | | | | |
| 9. Are these groups mentioned frequently and integrated into the material? | | | | | | | |
| 10. Does the material show the unique experiences and characteristics of these groups within the United States? | | | | | | | |
| 11. Are these groups shown as diversified and heterogeneous, with individuals portrayed in diverse life situations and occupations? | | | | | | | |
| 12. Are group members portrayed in a negative, patronizing, or stereotyped manner? Cite examples and give page numbers. | | | | | | | |
| 13. Are members of these groups portrayed as active or problem solving? | | | | | | | |
| 14. Are the contributions of these groups to society presented or discussed? | | | | | | | |
| 15. Are the problems faced by these groups presented or discussed? | | | | | | | |
| 16. Does the material provide perspectives of and expressions by members of these groups? | | | | | | | |
| 17. Does the material provide a fair and accurate portrayal of these groups? | | | | | | | |

| **Multiethnic Perspective** (check [✓] and comment): | Yes | No | N/A |
|---|---|---|---|
| 18. Are opportunities provided for students to examine in depth the values, beliefs, points of view, and/or experiences of one or more ethnic groups? | | | |
| 19. Is the student encouraged to develop and examine his/her own opinions and values regarding diversity? | | | |
| 20. Does the material foster appreciation of ethnic and cultural diversity as a positive value? | | | |
| 21. Are activities and experiences other than those common to the mainstream culture or white middle class included? | | | |
| 22. Does the treatment of ethnic groups show them as participating in the mainstream culture? | | | |
| 23. Are persons of different ethnic groups shown interacting as equals? | | | |
| 24. Are interrelationships among ethnic groups demonstrated? | | | |
| 25. Is the United States portrayed as having been developed by diverse groups in a pluralistic way? | | | |

| **Multiethnic Perspective** (check [✓] and comment): | Yes | No | N/A |
|---|---|---|---|
| 26. Is the United States portrayed as a nation of differing groups that sometimes compete or conflict with each other? | | | |
| 27. Is the subject of prejudice or discrimination against various groups portrayed or discussed? | | | |
| 28. If inequities are portrayed, are the causes of inequities clearly portrayed? | | | |
| 29. Are the cultural differences of ethnic groups shown as having their own value and as making contributions to society? | | | |
| 30. Is the material consistent throughout in portraying different ethnic groups fairly and accurately? | | | |

| **Biases in the Material** (check [✓] and comment): | Yes | No | N/A |
|---|---|---|---|
| 31. Does the material reflect any religious bias? | | | |
| 32. Does the material reflect any gender bias? | | | |

| **Biases in the Material** (check [✓] and comment): | Yes | No | N/A |
|---|---|---|---|
| 33. Are any other biases apparent that would make the material less useful (e.g., sectional, occupational, socioeconomic, disability role stereotypes, or physical stereotypes)? <br><br>_____ <br><br> _____ | | | |

| **Teacher Materials** (check [✓] and comment): | Yes | No | N/A |
|---|---|---|---|
| 34. Does the teacher's guide or lesson plan help the teacher clarify the material for the student? (If deficiencies exist in the student material, do the teacher materials make up for such defects?) <br><br>_____ <br><br> _____ | | | |
| 35. Are the activities appropriate to the material and the suggested student population? (Would they also be appropriate to differing ethnic, cultural, or socioeconomic groups?) <br><br>_____ <br><br> _____ | | | |

| **Teacher Preparation** (check [✓] and comment): | Yes | No | N/A |
|---|---|---|---|
| 36. Before this material is used for the first time, would the teacher have to spend a long time preparing for use? (How long? Would special training be needed?) <br><br>_____ <br><br> _____ | | | |
| 37. Would using the material on a day-to-day basis require much preparation time by the teacher? (How much?) <br><br>_____ <br><br> _____ | | | |

**Evaluation Techniques** (check [✓] and comment):

| | Yes | No | N/A |
|---|---|---|---|
| 38. Does the material provide any method of assessing the students' prior knowledge? | | | |
| 39. Does the material provide any method of assessing the progress made by the student or his/her current knowledge? (Do these evaluation techniques cover only the basic subject matter, only his/her concepts of ethnic heritage, or both? | | | |

**Summary** (check [✓] and comment):

| | Yes | No | N/A |
|---|---|---|---|
| 40. Does the material appear to make use of the correct methods, scope, and sequence to achieve the instructional goals and objectives of the author? | | | |
| 41. Do the suggested activities promote a multiethnic, multicultural perspective? | | | |
| 42. Do the evaluation techniques appear to be sufficient? (Do they measure the degree to which the student has mastered the goals and objectives of the material?) | | | |

**Final Recommendation** (check [✓] and comment):

| | Yes | No | N/A |
|---|---|---|---|
| 43. Do you recommend the use of the material? If so, for what instructional purposes? <br><br> _____ <br><br> _____ | | | |
| 44. Do you have reservations about the use of this material? If so, please explain. <br><br> _____ <br><br> _____ | | | |

45. Please justify your final recommendation. (You may wish to do so by comparing this material with other materials on the same theme.)

_____

_____

_____

_____

_____

# CHECKLIST FOR EVALUATION OF SEXISM IN MATERIALS

Identify the materials you are planning to use and examine them for the points listed below.

1. Number of stories where main character is     Male     Female

2. Number of illustrations of     Male(s)     Female(s)

3. Number of times children are shown     Male(s)     Female(s)
    a. in active play
    b. using initiative
    c. being independent
    d. solving problems
    e. earning money
    f. receiving recognition
    g. being inventive
    h. involved in sports
    i. being passive
    j. being fearful
    k. being helpless
    l. receiving help
    m. in quiet play

4. Number of times adults are shown –     Male(s)     Female(s)
    a. in different occupations
    b. playing with children
    c. taking children on outings
    d. teaching skills
    e. giving tenderness
    f. scolding children
    g. biographically

5. Ask these questions:
    a. Are boys allowed to show emotions?
    b. Are girls rewarded for intelligence rather than for beauty?
    c. Are there any derogatory comments directed at girls in general?
    d. Are women shown working outside the home?
    e. What kinds of jobs?
    f. Are there any stories about one-parent families?
    g. Are there any stories about families without children?
    h. Are child care attendants shown?
    i. Are females and males of color and ethnic groups treated naturally instead of gender stereotypically?

6. What other questions would you add?

# CULTURAL BIAS IN MATERIALS

Directions: The responses to these questions are intended to reflect the attitudes that the materials described would arouse in a reader. If you believe a reader would have a positive or negative response based upon the material, make a mark in the appropriate column.

Title of Material:

Author:

Publisher:

Type of Material:

<u>Yes</u>   <u>No</u>

1. Would this help a student of color identify with and be proud of his/her heritage?

2. Does this affect the European-American reader's image of people of other ethnic groups?

3. Does it foster a positive or a negative image of American ethnic and cultural groups?

4. Does this book express diverse groups' values?

5. Might this book help a reader of color to reconcile his/her own values with conflicting ones?

6. Is the book sympathetic to the distinctive characteristics of diverse cultures?

7. In terms of whose attitudes is the culture being evaluated? (His/her own or those of another culture?)

8. Do the illustrations authentically depict culturally differing ways of life?

9. Is the image of the group's member that is presented one of a real human being, with strengths and weaknesses, who acts in response to his/her own nature and his/her own times?

10. Does the person also react in a way, which will foster a positive image in the light of contemporary developments?

11. If fictional, are the characters realistically developed? Are situations true or possibly true to life?

12. Are the images of the persons of color or others stereotyped?

13. Does this item present both sides of the event, issues, problem, etc.?

14. Does it contain any factual errors or misleading information?

15. Does it perpetuate myths about ethnic, racial, religious, gender or cultural groups?

16. Are loaded words (i.e., chief, savage, buck, squaw, red skin, honkie, red neck, slave, master, polak, spic, etc.) used in such a way as to be offensive, insensitive, or inappropriate?

17. Does this item put the contributions that persons of color have made to the American Experience in rightful and accurate perspective?

                                                                              <u>Yes</u>   <u>No</u>

18. Is the author qualified to write on this topic?

19. Is the illustrator qualified to illustrate on this topic?

20. Has this item been reviewed or evaluated by a person who is knowledgeable of the topic as well as the particular group being portrayed?

21. What additional information might be needed to make this more relevant, useful, or to present both sides?

22. Is comparable information presented more effectively elsewhere?

23. When and how might this item be used in a school curriculum to increase awareness and understanding of American ethnic groups, racial, cultural, religious, economic, or other?

*General: For 24 through 30 respond with: great extent, some extent, or no extent and clarify why.*

24. To what extent does this material consistently and naturally depict the multi-ethnic dimensions of the factual and idea content under consideration?

25. To what extent does the material emphasize the values of a pluralistic society?

26. Does the material afford ample opportunity for the learner to challenge common stereotypes?

27. To what extent does the material reflect a clear and accurate understanding of those concepts useful in explaining group and intergroup behavior?

28. To what extent does the material examine socioeconomic diversity?

29. After careful consideration of all the above, is this item appropriate for use in schools?

30. Other considerations:


Comments/Overall Assessment:

# EVALUATION CRITERIA

Following is a list of criteria by which educators can evaluate most if not all curriculum materials. While not all 15 criteria will be applicable in every case, the questions raised by them do focus upon basic considerations in the materials that are used in the education. Do the curriculum materials –

1. Give evidence on the part of writers, artists, and editors of a sensitivity to prejudice, to stereotypes, and to the use of offensive materials?

2. Suggest, by omission or commission, or by overemphasis or under-emphasis, that any racial, religious, economic, ethnic or gender segment of our population is more or less worthy, more or less capable, more or less important in the "mainstream" of American life?

3. Provide abundant, but fair and well-balanced, recognition of children and adults of a variety of groups by placing them in positions of leadership and centrality?

4. Exhibit fine and worthy examples of mature American types from a variety of groups in art and science, in history and literature, and in all other areas of life and culture?

5. Present a significant number of instances of fully integrated human groupings and status and non-segregated social relationships?

6. Make clearly apparent in illustrations the group representation of a variety of individuals - e.g. European American/Caucasian, Blacks or African American, Native American/American Indian, Asian-American/Pacific Islander, Hispanic/Latino(a)-American, etc. - and not seek to avoid identification by such means as smudging some color over facial features?

7. Delineate life in contemporary urban environments, as well as rural or suburban environments, so that today's city children can also find significant identification for themselves, their problems, and potential for life, liberty, and the pursuit of happiness?

8. Portray racial, religious, gender, ability, economic, and ethnic groups, with their similarities and differences, in such a way as to build positive images?

9. Emphasize the multi-ethnic character of our nation as having unique and special value, which we must esteem and treasure?

10. Assist students to recognize clearly and to accept the basic similarities among all members of the human race, and the uniqueness and worth of every single individual, regardless of race, ability religion, gender, ethnicity, or socioeconomic background?

11. Help students appreciate the many important contributions to our civilization made by members of the various groups, emphasizing that every human group has its list of achievers, thinkers, writers, artists, scientists, builders, and leaders?

12. Supply an accurate and sound balance in the matter of historical perspective, making it perfectly clear that all ability, gender, racial, religious, and ethnic groups have mixed heritages, which can well serve as sources of both group pride and group humility?

13. Clarify or present factually the historical and contemporary forces and conditions that have operated in the past and that continue to operate to the disadvantage of many groups?

14. Analyze intergroup tension and conflict fairly, frankly, objectively, and with emphasis upon resolving our social problems in a spirit of fully implementing democratic values and goals in order to achieve the American dream for all Americans?

15. Seek to motivate students to examine their own attitudes and behaviors, and to comprehend their own duties and responsibilities as citizens in a pluralistic democracy – to demand freedom and justice and equal opportunity for every individual and for every group?

16. What would you add to this questionnaire?

17. What is your overall assessment?

# IN THE CLASSROOM

1. "Level" with the students in your classroom. Point out the bias of books or materials. Help them learn to identify sources of bias and important omissions in the materials.

2. Develop classroom activities around identifying bias found in television, textbooks, movies, library books, magazines, etc.

3. Incorporate the development of critical reading skills as an instructional objective for all your teaching, not just when special efforts are being made to identify bias in materials.

4. Identify or develop supplementary materials, which can help "correct" some of the bias of available materials.

5. Design student research projects. These might include a study of their own textbook materials or their identifications of supplementary materials.

6. Assign student papers, themes, term papers, or other activities on topics or persons not usually covered in textbooks or materials.

7. When students have completed activities identifying bias, have them write letters and send reports to administrators, publishers, community groups, and organizations working to reduce bias in textbooks.

8. Invite local resource persons into your classroom to provide additional information and work with students on special projects and activities.

9. Ask students to rewrite materials or write their own materials on subjects omitted from the textbook or write the material from another person's point of view.

10. Use bulletin boards, posters, pictures, magazines, and other materials to expose students to information commonly excluded from traditional materials.

11. Develop a classroom collection of nonracist, nonsexist reading materials for students. Identify books that students may be encouraged to seek out in their personal reading.

---

**Reflection/Discussion Items:**
1. Form small groups and discuss these and other options for addressing these issues in classes. Be prepared to share your responses.

2. Be prepared to share your responses with the class.

# DIFFERENT VIEWS OF AMERICA'S ETHNIC COMPOSITION

Directions: Each of the following items presents a particular view of the nature of American society with regard to its ethnic composition. Beside each item, place a number from the continuum to indicate your perception of America's ethnic character presented in that item.

1-Melting Pot     2-Anglo Conformity     3-Separatism     4-Cultural Pluralism/Multicultural

1. My parents decided never to teach us Slovak. They hoped that thereby we would gain a generation in the process of becoming full Americans.

2. Our blood is as the flood of the Amazon, made up of a thousand noble currents all pouring into one. We are not a nation so much as a world.

3. The reliance of our race upon the progress and achievements of others for a consideration in sympathy, justice and rights is like a dependence upon a broken stick, resting upon which will eventually consign you to the ground... The Negro needs a nation and a country of his/her own, where he/she can best show evidence of his/her own ability in the art of human progress.

4. Outwardly I lived the life of white society; yet all the while I kept in direct contact with tribal life. While I learned all that I could of the white's culture, I never forgot that of my people. I kept the language, tribal manners and usages, sang the songs and danced the dances.

5. That's right – I was ashamed of my name. Not only that, I was ashamed of being a Jew. There you have it. Exit Abraham Isaac Arshawsky. Enter Art Shaw! You see, of course, how simple this little transformation was. Presto, Change-O! A new name, a new personality. As simple as that.

6. We believe this is the time in history for the separation of the so-called Negroes and the so-called white Americans. We believe the black people should be freed in name as well as in fact. By this we mean that they should be freed from the names imposed upon them by their former slave masters.

7. Indian children are taught "to be like a white and think like a white." They completely lose their self-identity as Navajos.

8. There are plenty of rich Italians here who a few years ago had nothing and now have so much money that they could not count all their dollars in a week. The richest ones go away from the other Italians and live with the Americans.

9. There are many sections of the United States in which even the third generation of immigrants does not speak English.

28. The result was that the new immigration contained a large and increasing number of the weak, the broken and the mentally crippled of all races drawn from the lowest stratum of the Mediterranean basin and the Balkans, together with the hordes of the wretched, submerged populations of the Polish Ghettos. Our jails, insane asylums and alms-houses are filled with this human flotsam, and the whole tone of American life, social, moral and political has been lowered and vulgarized by them.

11. What I should like to do is come to a better and more profound knowledge of who I am, whence my community came, and whither my son and daughter, and their children's children, might wish to head in the future. I want to have a history.

12. I only ask of the Government to be treated as all other people are treated. If I cannot go to my own home, let me have a home in some country where my people will not die so fast...

13. It makes no difference to me whether my students are black, white, brown, green, red, yellow or purple. They are students and I treat them all the same. After all, we are all human beings. Why can't we forget about color entirely and just treat each other like human beings.

14. The survival and development of the people (the tribe or nation) is generally a paramount goal. Educational programs must contribute to the continued existence of the nation.

15. Teachers must have deep knowledge of the characteristics of economically different people and also of the cultural traits of the Puerto Rican population and be able to distinguish between the differences in the cultural strata.

16. Michael, my boy, you are beginning to understand our American ways, and the sooner you drop your Serbian notions the sooner you will become an American.

17. There is nothing wrong with the Black race except that the majority of them will not accept the standards, rules, and ways given to them by the Whites, and I do believe these rules are equal and fair to both Black and White.

18. Children in bilingual education programs develop a sure understanding and respect for their mother tongue and the culture associated with it. This understanding and respect lead to a more positive self-image and better social and personal adjustment.

19. Where inability to speak and understand English excludes Spanish-speaking children from effective participation in the educational program offered by a school district, the district must take affirmative steps to open its instructional program to these students.

20. The Japanese race is an enemy race and, while many second and third generation Japanese born on United States soil, possessed of United States citizenship, have become "Americanized," the racial strains are...[unchanged].

21. More and more, I think in family terms, less ambitiously, on a less than national scale. The differences implicit in being Slovak, and Catholic, and lower-middle class seem more and more important to me.

22. Americans who do not speak English should learn it to fit better into American life.

23. Other immigrant groups have in time learned English. Puerto Ricans have been slower to do this. Spanish is their language. Why give up Spanish when you may at any time return to Puerto Rico? Why give up Spanish when you need it to get along in your neighborhood?

24. We demand that ... Spanish be the first language and the textbooks be rewritten to emphasize the heritage and the contributions of the Mexican-American or Indio-Hispano in the building of the Southwest.

25. The Ohio Board of Education ruled that two Amish secondary schools, ... would have to measure up to state standards or close. The Amish schools, the Board said, have no graded courses in geography, American history, natural sciences, government, and other required subjects. Some teachers, the board added, have no more than an eighth grade education.

26. We ... demand the teaching of the contributions and history of [all] who have ... helped build this country.

27. Each year a few thousand boys and girls were sent to "Indian schools," where they were taught English and other subjects thought important to make them give up their old ways of living. Most of these children left school as soon as they could. Their different culture made most of what they were taught meaningless to them.

28. The Amish want to keep to themselves – a separate people. They are tied together by their religion and its values, by kinship (most of them are related), and by customs that make them seem different from everyone else.

# SCHOOL CHECKLIST FOR ASSESSING THE EFFECTS OF RACISM AND SEXISM

*I. Objective*

For participants to increase their awareness of many forms of racism and sexism in education.

*II. Rationale*

Since no school within a racist and sexist society can be free of these manifestations, examining one's own school can help participants to clarify what they would like to change or improve.

*III. Time Allotment*

Variable.

*IV. Materials*

Paper, pencil and checklist.

*V. Activity*

1. Reads all of enclosed materials.

2. Gather as much advance information as possible on information sheet.

3. Presents the information gathered.

4. Use CHECKLIST and then write next to each number:

**A** – meaning, "Yes, always."   **C** – meaning, "Rarely."
**B** – meaning, "Sometimes."     **D** – meaning, "No, never."

Answers are to reflect each assessment of school.

5. When all questions have been answered, with or without discussion after each one, tally number of A's, B's, C's and D's. If participants are from the same school, trainer should see if there is any great divergence in appraisals and, if there is time, allow discussion of differences and appraisals. If participants represent many schools, then any wide divergence in school ratings should provoke discussion of what factors result in greater pluralism at one school than at another.

6. When time is set aside to discuss change strategies, see that participants start with an analysis of the existing power set-up, existing control of resources and existing decision-making about values and norms in their schools. After such an analysis, change should be structured around practical ways to achieve more equitable sharing of power and resources and more equitable decisions about values and norms.

*VI. Cautions*

If you wish to work for change, it is important to arrange for participation by all groups on goals and methods. It is also important that change be based upon realistic assessments of what can be tackled first, what support can be mustered, etc. Step-by-step organization for the goal decided upon is at least as important as a change in agent's good intentions.

This SCHOOL CHECKLIST owes much to previous checklists produced by (1) the Civil Rights Commission (unpublished); (2) Integrated Education Associates; (3) the United Church Press; and (4) a much more thorough checklist prepared by Dr. Claire Halverson for the EEO Center of the National College of Education.

Information Sheet on School District

Note: Gather information for your school, if not available for your entire district.

All of the information, which can be gathered on this sheet prior to group use of the SCHOOL CHECKLIST, will enhance the usefulness of the activity. The trainer may wish to gather this information, or may assign this responsibility to some participants in advance.

1. What is racial breakdown of the community serviced by the district?
   - Percentage European American/Caucasian        _____
   - Percentage Blacks/African American            _____
   - Percentage Hispanic/Latino(a) American        _____
   - Percentage Native American/American Indian    _____
   - Percentage Asian American/Pacific Islander    _____
   - Percentage Bi-racial or multi-racial          _____
   - Percentage other (add other categories)       _____

2. Of high-income residents, what percentage is each group?
   Of middle-income residents, what percentage is each group?
   Of low-income residents, what percentage is each group?

3. Are all the economic, religious and other groups well integrated in each school in the district?

|  | Total | European American | and Persons of Color by category |
|---|---|---|---|
| Category | Female/Male | Female/Male | Female/Male |

School Board

Superintendent

Principals (High School)

Principals (Junior High)

Principals (Elementary)

Other Administrators

Guidance Staff

Teaching Staff

Support Staff/ Paraprofessionals

Maintenance Staff

Lunchroom Staff

**Checklist On Racism**

For all questions respond with     A    B    C    D    F

*Community*

1. Are parent/guardian meetings held at suitable times for working parents/guardians to attend?

2. Is language used at meetings understandable to all or translated as necessary for some?

3. Are all parents/guardians made to feel welcome and comfortable when they visit a school?

4. Are parents/guardians of all racial, cultural, religious, economic and ethnic groups encouraged to participate and contribute to school programs and learning?

5. Are people of color and parents/guardians with limited incomes represented as advisors:
    To school board?
    To administrators of each school?
    To curriculum committees?

*School Board*

6. Does the school board reflect the make-up of the community?

7. a) If board members are selected, are various racial, religious, gender, ethnic, and economic viewpoints involved in the selection process?

        *or*

b) If board members are elected, is it on a district basis that reflects the racial/ethnic and socioeconomic levels of the community, rather than on a city-wide basis in which a European American, middle-class majority can predominate?

8. Does the school board encourage and facilitate meaningful participation of students and parents/guardians from all groups in decision-making?

9. Does the school board get involved in community affairs related to housing, jobs, police and other matters directly tied to schools and racism?

10. Are the age, quality, facilities and maintenance of the school buildings that are attended by the greater proportion of the students of color as good as those attended by a lesser proportion of students of color?

11. Is the per pupil expenditure the same for students from all racial/ethnic groups in all districts in your community? (This does not include federal money.)

12. If not, do the schools that expend more money per student have a higher percentage of groups of color?

13. In negotiating contracts, is past discrimination against people of color recognized and compensated for in considerations of promotion or lay-offs, rather than using seniority, which results in "last hired, first fired" and counteracts affirmative action and equal employment efforts?

14. Does a good share of the school system's business contracts go to contractors and to contractors of color whose hiring and personnel policies encourage racial/ethnic and gender equity?

*Administration*

15. a) Is racial make-up of administrative and guidance staff similar to racial make-up of student body?

or

15. b) If student body is mainly European American, does administrative staff represent racial diversity of this nation?

16. Do administrators of color, including women of color, hold positions of general authority rather than mainly positions relating more specifically to special federal programs, concerns or relations involving people of color?

17. Are administrators and teachers encouraged to live or participate in the community where they teach?

18. When new administrators are hired, is their ability to relate to the community one important qualification?

19. Do administrators place high priority on creating and enforcing policies and practices, which are aimed at achieving cultural pluralism?

20. Does the administration make decisions based on input from all students, parents/guardians, teachers and their viewpoints?

21. Are good academic grades for students of color a topic of serious concern?

22. Are school songs, symbols, decorations and holidays chosen to reflect all cultures and viewpoints?

23. a) Are school announcements sent in the language that parents can understand?

or

23. b) Are parent meetings conducted or translated so parents can understand?

24. If busing is practiced for desegregation, are European American students bused in equal numbers to students of color?

*Teachers*

25. a) Is the racial make-up of the teaching staff similar to racial make-up of student body?

    *or*

    b) If student body is mainly European American, does racial make-up of teaching body reflect racial diversity of this nation?

26. When new teachers are hired, is strenuous effort made to find members of all groups?

27. When teachers are interviewed for hiring, is it policy for the personnel committee to contain staff and parents of color?

28. a) Are in-service courses required of the entire teaching staff to enable them to increase their awareness of racism in our society and to acquaint them with the culture, history and viewpoints of diverse groups?

    *or*

    b) Is this true even if school is predominantly European American?

29. Are teachers encouraged to learn to understand the language spoken by their students?

30. Are interpreters readily available?

31. Do teachers clearly demonstrate that their behavioral and academic expectations are high for all students in all classes?

32. Do teachers routinely assign work by authors of color (both male and female) for reading homework to all pupils?

33. Do teachers encourage diversity of values, styles and viewpoints, even when these run counter to the teacher's own preferences?

34. Do teachers make special help accessible and comfortable for all students?

35. Do teachers encourage full participation in all classes and extracurricular programs by students of color?

36. Do teachers contact administrators, school board, and publishers to complain about stereotypes, bias and omission in materials and lack of multicultural materials?

37. Do teachers confront statements made by students and other teachers that are racially or culturally biased or prejudiced?

*Guidance*

38. Are women and men of color represented on the counseling staff in proportion to their representation in the student body, or, in predominantly European American schools, in relation to their proportion in U.S. society?

39. Are guidance counselors required to attend in-service courses to enable them to increase their awareness of racism and sexism in our society, and to re-examine their views of racial/ethnic and culturally different students, including expected behavior traits, social mores, achievement potential, etc? Is this true even if the school is predominantly European American?

40. Are students assigned guidance counselors who can communicate with students and parents in the language used at home?

41. Do guidance counselors arrange night or weekend hours to meet with working parents?

42. Do guidance counselors encourage high academic goals for students from all groups?

43. Do guidance counselors provide those students who have decided to enter the work force after college with effective career options rather than channeling them into low-paying service jobs?

*Students*

44. Do students from all groups have equal access to the school of their choice?

45. If standardized achievement tests are used, are they offered in the language in which each student is most proficient?

46. Are teachers, parents and students given a clear-cut explanation of the cultural and class bias inevitably built into all such tests?

47. Are student performance and interest given equal or greater emphasis than test scores in decisions on placement of students?

48. Are discussions with medical and psychological professionals, as well as with a child's parents, given equal to greater weight than scores in the decision to place students into special education classes?

49. If your school maintains tracked classes, does the racial and gender breakdown in each class roughly reflect the racial breakdown of the school student body?

50. Are students regularly moved from track to track, rather than frozen into the same track for most of their school life?

51. Is the proportion of (both male and female) students of color in both college bound and vocational/technical courses equal to the proportion of students of color in the school (or system)?

52. Are students in non-college prep courses provided counseling, training and worthwhile options that reflect changing economic and technical patterns in our society and lead to well-paying careers with good advancement potential?

53. Are students encouraged to learn to understand and respect each other's language, dialect or expressions?

54. Is bilingual, bicultural education available to all students who request it?

55. Do students feel that all discipline rules are fairly and equitably applied?

56. Have students of color (both male and female) had input into creating discipline policies?

57. Is there a grievance procedure in which students feel free to bring complaints about sexual and racial matters to those having authority, whether that is student government, teachers, or administrators?

58. Does the racial breakdown of students expelled or suspended reflect the proportions of the student body?

59. Are students encouraged to discuss school events and current events, which relate to race?

60. Are students made to feel that their cultural group's dress and speech styles are as acceptable as are European American middleclass styles?

61. Does food served in cafeteria reflect the tastes of all racial and ethnic groups?

62. Is care taken to prevent students receiving free or reduced price lunches from feeling self-conscious in any way because they are identified by the school and their peers?

63. Do students of limited income receive some funds or scholarships to participate in extracurricular activities?

64. Does the school recognize the need for and facilitate the arrangement of self-segregation among students at times in the classrooms, extracurricular activities and leisure periods?

65. Are all students encouraged to participate in extracurricular activities such as drama, arts and crafts, musical groups, dance groups, athletics, and student government?

66. Do school groups and clubs include activities representing the diversity of racial and ethnic cultural contributions, to provide positive experiences for all students?

*Curriculum*

67. Are instructional materials as anti-racist and anti-sexist as possible?

68. Does a curriculum committee, composed of school professionals, community representatives (including all groups) and student representatives (age permitting), screen all instructional materials prior to purchase?

69. When ideal materials cannot be found, are teachers trained to detect – and to guide their students to detect – both overt and subtle manifestations of racism, and sexism within race?

70. If materials aren't representative of our multi-racial, multi-cultural society, do teachers supplement them with materials that are?

71. a) Do materials, resources and media available in the library, media center and guidance offices reflect the racial and ethnic diversity of the nation, and contributions and achievements of people of color

      or

b) Project anti-racist images and concepts?

72. Do materials on classroom walls depict the racial diversity (both women and men) of this nation?

73. Is it a requirement that curriculum for all students present the true nature of both historical and present-day racism (both men and women)?

74. Is it a requirement that curriculum for all students include the culture, contributions and history of all racial groups, and of women of color?

75. Does the curriculum make room for open discussion of racial conflicts in the larger society, the community and the school?

76. Does the curriculum teach how values differ in our society?
Are all values presented as equally valid?

77. Are students encouraged to mold their future by becoming active participants in working for social justice in the school and community?

## Checklist on Sexism

*Community*

1. Are feminist groups in the community encouraged to assist the schools in combating sexist practices?

2. Do schools perceive both mothers and fathers whether married or not, as equally concerned and responsible for children, and communicate with both in notices, in requesting parent-teacher meetings, in encouraging parental/guardian involvement in school related affairs?

3. Do fathers/male guardians participate equally in PTA activities such as organizing, planning events, record keeping, baking, etc.?

*School Board*

4. Are approximately one-half the members of the Board female?

5. When drawing up contracts, is past discrimination against women recognized and compensated for in considerations of promotion or lay-offs, rather than using seniority which results in "last hired, first fired" and counteracts affirmative action and equal employment efforts?

6. Are fringe benefits such as retirement plans, maternity and/or family, insurance benefits, and sabbatical and training opportunities equal for females, males, and partners?

7. Does the school system attempt to direct its business contracts to female contractors and to contractors whose hiring and personnel policies encourage gender equity?

8. Are all specialized, technical and academic schools in your district open to both females and males equally?

9. Has the board elected as many female as male board chairs?

*Administration*

10. Are women equally represented in the administrative positions of decision-making and high salary in both the central administration and the individual schools? (i.e., assistant superintendents, principals, assistant principals, department heads, etc.)

11. Do administrators place high priority on creating and enforcing policies and practices that are aimed at achieving gender equity and anti-sexist education?

*Teachers*

12. Are male teachers as numerous as female teachers in the primary and elementary grades?

13. Are female teachers employed in equal number to male teachers in high schools?

14. Are in-service courses required of the entire teaching staff to increase their awareness of sexism and heterosexism in our society, and to re-examine their views of behavior traits, role expectations, achievement potential, etc. in regard to female and male students?

15. Are the average salaries of female and male teachers equitable?

16. Do teachers contact administrators, school board and publishers to complain about sex role stereotypes, bias in materials and the lack of materials by and about women's and women of color's significant role in our society?

17. Do teachers confront statements made by student and other teachers that are sexist or reflect stereotypes about females?

18. Do teachers discuss the implication of – and avoid using – terms like "man" or "mankind" to refer to people or humankind; "he" or "him" when referring to an unknown individual; "chairman" or "congressman" when referring to a chairperson or congressperson, etc?

19. Do teachers avoid imposing such sex role expectations of femininity and masculinity on children as "girls love reading and hate math and science," "boys shouldn't cry," or that boys can be loud and noisy while girls must learn to control themselves?

20. Do teachers avoid separating females and males when forming a class into lines, asking for student assistance in classroom duties (i.e., operating equipment vs. cleaning), or other activities?

*Guidance*

21. Are female counselors employed in equal numbers to male counselors?

22. Are counselors informed on the realities of gender discrimination in employment and in turn do they provide such information to all students?

23. Do counselors encourage and counsel female students to strive for skills and training that will equip them to compete for good careers in any field, rather than assume that "most girls get married" or become secretaries after high school?

24. Do guidance staff members avoid gender role stereotyping in all advice given?

25. Are females encouraged in math, science, sports and technology, and males in family consumer science and commercial classes?

26. Is similar behavior encouraged from girls as from boys?

27. a) Are females who are pregnant, whether married or not, encouraged to continue schooling in the regular school?

    and

b) Are child care facilities available?

28. Can girls and boys wear any comfortable, clean clothing they desire?

29. Are females and males equally encouraged to participate and equally represented in (extracurricular) activities such as drama, arts and crafts, musical groups, dance groups, athletics and student government?

30. Do females have equal access in terms of times available and equipment to all athletic facilities in the school?

31. Does the school encourage programs that are most conducive to co-educational practices?

32. Are equitable amounts of money expended on boys' and girls' athletics?

*Curriculum*

33. Are instructional materials as anti-sexist as possible?

34. When ideal materials cannot be found, are teachers trained to detect – and to guide their students to detect – both overt and subtle manifestations of sexism?

35. Does a curriculum committee, composed of school professionals, parent/guardian representatives (including females from diverse groups) and student representatives (age permitting), screen all instructional materials prior to purchase for sexist stereotyping, omissions and distortions?

36. If materials omit the contributions and struggles of women in our society, does the teacher supplement them with materials that can provide this information?

37. a) Is literature by women authors, literature about women, and literature with women as central characters in non-stereotyped roles equally represented in the curriculum?

    and

b) Does this include women of color?

38. Do materials on classroom walls depict males and females in nontraditional, and non-stereotyped roles?

39. Is a conscious effort made to bring in outside people who counteract traditional sex roles such as female scientists, engineers, dentists and plumbers or male nurses and secretaries?

40. Does your library/media center avoid special sections listed "especially for girls" or "especially for boys?"

What other suggestions do you have?

---

**Reflection/Discussion Items**

1. How does you school and/or district report card look?

2. What suggestions do you have for your school and/or school district?

3. How can low-rated items be addressed in your school and community?

4. What are items that must be overcome to achieve equity?

# SECTON XI

# MISCELLANEOUS READINGS, REFERENCES, AND RESOURCES

# MINNESOTA PUBLIC SCHOOL GUIDELINES

**Purpose of Guidelines**

1. Establish and maintain, uniformly, complete religious neutrality in the Minnesota Public Schools (MPS).

2. Provide a climate in the MPS that does not undermine the religious belief or disbelief of any child.

3. Eliminate the use of substitute cultural symbols* that serve to undermine more meaningful religious interpretations of Christmas.

>   *Santa Claus, Rudolf the Rednose Reindeer, etc.

**Guidelines**

The MPS should be religiously neutral. It should refrain from promotion of any religion or showing preference of one religion over another.

1. Vacations. The vacation period, occurring in December, should be used as the "year-end break," "winter vacation" or some other title that does not suggest this time as a time given to observe a religious holiday. No time, facilities or funds should be used for religious purposes.

2. Celebrations. There should be no celebrations held in observance of Christmas or any other religious holidays (as Easter or Chanukah). Comparative religions can be taught to educate students.

An observance is the act or practice of keeping a custom through ceremonies or rites. The question of whether this observance is practiced with strict religious (sectarian) orientation or a cultural (secular) one is irrelevant because both disrespect religious neutrality in the sense that they are practices that keep the custom of celebrating the birthday of Christ. This makes it a religious sectarian observance any way the celebration is practiced.

Christmas and Easter parties, concerts, plays, gift exchanges and Christmas tree decorating activities are some of the major violations of religious neutrality in the public schools.

3. Music. There should be no music programs or concerts planned for the celebration of Christmas or any other religious holidays.

As religious music is an integral part of the study of good music and the history of music, it should be studied with the musical content in mind that is not to be used for programs that are in observance of a religious holiday.

4. Art. Religious art displays should not be planned for use during the religious seasons.

As religious art is an integral part of the study of "good art" and the history of art, it should be studied with the art content in mind and not the religious content.

The cultural symbols* of the religious holidays should not be chosen for art projects during these holiday seasons.

>   *Examples of cultural symbols are Rudolph the Rednose Reindeer and the Easter Bunny.

5. General Classroom Activities. In this area in the MPS, with particular reference to the traditional Christmas and Easter celebrations, there should be no directive to the students to create pictures, artifacts, decorations or to assign the students projects asking for their expression of the season and its meaning. However, it must be understood that

the spontaneous creations of children during these seasonal periods will often reflect these celebrations. They should in no way be criticized but rather respected as an unsolicited expression of their cultural or religious tradition.

6. Christmas Trees. The school cannot use public funds to purchase or decorate a Christmas tree. This is in violation of religious neutrality in public education.

Although it should not be encouraged, should a parent or group independent of the MPS donate a tree to a school and decorate it, it should be allowed to stay. This is not to suggest that a tree should be solicited in this manner or even suggested, but this is a way to deal with the problem should it be presented. Future presents of trees would be discouraged.

7. Nativity Scenes and Other Religious Objects. Nativity scenes and other religious objects should not be allowed on display in the school or on the grounds of the public school.

8. Stories and Poems. It is in the best interest of promoting religious neutrality to discourage group readings of any story or poem that has strong religious content. Stories with cultural (secular) content should be left to the discretion of the teacher. These stories should not violate any of the objectives listed in these guidelines.

9. Prayers. There shall be no prayer or Bible readings or recitations in the MPS.

10. Use of School Premises by Religious Groups. Normally during school hours, public school buildings should not be used by sectarian groups. After hours, however, if civic groups and other groups are allowed to meet there, then sectarian groups should also be allowed to.*

*Subject to the approval of the Superintendent, area director, building principal and school board policy, use of the building during school hours may be permitted as long as it does not interfere with school activities.

11. Teaching of Religion. A study of comparative religions can be offered as a credit course being careful not to condone or sanction one specific religion or religious orientation.

---

**Reflection/Discussion Items**

1. What is your initial reaction to these items?

2. How are public and private school similar?

3. How are public and private schools different?

4. What other questions of comments concerning this area do you have?

# BODY RITUAL AMONG THE NACIREMA
by Horace Miner

The magical beliefs and practices of a group of people known as the Nacirema are interesting because they are so unusual. The Nacirema have many magical beliefs, but the most interesting are those about their own bodies and how they should be cared for.

The Nacirema are a group of people who live in the territory north of the Tarahuamare people of Mexico. No one knows much about their origin, but traditional legends say they came from the east. Their customs have been studied for many years, yet their culture is still poorly understood.

The Nacirema have a highly developed market economy. They live in a rich natural habitat. The people devote much of their time to economic activity. However, a large amount of money and a great deal of time each day are spent on ceremonies. The subject of these ceremonies is the human body. The Nacirema are extremely concerned about the health and appearance of their bodies. They believe that certain rituals and ceremonies must be practiced to maintain and improve the condition of their bodies. Though it is not unusual for people to be concerned about their own bodies, the rituals practiced by the Nacirema are unusual and extremely time-consuming.

The main belief of the Nacirema appears to be that the human body is ugly and that the only way to prevent it from growing weak and diseased is to practice powerful rituals devoted to this purpose. Every household has one or more shrines devoted to this goal. The more powerful people in the society have several ritual shrine rooms in their houses. In fact, the wealth of the owners of the houses is often measured in terms of the number of such ritual shrine rooms in a house. The shrine rooms of the more wealthy people are walled with stone. Poorer families imitate the rich by applying pottery plaques to their shrine room walls.

While almost every family has at least one shrine in the home, the ritual ceremonies associated with it are not family ceremonies but are private and secret. The rites are normally discussed only with children, and then only during the period when they are being initiated into these mysteries. I was able, however, to make friends with the natives and they allowed me to examine the shrine rooms. Though they were reluctant to talk about them, they finally described the rituals to me.

The most important part of the shrine is a box or chest which is built into the wall. In this chest are kept the many charms and magical potions without which no native believes he could live. The natives get the charms and potions from specialized practitioners. The most powerful of these are the medicine men, whose assistance must be rewarded with generous gifts. However, the medicine men do not provide the curing potions for their clients, but decide what the ingredients should be and write them down in an ancient and secret language. This writing is understood only by the medicine men and the herbalists who, for another gift, provide the required charm.

The charm is not thrown away after it has served its purpose, but is placed in the charm-box of the household shrine. Since the people believe that a new material must be obtained each time a new problem arises, and since the real or imagined problems and diseases of the people are many, the charm-box is usually full to overflowing. The packets and containers of magical materials are so numerous that the people often forget what their purposes were and fear to use them again. While the natives are very vague on this point, we can only assume that the reason for keeping all the old magical materials is that their presence in the charm-box, before which the body rituals are conducted, will in some way protect the worshipper.

Beneath the charm-box is a small basin. Each day every member of the family, one after another, enters the shrine room, bows his head before the charm-box, mixes different sorts of holy water in the basin, and conducts a brief ceremony of ritual cleansing. The holy waters come from the Water Temple of the community, where the priests conduct elaborate ceremonies to make the liquid ritually pure.

The Nacirema have another kind of specialist whose name is best translated as "holy-mouth-man." The Nacirema have an almost extreme horror of and fascination with the mouth, the condition of which is believed to have a supernatural influence on all social relationships. Several times each day, the natives rub the insides of their mouths with a small bundle of hog bristles. Those who neglect this ritual are forced to visit the holy mouth man who, as punishment, digs holes in their teeth with sharp instruments. Though small children must be forced to undergo this punishment when they neglect the mouth ritual, adults willingly accept it. Were it not for the rituals of the mouth, they believe that their teeth would fall out, their gums bleed, their jaws shrink, their friends desert them, and their lovers reject them. I observed that those nearing marriageable age even decorated their teeth with strips of metal which are believed to improve their appearance.

A distinctive part of the daily body ritual is performed only by men. This is a rite which involves scraping the surface of the face with a sharp instrument. Special women's rites are performed only four times during each lunar month, but what they lack in frequency is made up in barbarity. As part of this ceremony, women bake their heads in small ovens for about an hour.

The medicine men have a special temple, or latipsoh, in every community of any size. The more elaborate ceremonies required to treat very sick patients can only be performed in this temple. The maidens who conduct the ceremonies move quickly about the temple chambers wearing special costumes and headdresses. No matter how ill the native may be or how serious the emergency, the guardians of many temples will not admit a client who cannot give a rich gift to the temple.

The people willingly go to the latipsoh even though they fear it. In fact, I observed that many people who went to the latipsoh for a cure died during the ceremonies, which appear to be very harsh. One curing ceremony which takes place at this temple involves allowing the medicine men to cut out and throw away parts of their bodies. The Nacirema believe that this ceremony will remove the evil from their bodies and improve their health. The medicine men who conduct these ceremonies own a large collection of special knives which the client is never allowed to see. The Nacirema also allow the maidens of the temple to place sharp wires in their bodies and to remove small amounts of their blood in order to cure them.

Our review of the ritual life of the Nacirema has certainly shown them to be a magic-ridden people. It is hard to understand how they have managed to exist so long under the burdens they have imposed upon themselves.

**Reflection/Discussion Items**
1. After reading this article think about the ways this group is different from your own.

2. What types of activities does this group possess that are interesting?

3. Discuss these in a small group.

4. How does culture apply to this?

# APPENDIX A

**Multicultural Project**

Your project will be to turn in 10 typewritten pages of ideas regarding how you will integrate multicultural issues into teaching in your field, if you are not in teaching design a multicultural project related to your area. Please include ideas for addressing selected human relations/multicultural topics including intersecting variables from the following:

> Asian-Americans/Pacific Islanders – with attention to in-group diversity
> African-Americans/Blacks in America – with attention to in-group diversity
> Hispanic/Latino(a)-Americans – with attention to in-group diversity
> American Indians/Native Americans – with attention to in-group diversity
> Racism
> Women/Sexism
> Exceptionality
> Children/Ageism
> Homophobia/Heterosexism
> Religious Oppression
> Poverty and Class Issues
> Etc.

(NOTE: Don't forget to use intersecting variables or combinations of the above. For example, do not just deal with white women when addressing sexism or black men when dealing with Black and/or African Americans.

You may consider the following areas in making your curriculum multicultural.
1. School Atmosphere
2. Classroom Atmosphere
    a. Bulletin Boards
    b. Language
    c. The Mixing of Students for Group Work
    d. The "Hidden Curriculum" in the school and classroom
3. Objectives and Goals of Education
4. Teacher Behaviors
5. Texts, Materials, and Technology Content
6. Exercises, Activities, Games, Artwork, Field Trips, Discussions, etc.
7. Evaluation Methods
8. School Policies and Practices
9. Parent, Guardian, Family and Volunteer Involvement
10. Community and School Interaction
11. Etc.

You may present your ideas in almost any viable format you choose and you are encouraged to meet with others in your field to discuss ideas, but you must write up your own individual work. You written work should be clearly different from others and you may attach extra materials as an appendix. At a minimum include the following items

Introduce your topic and define what you will do and how it is multicultural.
Highlight areas you are focusing on and explain their use
Attach samples
Summarize
Enclose bibliography of print and electronic materials
Please enclose a self-addressed, stamped envelope or make a copy of your final project for yourself and turn in a copy.

# PLANNING

Lesson/Unit Plan with Learner Outcomes/
Multicultural Gender Fair Curriculum

*1. GENERAL INFORMATION*

NAME                           SCHOOL

SUBJECT                        GRADE LEVEL

UNIT TITLE                     LENGTH OF UNIT

LESSON TITLE                   LENGTH OF LESSON

*2. GROUPS YOU WILL ACCOMMODATE*
Each lesson/unit must include a MINIMUM OF THREE INTERSECTING VARIABLES and be multicultural/gender/disability fair.

| | |
|---|---|
| Native American/American Indian | Racism |
| Asian American/Pacific Islander | Gender/Sexism |
| Blacks and/or African American | Harassment |
| Caucasians/European American | Exceptionality |
| Hispanic/Latino(a) American | Economics |
| Bi-cultural/Bi-ethnic | Homophobia |
| Other cultures/groups | |

*3. MEASURABLE LEARNER OUTCOMES*

*4. MAIN IDEA(S) OF LESSON*
State the focus of the lesson. It is to be inclusive of the groups indicated above.

*5. INSTRUCTIONAL OBJECTIVES*
State what the student will be able to do as a result of the lesson. Include higher order thinking skills. Objectives should reflect the groups named above and the identified learner outcomes.

*6. TEACHING PROCEDURES/STUDENT ACTIVITIES*
Explain activities and teaching procedures in which students will be involved. These procedures and activities must result in the attainment of the instructional objectives and the measurable learner outcomes. Teaching/classroom procedures must integrate students by race, gender, and ability in large group instruction; small group instruction; peer teaching; work group and/or lecture/discussions.

*7. RETEACHING*
Outline procedure/activities for students who did not attain the instructional objectives.

*8. ENRICHMENT*
Outline procedures/activities for students who need additional challenge.

*9. EVALUATION PROCEDURE*
List an activity to be done with students that will measure how well they learned the instructional objectives.

*10. INSTRUCTIONAL MATERIALS*




*11. BIBLIOGRAPHY*




*12. CONTEXT*
What is the context in which this instruction will occur?
What do you know about the students and community?



*13. OTHER ITEMS AND/OR COMMENTS*

# SAMPLE LESSON PLAN

READING  LANGUAGE ARTS  SPELLING  MATH  SCIENCE  SOCIAL STUDIES  OTHER

TOPIC

LEARNER
OUTCOMES

OBJECTIVES

SKILLS
PROCESSES
THINKING

(Student Activities)

PROCEDURE
RESOURCES

(Teaching Strategies)

Education that is Multicultural

PRODUCT
EVALUATION
OUTCOME

# APPENDIX B

## Sample of Sources for Under-Represented People

Adair, G., (1989), George Washington Carver: Botanist, Chelsea House Pub., 1-55546-577-3.
Altman, L.J., Women Inventors, 0-8160-3385-4.
Altman, S., Extraordinary Black Americans: From Colonial to Contemporary Times, 0-516-00581-2.
American Mothers Committee, Mothers of Achievement in American History 1776-1976, 0-8048-1201-2.
Avery, S., Extraordinary American Indians, 0-516-00583-9.
Blasser Riley, G., (1995), Wah Ming Chang: Artist and Master of Special Effects, Enslow Pub., 0-89490-639-9.
Blue, R., (1991), Colin Powell: Straight To The Top, Millbrook Press, 1-56294-052-X.
Brown, T., (1991), Lee Ann: The Story of a Vietnamese-American Girl, G.P. Putnam's Sons, 0-399-31842-4.
Dallard, S., (1990), Ella Baker: A Leader Behind the Scenes. Silver Burdett Press, 0-382-09931-1.
Gilpin, D., Mothers of Invention: Women of the Slaveholding South in the American Civil War, 0-8078-2255-8.
Gleasner, D.C., Breakthrough: Women in Science, 0-8027-6501-7.
Gornick, V., Women in Science: Portraits From a World in Transition, 0-6712-41738-X.
Griffin, L., The Book of Women: 300 Notable Women History Passed By, 1-55850-10601.
Hargrove, J., (1993), An Wang: Computer Pioneer, Children's Press, 0-516-03290-9.
Haskins, J., (1974), Ralph Bunche: A Most Reluctant Hero, Hawthorne Books, 73-9311
Haskins, J., One More River to Cross: The Stories of Twelve Black Americans, 0-590-42897.
Herda, D.J., (1995), Thurgood Marshall: Civil Rights Champion, Enslow Publishers, 0-89490-557-0.
Herstory, Women Who Changed the World, 0-670-8543-4.
Holmes, B., (1995), Paul Robeson: All American, Gallin House, 0-8114-2381-6.
Igus, Ellis, Patrick, Wesley, Great Women in the Struggle: Book of Black Heros, Volume Two, 0-590-46629-1.
Johnson, R., (1991), Jim Abbott: Beating the Odds, Dillon Press, 0-87518-484-7.
Johnston, J., They Led the Way: 14 American Women, Original Title: Women Themselves), 0-590-44431-X.
Keenan, S., Scholastic Encyclopedia of Women in the United States, 0-590-22792-0.
MacDonald, A.L., Feminine Ingenuity: Women and Invention in America, 0-345-35811-2.
McGovern, A., Wanted Dead or Alive: The True Story of Harriet Tubmasn (original title: Runaway Slave), 0-590-44212-0.
McKissack, P. & McKissack, F., (1991), The Story of Booker T. Washington, Children's Press, 0-516-04758-2.
McKissack, Sojourner Truth Ain't I a Woman?, 0-590-44691-6.
Meltzer, M., Mary McLeod Methune: Voice of Black Hope, Viking Krestal Pub., 0-670-80744-3.
Miller, D., (1988), Frederick Douglass: And The Fight For Freedom, Facts on File Pub., 0-8160-1617-8.
Morey, J. & Dunn, W., (1992) Famous Asian Americans, Cobblehill Books, 0-525-65080-6.
Morey, J. & Dunn, W., Famous Asian Americans, 0-525-65080-6.
Morse, M., Women Changing Science: Voices From a Field in Transition, 0-306-45081-X.
Nicholson, L., (1994), Oprah Winfrey: Entertainer, Chelsea House Pub., 0-7910-1886-5
Nies, J., Seven Women: Portraits from the American Radical Tradition, 0-1400-4792-1.
Press, D.P., A Multicultural Portrait of Professional Sports, 1-85435-661-5.
Rollins, C., (1965), Famous Negro Poets, Dodd, Mead & Company, 65-11811.
Rossiter, M.W., Women Scientists in America: Struggles and Strategies to 1940, 0-8018-2443-5.
Simon, C., (1991), Wilma Mankiller: Chief of The Cherokee, Children's Press, 0-516-04181-9
Simon, C., (1994), Evelyn Cisneros: Prima Ballerina, Children's Press,0-516-04276-9.
Sinnott, S., Extraordinary Asian Pacific Americans, 0-516-03052.
Sinnott, S., Extraordinary Hispanic Americans, 0-516-00582-0.
Smith, J.E., Black Firsts: 2000 Years of Extraordinary Achievement, 0-8103-9490-1.
Stille, D.R., Extraordinary Women Scientists, 0-516-00585-5.
Vare, E.A. & Ptacek, G., Mothers of Invention: From the Bra to the Bomb: Forgotten Women and Their Unforgettable Ideas, 0-688-06464-7.
Vare, E.A., Women Inventors & Their Discoveries, 1-881508-06-4
Westridge Young Writers Workshop, Kids Explore America's Afro-American Heritage, 1-56261-090-2.
Yep, L., (1991), The Lost Garden, Simon and Schuster Pub., 0-671-74159-4.
Yount, L., Twentieth-Century Women Scientists, 0-8160-3173-8.

# APPENDIX C

# Sample of Community Resources and Community Services

(As a courtesy please call ahead)

AFRICAN-AMERICAN CULTURAL ART CENTER – 612-332-3506
2429 South 8th Street, Minneapolis, MN 55454. Provides visual art, music, poetry, drama for Blacks, Chicanos American-Indians, Asians. Promotes cultural heritage and historical legacy. Art shows, music performances, tours. Primarily for Black community but attempts to promote communication among people of all cultures. Tours available on basis of goals, etc. Pre-school through college. No larger than 30. 1 hour or more. Charge.

AMERICAN INDIAN BUSINESS DEVELOPMENT CORPORATION – 651-874-8482
1308 East Franklin Avenue, St. Paul, MN.

AMERICAN INDIAN CENTER – 612-776-8592
1001 Payne Avenue, St. Paul, MN 55101. Established to foster, maintain, and preserve Native American culture. Provides employment training and referral services; emergency assistance for food, clothing, transportation and budget counseling; a variety of youth services; senior Native American program; legal services; cultural programs; and chemical dependency counseling and therapy. Acts as a resource center for the non-Indian community on customs and cultural differences.

AMERICAN INDIAN CHEMICAL DEPENDENCY DIVERSION PROJECT – 612-872-1020
808 Franklin Street, Minneapolis, MN.

AMERICAN INDIAN CULTURAL RESOURCE CENTER – 651-224-0315
90 Western Avenue South, St. Paul, MN.

AMERICAN INDIAN HEALTH CARE ASSOCIATION – 612-870-3504
1925 Nicollet Avenue, Minneapolis, MN.

AMERICAN INDIAN OPPORTUNITIES INDUSTRIAL CENTER – 612-379-1540
1845 Franklin, Minneapolis, MN.

AMERICAN INDIAN SERVICES, INC. – 612-871-2175
735 Franklin Avenue East, Minneapolis, MN.

ASIAN-AMERICAN CENTER – 651-488-8051
St. Paul, MN. North Inn School, 27 East Geranium Avenue, St. Paul, MN 55117.

BLACK RESOURCE CENTER – 651-224-4851
Maxfield School, 380 North Victoria Street, St. Paul, MN 55104.

BIG BROTHERS (and BIG SISTERS) – 651-224-7651
711 Empire Building, 360 Robert Street, St. Paul, MN 55101. Basically, they serve all races and cultures. About 15% would be people of color. They will send out speakers. They enable fatherless boys, ages 8-17, to develop a one-man, one-boy relationship and receive guidance, understanding, and companionship.

BILINGUAL CENTER – 612-623-3003
Sheridan School, 1201 University Avenue NE, Minneapolis, MN 55413.

BUREAU OF INDIAN AFFAIRS – 612-725-2911
15 South 5th Street, Minneapolis, MN. Provides social and employment services, education information, credit help, and tribal operations services. Call before going.

CASA de ESPERANZA – 651-772-1723
P.O. Box 75177, St. Paul, MN 55175.

CENTRO LEGAL – 651-291-0110
179 E. Robie, St. Paul, MN 55107.

CHICANO LATINO AFFAIRS COUNCIL – 651-296-9587
555 Park Street, Suite #210, St. Paul, MN 55103. Works to advise the governor and state legislature. Publishes monthly newsletter and resource directory.

CHICANOS LATINOS UNIDOS EN SERVICIOS (CLUES) – 651-292-0117
220 S. Robert St., Suite 103, St. Paul, MN 55107.

CHICANO STUDIES DEPARTMENT – 651-373-9707
489 Ford Hall, University of Minnesota, Minneapolis, MN. Call for more information.

ETHNIC CULTURAL CENTER – 612-348-6130
807 NE Broadway, Minneapolis, MN 55413. They offer resources to teachers on all ethnic groups. Make an appointment for an interview or for a visit.

Families Like Mine – 612-362-3389
A local web site for people with GLBT parents. http://www.familieslikemine.org/

GUADALUPE AREA PROJECT – 651-222-0757
381 E. Robie St., St. Paul, MN 55107.

Gay, Lesbian, and Straight Educators Network (GLSEN) – 952-996-8936
P.O. Box 21187 Minneapolis, MN. Coalition of educators working to support GLBT youth.

HEART OF THE EARTH SURVIVAL SCHOOL – 612-331-8862
1209 SE 4th St., Minneapolis, MN.

HISPANOS IN MINNESOTA – 651-227-0831
179 E. Robie Street, St. Paul, MN 55107. Ricardo Flores, Director. Multi-social service organization.

HOLLAND SCHOOL – 612-627-3059
1534 NE 6th Street, Minneapolis, MN 55413. Provides educational assistance for Hmong students. Excellent for students to visit and participate.

INTERNATIONAL INSTITUTE OF MINNESOTA – 651-647-0191
1694 Como Avenue, St. Paul, MN 55108. Provides English classes for refugees, foreign language classes, and weekly international dinners. Sponsors Festival of Nations in May. Our students could conduct projects, tutor. Also has gift shop. Classes at reduced rates to members. Call ahead for appointment for interview.

JEWISH COMMUNITY CENTER OF ST. PAUL – 651-698-0751
1375 St. Paul Ave., St. Paul, MN 55116.

JEWISH COMMUNITY RELATIONS COUNCIL – 612-388-7816
15 South 9th Street, Suite 400, Minneapolis, MN 55402. Speakers Bureau.

LAO FAMILY COMMUNITY OF MINNESOTA, INC. – 651-487-3466
976 W. Minnehaha Ave., St. Paul, MN 55104.

REGIONAL LEGAL SERVICES
530 Andrews, St. Paul, MN 55107. Provides free legal representation to low-income residents whose income falls within guidelines of Ramsey and Washington Counties in non-criminal matters. Legal services include: landlord/tenant, consumer, public assistance, food stamps, seniors problems, employment problems, default and delinquent mortgage counseling, family law, immigration migrant labor law, juvenile cases, education law, civil rights, American Indian law and many others.

Officina Legal – 651-291-2579

Migran Labor Law – 651-291-2837
Juan Lopez, Bob Hyman

MARTIN LUTHER KING – HALLIE Q. BROWN CENTER
270 North Kent Street, St. Paul, MN 55102. Provides family, employment, and senior citizens' services; recreation activities, day care, and summer day camp. Make arrangements to interview with Dorthea Burns ahead of time. Open M-F 8 AM to 10 PM. Fees vary with program.

MEXICAN-AMERICAN RESOURCE CENTER
Roosevelt Elementary School, Congress and Greenwood, St. Paul, MN 55107.

MINNEAPOLIS DEPARTMENT OF CIVIL RIGHTS – 612-348-7736
2649 Park Avenue, Minneapolis, MN. Handles complaints about acts of discrimination in employment, real estate, lending, public accommodations, public services, or education on the basis of race, sex, sexual preference, national origin, age, or dependence on public assistance. Open M-F 8 AM to 4:30 PM.

MINNEAPOLIS URBAN LEAGUE – 612-377-0011
1121 12th Avenue North, Minneapolis, MN. Provides social work and equal opportunity services to minority groups to help promote positive interracial relations. Open M-F 9 AM to 5 PM. No fee.

MINNESOTA DEPARTMENT OF HUMAN RIGHTS – 651-296-5667
Bremer Tower, Fifth Floor, East Seventh and Minnesota Streets, St. Paul, MN. Enforcement agency that handles complaints of illegal discrimination in Minnesota. Call to make arrangements for interviews.

MINNESOTA FOOD ACTION COALITION – 651-647-0286
1821 University Avenue, Room 365S, St. Paul, MN 55104. Works with welfare and food stamp recipients and low income people. Disseminate information on food issues through workshops. People can call them for information about different food programs. Students may call for more information.

Minnesota Men of Color – 612-671-1788
Group of men of color united to celebrate cultural and sexual identities.

NAACP – 651-224-4601
St. Paul Branch, 270 N. Kent St., St. Paul, MN 55102.

NATIONAL ORGANIZATION FOR WOMEN (Twin Cities Chapter) – 612-776-7195
P.O. Box 9629, Minneapolis, MN 55440. The oldest and largest of seven Twin Cities NOW chapters hold meetings the second Sunday of every month. Fifteen committees work on issues of concern to women. At this writing, their top priority is the proposed Equal Rights Amendment. For information on other chapters, contact Minnesota NOW, Box 3365, St. Paul, MN 55016. 651-298-0999. Membership open to men and women. Membership fee.

NATIVE AMERICAN RESOURCE CENTER – 651-224-0315
    Jefferson School, 90 Western Avenue South, St. Paul, MN 55102.

OutFront Minnesota – 612-822-0127
    310 East 38th Street, Suite 204, Minneapolis, MN 55409. Advocacy group for GLBT. Seeks support and equality for community members. http://www.outfront.org

PHYLLIS WHEATLEY COMMUNITY CENTER – 612-374-4342
    919 Fremont Avenue North, Minneapolis, MN. Provides recreation program, counseling, day care, nursery school, summer day camp, and latchkey program. Red Cross office in building. Fees based on ability to pay and vary with program. Will send brochure.

Rainbow Families – 612-827-7731
    711 West Lake Street, Suite 210, Minneapolis, MN 55409. http://www.rainbowfamilies.org

RED SCHOOL HOUSE – 651-488-6626
    643 Virginia, Street Paul, MN 55103. Alternative school for Indian children. Strong cultural reinforcement. Teaches "survival skills." K-12. Will come and speak. Can arrange interviews and students can visit at any time. Call first.

ST. PAUL AMERICAN INDIAN CENTER – 651-222-0690
    341 University Avenue, St. Paul, MN 55103.

ST. PAUL DEPARTMENT OF HUMAN RIGHTS – 651-298-4288
    515 City Hall, West Kellogg Boulevard at Wabasha Street, St. Paul, MN. Handles complaints about illegal discrimination in St. Paul. Open M-F 8 AM to 4:30 PM. No fee. May interview. Call supervisor for appointment.

ST. PAUL URBAN LEAGUE – 651-224-5771
    401 Selby Avenue, St. Paul, MN. Provides community services in cooperation with the Ramsey County Welfare Department, including housing and economic development programs. Make arrangements with David Rassman.

URBAN COALITION OF MINNEAPOLIS – 612-348-8550
    89 South 10th Street, Minneapolis, MN.

VIETNAMESE AMERICAN FRIENDSHIP ASSOCIATION – 651-690-1353
    1649 Juno, St. Paul, MN 55116.

WESA PROGRAM – 651-646-0520
    Hancock School, 1599 Englewood, St. Paul, MN 55104. Presently developing multi-media curriculum aids for teaching about minorities. Call for more information.

FOODS
There are numerous restaurants in the metropolitan area where you can sample cultural cuisine. If you choose to do this, learn something about the people and culture where this food originated. Remember, this is a relatively low level of development and it can be increased if it is done in a way to present and share relevant knowledge, not just as a fun time filler.

# APPENDIX D

## A Sample of Southeast Asian Resources

Asian American Press
417 University Ave, St Paul, MN 55103
651-224-6570

Asian American Student Cultural Center
University of MN, 159 Coffman Memorial, 300 Washington Ave SE, Mpls., MN 55455
612-626-7001

Asian Media Access
612-349-2549

Center for Asian and Pacific Islanders
1304 E Lake St, Mpls., MN 55407
612-721-0122

Council of Asian-Pacific Minnesotans
205 Aurora Ave, Suite 100, St Paul, MN 55103
651-296-0538

Fresh Air Radio (Hmong and Cambodian programs)
1808 Riverside Ave, Mpls., MN 55454
612-341-3144

Hmong American Partnership
450 N Syndicate #35, St Paul, MN 55104
651-642-9601

Hmong Catholic (St. Vincent's)
651 Virginia, St Paul, MN
651-488-6737

Hmong Media and Arts Society
217 MacKubin St, St Paul, MN
651-224-2712

Hmong National Organization
23 Empire St, St Paul, MN
651-290-2343

Hmong MN Pacific Association, Inc.
965 Payne Avenue S. Suite #102, St. Paul, MN 55102
651-778-2413

Hmong Pride Connection
1575 L'Orient St, St Paul, MN
651-488-9075

Kev Koom Siab (Hmong television program)
172 E 4th St, St Paul, MN 55101
651-229-1279

Lao Family Community of Minnesota
320 W University Ave, St Paul, MN 55103
651-221-0069

Southeast Asian Ministry
105 W University Ave, St Paul, MN 55103
651-293-1261

United Cambodian Association of Minnesota
1821 University Ave, Rm. 360S,
St Paul, MN 55104
651-645-7077

Vietnamese Social Services of Minnesota
1821 University Ave, St Paul, MN 55104
651-644-1317

Women's Association of Hmong and Lao
1544 Timberlake Rd, St Paul, MN 55117
651-488-0243

# APPENDIX E

# American Indian Resource List
(Courtesy of Indian Education, St. Paul Public Schools)

SAINT PAUL

Ain Dah Yung (Our Home) Shelter
1089 Portland Avenue
St. Paul, MN 55104
651-227-4184 / FAX 651-224-5136
Services: Emergency Shelter & Support
Services-American Indian Youth, ages 5-17

Children's Initiative
Saint Paul/Ramsey County
919 Lafond Avenue
St. Paul, MN 55104
651-642-4089 (Gen, Info.) / FAX 651-642-4068
Services: Health, Education, Child Development,
Family Functioning

American Indian Family Center
579 Wells Street
St. Paul, MN 55101
651-774-1888 / FAX 651-774-7708
Services: American Indian Family Support

Department of Indian Work,
  Council of Churches
1671 Summit Avenue
St. Paul, MN 55105
651-644-2768 / FAX 651-646-6866
Services: Early Childhood Education,
Social Services, Food Shelf

American Indian Family & Children's
  Services (AIFACS)
25 Empire Drive
St Paul, MN 55103
651-223-8526 / FAX 651-223-8529
Services: Foster Care Recruitment, Training Y
Licensing of American Indian Homes

Earthstar Project
1885 University Avenue, Suite 50
St. Paul, MN 55104
651-644-1173 / FAX 651-644-1887
Services: Family Support, Elders Program

American Indian Parenting Support
Early Childhood Family Education (ECFE)
North End Elementary
27 East Geranium Avenue
St. Paul, MN 55117
651-293-5346 / FAX 651-293-8798
or call 651-293-5191 / FAX 651-293-5193
Services: Parenting support for parents with children
– Birth-12 years

Indian Education Programs
Saint Paul Public Schools
1028 Van Slyke
St. Paul, MN 55103
651-293-5191 / FAX 651-293-5193
Services: Indian Student/Family Educational Support

American Indian Research & Policy Institute
  (AIRPI)
749 Simpson Street
St. Paul, MN 55104
651-644-1728 / FAX 651-644-0740
Services: American Indian research, educational
forums and discussions

Minnesota American Indian Bar Ass'n.
Fineday Law Office
P.O. Box 1136
Walker, MN 56484
218-547-3923 / FAX 218-547-2369
Contact: Anita Fineday
Services: Legal Areas

Children's Families and Community Initiative
633 University Avenue
St. Paul, MN 55104
651-291-1702 / FAX 651-291-0737
Contact: JoAnne Stately
Services: Funding grants for the communities of the
Summit-University
and Frogtown neighborhoods

Minnesota Department of Children, Family
  & Learning – Indian Education
740 Capitol Square Building
550 Cedar Street
St. Paul, MN 55101
651-296-6458 / FAX 651-297-7895
Contact: David Beaulieu
Services: Statewide Indian Education concerns
  ST PAUL (continued)

Minnesota Indian Affairs Council
1450 Energy Park Drive, Room 140
St. Paul, MN 55108
651-643-3032 or 643-3036
Services: Statewide Indian concerns

Saint Paul Technical College
235 Marshall Avenue
St. Paul, MN 55102
651-221-1300
Contact: Marcy Hart, American Indian Counselor – 651-221-1312

Mounds Park All Nations
American Indian Magnet School
1075 E. Third Street
St. Paul, MN 55106
651-293-5938 / FAX 651-293-5941
Services: Education K-8, Public School

St. Paul American Indians in Unity
1030 University Avenue
St. Paul, MN 55104
651-290-4849 / FAX 651-290-4785
Services: Community Education, Cultural Enrichment

Native American Special Project/
 Dreamcatchers
1030 University Avenue
St. Paul, MN 55104
651-290-4822 / FAX 651-290-4785
Contact: Wanda Weyaus
Services: GED Preparation, Brush-up Classes, American Indian Family Learning


MINNEAPOLIS (Agencies/Organizations)

Bureau of Indian Affairs (Mpls)
331 South Second Avenue
Minneapolis, MN 55401-2241
612-373-1000, 612-373-1065 ext. 1090
FAX 612-373-1186
Contact: Terry Portra
Services: Provide services for Indian tribes and organizations not individuals; information on boarding schools and Indian colleges

Minnesota American Indian Chamber of
 Commerce
212 Third Avenue North, Suite 567
Minneapolis, MN 55404
612-333-0500 / FAX 612-333-0330
Contact: Mike Bongo
Services: Assist in the development and referral to Indian owned businesses in Minnesota

Healthy Nations (Twin Cities)
1530 East Franklin Avenue
Minneapolis, MN 55404
612-879-1736 / FAX 612-879-1795
Contact: Tom Briggs
Services: Promotes wellness, strength, reduce substance abuse, mentoring, collaboration, cultural

NAES College – American Indian College
1305 East 24th Street. Minneapolis, MN 55404
612-721-1909 / FAX 612-721-7022
Hours: M-F, 8:30 a.m. - 4:30 p.m.
Contact: Sam Ardito

Native Arts Circle
1433 East Franklin Avenue, Suite 15
Minneapolis, MN 55404
612-870-0327
American Indian Artists

Minneapolis American Indian Center
1530 East Franklin Avenue
Minneapolis, MN 55404
612-871-4555 / FAX 612-879-1795
Services: Social Services, Cultural Areas

Upper Midwest Indian Center
1113 West Broadway
Minneapolis, MN 55441
612-522-4436 / FAX 612-522-8855
Contact: Ron Buckanaga
Services: Foster care; after school programs

TRIBAL OFFICES
(Minnesota Chippewa/Ojibwe Reservations)

Minnesota Chippewa Tribe
P.O. Box 217
Cass Lake, MN 56633-0217
218-335-8581 / FAX 218-335-6562

Mille Lacs Area Twin Cities Office
1433 E. Franklin Avenue
Minneapolis, MN 55404
612-872-2308

Bois Forte Reservation (Nett Lake)
Clint Landgren, Chairman
P.O. Box 16
Nett Lake, MN 55772
218-757-3261 / FAX 218-757-3312

Red Lake Reservation
Bobby Whitefeather, Chairman
Red Lake, MN 56671
218-679-3341 / FAX 218-679-3378

Fond Du Lac Reservation
Robert Peacock, Chairman
105 University Road
Cloquet, MN 55720
218-879-4593 / FAX 218-879-4146

Red Lake Area Twin Cities Office
1530 E. Franklin Avenue
Minneapolis, MN 55404
Contact: Pat Lussier: 612-871-4555 or 612-870-9004
10:00 a.m. to 2:00 p.m. Mon, Wed, Fri
Enrollment assistance and helps with business plans

Grand Portage Reservation
Norman Deschampe, Chairman
P.O. Box 428
Grand Portage, MN 55605
218-475-2277, 218-475-2279 / FAX 218-475-2284

White Earth Reservation
Eugene Bugger McArthur, Chairman

P.O. Box 418
White Earth, MN 56591
218-983-3285 / FAX 218-983-3641

Leech Lake Tribal Council
Eli Hunt, Chairman
Route 3, Box 100
Cass Lake, MN 55633
218-335-8200 / FAX 218-335-8309

TRIBAL OFFICES
(Minnesota Dakota Communities)

Lower Sioux Community
Roger Prescott, Chairman
R.R. #1, Box 308
Morton, MN 56270
507-697-6185 / FAX 507-697-6110

Shakopee-Mdewakanton Community
Stanley Crooks, Chairman
2330 Sioux Trail NW
Prior Lake, MN 55372
612-445-8900 / FAX 612-445-8906
233-4246

Upper Sioux Community
Dallas Ross, Chairman
P.O. Box 147
Granite Falls, MN 56241
320-564-2360 / 2550
FAX 320-564-3264
Board of Trustees 320-564-3853 / FAX 320-564-2547

Ho-Chunk (Wisconsin) Reservation Area Office
1885 University Avenue West
St. Paul, MN 55104
651-647-9498
Prairie Island Community
Curtis Campbell, Chairman
5636 Sturgeon Lake Road
Welch, MN 55089
612-385-2554 / FAX 612-388-1576
1-800-554-5473 / FAX 612-385-2548

# APPENDIX F
## Sample of Local Stores with Multicultural Resources

Amazon Bookstore Co-op
4432 Chicago Avenue S.
Minneapolis, MN

Birchbark Books
2115 W. 21st St.
Minneapolis, MN

Bookstore
1648 Grand Avenue
St. Paul, MN
651-699-0587

American Swedish Institute Associates
Museum Shop
2600 Park Avenue
Minneapolis, MN
871-3004

Ingebretsen Scandinavian Gifts
1601 East Lake Street
Minneapolis, MN
612-729-9333

Bear Hawk Indian Store
1219 East Franklin Avenue
Minneapolis, MN 55404
612-872-9166

Lerner Publications
241 First Avenue N
Minneapolis, MN
612-332-3344

Bookman, Inc.
525 North 3rd Street
Minneapolis, MN
612-341-3333

Minneapolis American Indian Center
1530 E Franklin
Minneapolis, MN 55404
612-871-4749, 612-871-4555

Borders Bookstore
3001 Hennepin Avenue S
Minneapolis, MN
612-825-0331

NAES College & Bookstore /American Indian Focus
1305 E 24th Street
Minneapolis, MN
612-721-1909

Central American Resource Center
Hispanic/Latino Focus
317 17th Avenue SE
Minneapolis, MN 55414
612-627-9445

Northland Poster Collective
1613 E Lake Street
Minneapolis, MN 55407
612-721-2273

Electric Fetus
Records Tapes
2010 4th Avenue S
Minneapolis, MN
612-870-9300

Northern Sun Merchandizing
Posters, T-Shirts, etc.
2916 E Lake Street
Minneapolis, MN
612-729-2001

Heart of the Beast Puppet Theater
1500 West Lake Street
Minneapolis, MN
612-721-2535

Uhuru Bookstore
African & African American Focus
1304 East Lake Street
Minneapolis, MN 55407
612-721-7113

Homestead Pickin' Parlor
Bluegress, Folk, Blues, Ethnic, Country Music
6625 Penn Avenue S
Minneapolis, MN
612-861-3308

Anderson Schools of Many Voices
Multicultural Laboratory Demonstration Site
2727 10th Avenue S
Minneapolis, MN 55407/612-627-22

# APPENDIX G
## Sample of Community Newspapers and Magazines

American Jewish World
4509 Minnetonka Blvd
Minneapolis, MN 55416
612-920-7000

LaPrensa De Minnesota
422 University Avenue, Suite 3
St. Paul, MN 55103
651-224-0404

Asian American Press
422 University Avenue, Suite 1
St. Paul, MN 55103
651-224-6570

Minneapolis Spokesman
3744 4th Avenue S
Minneapolis, MN 55409
612-827-4021

Asian Business/Community News
396 North Roy Street
St Paul, MN 55104
651-224-6570

MN Women's Press
771 Raymond Avenue
St. Paul, MN 55103
651-224-1510

Asian Pages, Box 11932
Minneapolis, MN 55411
612-869-1232

Nuestra Gente
7642 Lyndale Avenue S.
Richfield, MN 55423
612-243-1283

Colors
3123 East Lake Street, Suite 103
Minneapolis, MN 55406-2028
612-724-6685

The Circle
1530 East Franklin
Minneapolis, MN 55404
612-871-4555

Focus Point
PO Box 50188
Minneapolis, MN 55405
612-288-9001

The Recorder
59 Endicott Building
St. Paul, MN 55102
651-224-4886

Insight
422 University Avenue, Suite 8
St. Paul, MN 55103
651-227-8968

Visiones De La Raza
2201 Nicollet Avenue S
Minneapolis, MN 55404
612-874-1412

Latin Midwest
909 Selby Avenue
St. Paul, MN 55104
651-227-2589

Star Tribune
4325 Portland Avenue S
Minneapolis, MN 55488
612-673-4414

Other Useful Publications
American Visions
Magazine of Afro-American Culture
Warwick Communications
Carter G. Woodson House
Smithsonian Institute
Washington, D.C. 20560
202-462-1779

Native Peoples (Magazine)
5333 North 7th Street
Suite 224C
Phoenix, AZ 85014-2803
602-252-2236

Ebony (Magazine)
820 South Michigan Avenue
Chicago, IL 60605
312-322-9200

# APPENDIX H

# Sample of Internet Resources

(Selected Sites for any Age)


General Multicultural Sources

    This site provides an overview of issues relating to multicultural education
    Additional readings are available online through the links provided.
    http://http://www.ncrel.org/sdrs/areas/issues/educatrs/presrvce/pe3lk1.htm

Applied Research Center
    This site is a public policy and educational research center focussing on issues of race and social change. It also has several projects designed to foster worldwide and national awareness and action.
    http://www.arc.org

Teaching Tolerance
    This site is devoted to promoting tolerance and social justice.
    The Teaching Tolerance organization provides many useful resources free
    of charge, including a biannual journal and curriculum kits. The site also addresses
    current events and news topics related to tolerance.
    http://www/teachingtolerance.org

Arabs in America
    This site provides information with links to cultural and religious sites, film, current events, and chat rooms. It is also a search engine for more information specific to Arab sites.
    http://www.arabia.com/english/

Balch Institute for Ethnic Studies
    Multicultural library and educational center
    http://www.balchinstitute.org/

Educational Justice

    Curriculum resources
    http://www.edjustice.org/

    Facing History and Ourselves
    This site has information that examines history and legacies of prejudice and discrimination. It also has a teacher in-service component.
    http://www.facinghistory.org/facing/fhao2.nsf

    Teaching for Change
    Resources to help integrate diverse cultures into the curriculum
    http://www.teachingforchange.org

Cultural Diversity

    Check this site for loads of links about African Americans, Latinos, Asian Americans, Native Americans, and more. Parental warning: preview links, this site changes often.
    http://latino.sscnet.ucla.edu/diversity1.html

Rethinking Schools
This site is devoted to reforming urban schools and is committed to equity.
http://www.rethinkingschools.org

African American

Drum Web Server Home Page
Here you'll find links to the arts, historical sources, entertainment, and much more. Read Dr. Martin Luther King's "I Have a Dream" speech, or the words of Malcolm X. Explore the civil rights resources and think about Maya Angelou's poem.
http://drum.ncat.edu/

Melanet On-Line African Wedding Guide
You'll find information on choosing African fabrics, using symbols, and incorporating African traditions.
http://www.melanet.com/melanet/wedding/

Selections from the African-American Mosaic
The Library of Congress is in Washington, D.C., and it has a huge collection of materials, some of which cover about 500 years of African history in the Western Hemisphere. They have books, periodicals, prints, photographs, music, film, and recorded sound. This exhibit samples these kinds of materials in four areas--Colonization, Abolition, Migrations, and the Work Projects Administration period.
http://lcweb.loc.gov/exhibits/African.American/intro.html

African American inventors, inventions, and patent dates
This is a list of some African American inventors and their patented inventions. These include a pencil sharpener, refrigeration equipment, elevator machinery, and railroad telegraphy discoveries.
http://www.ai/mit.edu/~isbell/HFh/black/event-s_and_people/009.aa_inventions

African American On-line Exhibit Homepage
Profiles of significant African Americans in science, medicine, and technology. There is also a great timeline of events, inventions, and people, and you'll find educational opportunities and organizations in support of African Americans pursuing a career in the sciences.
http://pitcairn.lib.uci.edu/AA/AAhomepage.html

African Americans in History
This site provides information on key African Americans in history
http://www.uga.edu/~iaas/History,html

Asian American

A. Magazine
"Inside Asian America" gives you a few articles from the print version of the magazine, as well as links to other Asian American sites on the Net. You'll find links to Asian music, newsgroups, and more!
http://www.amagazine.com/

Asian Astrology
Find out about Chinese, Vietnamese, and Tibetan calendar and astrological systems here. There are also calendar conversion utilities and information on Asian divination. There is also an informative FAQ on Feng Shui , the art of locating buildings according to the most favorable geographic influences.
http://www.deltanet.com/users/wcassidy/astroindex.html

Hmong Textiles
> The Hmong people of Vietnam and Laos have a language, but is was a spoken language, not a written one. Their culture passes down its stories by telling them orally, or by telling them in cloths. Here are some cloths made by Hmong Americans and native Hmong.
> http://www.lib.uci.edu/sea/hmong.html

WWW Hmong Homepage
> The Hmong came from China, Thailand, and Laos. This is a collection of resources relating to the history, culture, and language of the Hmong people. many of whom have immigrated to the U.S. Check the photographic archives and the news links to read current information about the Hmong.
> http://www.stolaf.edu/people/cdr/hmong/

Latino/Hispanic American

Azteca Home Page
> Did you know many kids in the United States are of Mexican descent? They are proudly called Chicanos y Chicanas. Understanding what it means to be a Chicano means many things. It's music, history, culture, and language. For anyone wanting to understand about being Chicano, the Azteca Home Page is a good place to start.
> http://www.directnet.com/~mario/aztec/

LatinoWeb
> BIENVENIDO! That's Spanish for "Welcome," one of the first things you'll see on the LatinoWeb, one part of the Internet set aside for things Latino. LatinoWeb has much to see. News, music, etc.
> http://www.catalog.com/favsion/latnoweb

Chicano Mural Tour
> Murals are paintings on buildings, and they turn the outdoors into an art gallery. Some of the best mural artists are Latino.
> http://latino.sscnet.ucla.edu/murals/Sparc/sparctour.html

Hispanos Famosos
> What do Roman Emperor Hadrian, Nobel Prize-winning scientist Luis Leloir, and painter Pablo Picasso have in common? They are all famous Hispanics--people with a Spanish heritage. Throughout history Hispanic people have been great scientists, soldiers, political leaders, artists, and musicians. Read about many famous and accomplished Hispanics here--both English and Spanish!
> http://www.clark.net/pub/jgbustam/famosos/famosos/html

Hispanic American History and Literature for K-12
> This site offers a comprehensive list of resources for teachers.
> http://www.falcom.jmu.edu/~ramseyil/hispan.htm

Native American/American Indian and Other Indigenous Peoples

Arctic Circle: History and Culture
> You'll find information here about many people who are native to the Arctic Circle region of the world. You'll not only learn about the Cree of Northern Quebec and the Inupiat of Arctic Alaska, but also the Nenets and Khanty of Yamal Peninsula, Northwest Siberia, and the Sami of Far Northern Europe. Find out why the concept of "wilderness" is unknown to these people who live in harmony with their natural surroundings.
> http://www.lib.uconn.edu:80/ArcticCircle/HistoryCulture/index.html

A Guide to the Great Sioux Nation

The people of the Sioux Nation prefer to be called Dakota, Lakota, or Nakota, depending on their language group. On this South Dakota home page, you can learn about the languages, legends, and rich cultural traditions of these proud peoples. You'll see beautiful costumes and a calendar of annual events.
http://www.state.sd.us/state/executive/tourism/sioux/sioux.htm

National Museum of the American Indian
This particular Smithsonian Museum is in New York City, not Washington, D.C. Most of the one million objects in its collection represent cultures in the United States and Canada, although there are also items from Mexico and Central and South America. You can see many artifacts of ancient and contemporary native culture through the on-line exhibits of clothing, baskets, beadwork, and other objects.
http://www.si.edu/organiza/museums/amerind/nmai/start.htm

Native Village
Information about indigenous cultures in the world.
http://www.nativeweb.org

Virtual Library on Native Americans
This site provides a comprehensive index of teaching resources.
http://www.hanksville.org/Naresources/

NativeWeb Home Page
There are hundreds of federally recognized Nations within the United States. Learn more about Native Americans at this site which collects info on art, culture, government, languages, music, religious beliefs, and current tribal issues.
http://web.maxwell.syr.edu/nativeweb/

Web Pages and Other Resources for Indian Teachers and Students
This page offers annotated links to Mayan, aboriginal, and other resources.
http://indy4.fdl.cc.mn.us/~isk/

Booklist by the American Library Association
Reviews of current books for all levels of readers and audiovisual materials. Published twice monthly.
http://www.ala.org/booklist

Miscellaneous

Arabs in America
Links to cultural sites, religions, information, and other specific topics on Arab sites.
http://www.arabia.com/english/

National Indian Telecommunications Institute (NITI)
The Native founded and run organization in Sante Fe, New Mexico, strives to employ advanced technology to serve American Indians and Alaska Natives. Areas targeted include education, language and cultural preservation, and self determination. The site provides information on training facilities and classes offered at the NITI computer laboratory in Sante Fe. Information is available on NITI's internship program for American Indian and Alaska Native students. The Native American Web Pages section gives links to sites on Native languages, music, organizations, and tribal information. Also supplied are links to organizations affiliated with NITI, including the National Science Foundation, Los Alamos National Laboratories, and the Prairie View A&M University's Network Resources Training Site.
http://numa.niti.org/

Mancala
This Web site is a computer version of the ancient African game Mancala, also known as Kalaha. The physical game board has 12 playing pits, each containing 3 seeds. Each seed in the pit is then placed, one at a time, into successive pits, moving counterclockwise around the board. Points are earned by placing seeds in a scoring pit. The game ends when all of the pits on one side of the board are empty. There are two difficulty levels available, as well as a hint button that suggests moves for the player.
http://imagiware.com/mancala/

Varieties of Multicultural Education: An Introduction
This ERIC/CUE (Clearinghouse on urban Education) Digest article classifies multicultural education programs into three broad groups: content-oriented, student-oriented, and socially-oriented. The content-oriented programs attempt to infuse information about different cultures into the curriculum. Student-oriented programs address the academic needs of different groups by offering special programs based on different learning styles. The programs that seek the broadest reform are the socially-oriented; these aim to reform both schooling and the cultural and political contexts of schooling, thereby increasing cultural and racial tolerance and reducing bias.
http://eric-web.tc.columbia.edu/digests/dig98.html

Multicultural Pavilion
Developed for K-12 educators, this Web site offers resources about multicultural education and provides a forum for online discussion. The site features an article that describes the concept of multicultural education, including a working definition, components, and goals. The Teacher's Corner provides online resources for teachers, including reviews of children's music, multicultural activities, and online literature archives. In the Research and Inquiry section, users can find research resources such as statistical data archives, online article archives, and links to online libraries, electronic journals, and research organizations. Classroom discussion activities are provided to heighten multicultural and diversity awareness. The site also includes a collection of online networking strategies, Web tutorials, and links to other multicultural sites. This site has been named a Magellan 3-Star site and has been a weekly selection of Suite 101.
http://curry.edschool.Virginia.EDU/go/multicultural/

Encyclopedia of Women's History
http://www.teleport.com/-megaines/women.html

Sojourn to America
http://library.thinkquest.org/2792
Sojourn to America is a forum through which students share stories about how and why they, or their relatives and ancestors came to America.

Cybrary of the Holocaust
http://www.emulateme.com/
This site is an online multimedia library of resources pertaining to the Holocaust.

National Civil Rights Museum Interactive Tour
http://www.midsouth.rr.com/civilrights/
A small sampling of the 100,000 square feet of documents and other media housed at the actual museum in Atlanta.

Multicultural Passport
http://204.98.1.2/passport/index.html
Passport houses a compendium of multicultural lesson plans and ideas arranged by subject area, region, and identity dimension.

A Celebration of Women Writers
http://digital.library.upenn.edu/women/

This site was created in conjunction with the Online Books Page to celebrate the contributions and voices of women.

SI SE Puede! Cesar E. Chavez and His Legacy
http://clnet.ucr.edu/research/chavez/
This site was developed at UCLA to commemorate the life and work of Chavez, who led the first successful farm workers' union in U.S.

A Deeper Shade of History
http://www.ai.mit.edu/-isbell/HFh/black/bhist.html
This site serves as a clearinghouse for Black History resources.

Disability Social History Project
http://http://www.disabilityhistory.org/
This site represents an attempt by people with disabilities to reclaim their own history and to highlight the contributions of disabled people in the history of the world.

First Nations Histories
http://www.dickshovel.com/Compacts.html
This site provides an examination of history by and about First Nations peoples.

Transsexual, Transgender, and Intersex History
http://www.transhistory.org/
This site provides historical information by and about people whose gender identities do not fit neatly into the male/female dyad.

American Studies Web: Reference and Research
http://www.georgetown.edu/crossroads/asw/
The American Studies Department at Georgetown University maintains this extensive list of related sites with subtopics that include "Race and Ethnicity," "Gender and Sexuality," and "Sociology and Demography."

Diversity Database
http://www.inform.umd.edu/Diversity
Developed by a team of content and technology experts at the University of Maryland, College Park, the Diversity Database is a compendium of resources organized by identity dimensions including age, class, race, gender, ability status, religion, and sexual orientation.

Gay, Lesbian, and Straight Education Network
http://www.splcenter.org/teachingtolerance/tt-index.html
GLSEN is a national organization consisting of educators, students, parents, and others working together to address heterosexism and homophobia in schools.

Multicultural Approaches to Art Learning
http://www.artsednet.getty.edu/ArtsEdNet/Resources/Chalmers/designing.html
This ArtsEdNet site describes strategies for creating and implementing effective multicultural arts curricula.

African American Holocause
http://www.maafa.org/
Atrocities African Americans have faced in the United States.

Documenting the Southeast Asian Refugee Experience
http://www.lib.uci.edu/new/seaexhibit/index.html
Exhibit of the experiences, trials, and tribulations of southeast Asian refugees to the U.S.

The Japanese American Internment
http://www.geocities.com/Athens/8420/main.html
Photographs, articles, and intriguing quotes make this an interesting educational journey into a too-often not-talked-about piece of American History.

Native American Website for Children
http://www.nhusd.k12.ca.us/ALVE/NativeAmerhome.html/nativeopeningpage.html
This site actively engages students in a multimedia adventure as they learn about the lives, cultures, and histories of Native American tribes.

4000 Years of Women in Science
http://crux.astr.ua.edu//4000ws/4000ws.html
This site houses photographs, biographies, and references for women who contributed to the field of science.

Annotated Bibliography of Multicultural Perspectives in Mathematics Education
http://jwilson.coe.uga.edu/DEPT/Multicultural/MEBib94.html
Extensive annotated listing of resources related to multicultural education in the math classroom.

Barrier Free Education
http://barrier-free.arch.gatech.edu/
The aim of Barrier Free Education is to help students with disabilities gain access to math and science education.

The Faces of Science: African Americans in the Sciences
http://www.lib.lsu.edu/lib/chem/display/faces.html
This virtual encyclopedia highlights African American scientists and their work and accomplishments.

Integrating Gender and Equity Reform in Math, Science, and Engineering Instruction
http://www.coe.uga.edu/ingear/
The site includes specific teaching strategies, online publications and articles, and a collection of classroom activities that address gender issues.

Game Central Station
http://www.gamecentralstation.com/gcshome.asp
This site features over 350 descriptions of Physical Education activities for K-12 teachers and students.

# APPENDIX I

# CASE STUDIES

Write a case study to better assist in examining the factors involved in interactions in the school and community. Include the following elements in your case study and take time to discuss this with a trusted colleague whose culture/ethnicity differs from yours in several ways. This will afford the greatest learning opportunity for you. Cases have often been defined as narrative stories containing events such as stories describing classroom or school-related events. Good cases have possibilities for multiple levels of analysis and are sufficiently complex to allow multiple interpretations (Redman, 2003). Write your case study and have others analyze it to provide insight into the situation.

Title

Grade Level

Subject Matter

Teaching Topic w/in subject

Contextual Factors

Community Factors

Classroom Factors

Teacher Characteristics

Student Characteristics

Characteristics of Curriculum

Story/case

Questions for Reflection

Activities for Extended Thinking

Criteria for Assessing Responses

List acceptable and unacceptable responses

**References**
Redman, G. (2003). A casebook for exploring diversity, 2$^{nd}$ ed. Boston, MA: Allyn & Bacon.
Taylor, L. & Whittaker, C. (2003). Bridging multiple worlds: Case studies of diverse educational communities. Boston, MA: Allyn & Bacon.

# NOTES

# NOTES

# NOTES

# NOTES

NOTES

# NOTES